SPEECH

ITS FUNCTION AND DEVELOPMENT

SPEECH

Its Function and Development

By

Grace Andrus de Laguna

Associate Professor of Philosophy
Bryn Mawr College

New Haven: Yale University Press

London: Humphrey Milford: Oxford University Press

1927

CONTENTS

CONTENTS

PREFACE

IT is common enough to regard language, as distinguished from the act of speaking it, as a social phenomenon comparable to art or religion, and to study it by the historical and comparative methods of anthropology and philology. But the activity of speech has always been regarded as a phenomenon of individual life and treated from the standpoint of individual psychology. Yet it is evident that, while it is the individual who speaks, speech itself is as much a part of the organized life of society as is buying or selling or bearing arms. I have attempted in this book to investigate speech from this point of view, and to inquire first of all what specific function it performs in society, and how speaking as a social enterprise is related to other forms of group activity. In doing this it has been my hope that fresh light might be thrown on the vexed problem of the origin of speech, and that at the same time the way might be prepared for a more fruitful study of speech as a phenomenon of individual psychology.

The first part of the book, accordingly, deals with the social function of speech. It compares speech in this respect with the animal cry, and offers a tentative and partial theory of the evolution of the one from the other. Different as they are in important characteristics, they are both found to perform the same fundamental function of *coördinating the activities of the members of the group.* The evolution of the one from the other thus becomes comprehensible, as it is not if speech is regarded, in the traditional fashion, primarily as the expression of ideas, and the cry as the expression of emotion. The chief factors determining this evolution are found to lie in conditions affecting primarily the maintenance of the group as a group, and through it the lives of its members. More specifically it is argued that the change from arboreal life to ground-dwelling must have made a more flexible type of group organization highly advantageous, if not indeed necessary, and that it was probably in serving this end that speech developed.

No account of speech can, of course, avoid dealing to some extent with the structure of the language which is spoken. If the primary function of speech is, as is here assumed, the coördination of group activities, and if its evolution from the cry has been determined by the necessity for the enlargement and specialization of this function, then the structure of language must bear evidence to this fact. Examination shows that this is the case. The basic structure, which all languages possess in common, is analyzed in the light of the social function of speech, and is found to be specifically adapted to its performance. No attempt is made, however, to examine the comparative structure of different types of language. This lies wholly outside the purpose of the present investigation.

The remainder of the book is psychological. Part III, to mention that first, deals with the function of speech in the life of the individual, and, in particular, with its relation to the higher forms of intellectual life. But before these topics, which are very complex, could be discussed intelligibly, it seemed necessary to give some preliminary account of the general psychological scheme into which they were to fit. Psychology at the present day is in a very confused state. There is no general system which can be taken for granted as definitively established. Certainly the behavioristic position which is developed in Part II, at the expense, perhaps, of a certain unity in the book, could not be assumed without explicit formulation. It is far from being generally accepted, or even understood; and it differs in essential respects from the better known behaviorism of the Watson school. Yet it is, as I try to show, absolutely fundamental to the whole treatment of speech. It is presented under the heading, "Aspects of Mental Evolution," partly because I found a genetic treatment indispensable to the sort of analysis I wished to make, and partly because it is one of the essential aims of the book to show that the appearance of speech is not an inexplicable mystery, as it has appeared in the light of traditional psychology, but that it is of a piece with the evolution of mind generally. Consequently the discussion in Part II prepares for the specific treatment of speech as a form of individual behavior in Part III, and is intended to supplement the evolutionary theory of Part I.

In Part III the threads of the argument of both preceding parts are drawn together. The analysis of speech as a form of individual behavior is guided throughout by the earlier treatment of its social function. At the same time speech is seen to be a further extension of the indirectness in the attainment of individual ends which has marked the development of intelligent behavior from the beginning. The higher mental activities

—conception and purpose, memory and imagination, belief and thought—so far as these are distinctively human, are found to be closely dependent on speech. They
are fundamentally social in origin, being due indirectly
to the development of *conversation*, which, it is argued,
has the primitive function of preparing for concerted
group action, much as distance-perception prepares the
immediate response of the individual. Conversation is
shown to have a characteristic structure, adapted to its
function, and it is this structure which makes possible the
organized activity of thought, in which it is reflected.

I wish to acknowledge my indebtedness to my col-
leagues, Professor James H. Leuba and Professor Theo-
dore de Laguna, both of whom have read the entire
manuscript and have made valuable criticisms and sug-
gestions. A debt of another sort I owe to the philosophi-
cal writings of Professor Edgar A. Singer, Jr., of the
University of Pennsylvania. How far I have been directly influenced by him I do not know, nor how far he
himself would be willing to recognize in my work the
marks of such an influence. But the general behavioristic
position adopted in the present inquiry is, I venture to
believe, substantially the same as that which he was the
first to formulate and which he has so brilliantly de-
fended.

Bryn Mawr College,
    January, 1927.

PART I

The Rôle of Speech in Society

Speech: Its Function and Development

CHAPTER I

The Problem of Origin

INTEREST in the problem of language is no new thing in the history of speculative thought. It was the Sophists who may be said to have "discovered" language along with morality and other social phenomena, and it was they who first speculated whether it was due to "nature" or "convention." Later on we find the issue joined between the Epicureans and the Stoics over the question whether language had its origin in mere natural cries which gradually became associated with specific natural objects, or whether it arose through a more or less conscious attempt to imitate the sounds of objects. While interest in the subject has not always been equally intense, it has been perennial. At the beginning of modern times it was the relation of language to thought which chiefly exercised men's minds, and especially the dangers to clear thought which lurk in the use of words: the Idols of the Market-place. It was the growing appreciation of this danger, and with it the fuller realization of the intimate dependence of thought on language, that inspired the project, so characteristic of the Enlightenment, of founding a universal language of exact symbols which should be the adequate instrument of universal and exact science. The succeeding period, with its riot of speculative theories of social evolution, and its soberer descent to historical

3

research, revived again the ancient interest in the origin and evolution of language, and saw the rise of the science of comparative philology.

Difficulties of the Problem.

IT is not our purpose to trace, even schematically, the course of speculation on the subject of language. It would be a long and interesting history, but chiefly instructive, perhaps, in the seeming futility which it reveals. For although it has occupied men's thoughts throughout so many centuries, the problem of the origin of human speech, and even of its relation to human reason, is apparently as far as ever from solution. The notorious attempts nicknamed by Max Müller "the pooh-pooh theory" and "the bow-wow theory," and his own "ding-dong theory" as well, are not on a much higher level than their ancient prototypes; nor is the more recent contribution of Noiré, or even that of Jespersen, to be regarded as a serious scientific hypothesis. It is not difficult to understand or sympathize with the decision of the French Société linguistique to accept no more contributions on the subject of the origin of language. The part of wisdom has seemed to be to put the problem of origin aside indefinitely and to devote attention to the analysis and comparison of existing languages on the one hand, and to anthropology and psychology on the other.

A number of causes, besides the ill-success of previous adventurers, have contributed to bring the enterprise of explaining the origin of language into disrepute. The first of these is the realization of the actual lack of data on which to build a really scientific theory. Speculation in fields where empirical verification of theories is not feasible, is frowned upon more effectively in these days of solid scientific achievement than it ever was before. Then, too, the advances which have been made in anthropology generally, and in philology in particular, have served to reveal how vast our ignorance is, and is likely to be, in regard to essential matters of fact about primitive conditions of humanity. The origins of culture have receded steadily into the obscurity of distance as we have advanced in our understanding of existing cultures. For no existing culture and no existing language is anywhere near primitive. The language of the lowest savages is ages old and bears in its structure the marks of an age-old evolution. The former hope of philologists, that they might by the comparison of different types of languages be able to place them in a developmental order, and so to trace a curve of evolution which could be followed back to its origin, has been wholly abandoned. Indeed, so far has the pendulum swung in the other direction, that a careful anthropologist like Boas not only denies that any language is superior to any other, but also seems to doubt that any existing language is more primitive in its structure than any other. We may be able in the future, from the now rapidly accumulating archaeological remains of early man, to reconstruct primitive culture in its essential outlines; but primitive language, unfortunately, leaves no record, being limited to the winged word, eked out perhaps by the no less fleeting gesture. It seems beyond the limits of the most sanguine hope to suppose that we shall ever have any direct evidence as to how primitive men spoke in the dawn of culture.

It has sometimes been thought that in the gesture-language used by deaf-mutes and as a means of inter-tribal communication by the American Indians, for example, one might discover the form of primitive language. But there is no ground for supposing that gesture *preceded* vocal utterance as a form of language, although it is highly probable that gesture and voice coöperated more than they usually do now. Much is doubtless to be learned from the study of gesture-language. The fact that it has substantially the same form wherever it grows up is highly significant. But gesture-language is still a *language;* that is, it exhibits what may be regarded as the minimum essential of a language—predication. And it has distinct *words, i.e.,* conventional symbols which function as separable elements in a sentence. By what stages and under what conditions such cries and gestures as we find among the higher animals became gradually modified into conventional symbols —above all, how predication arose—is the crucial question.

There remains, of course, the evidence to be gleaned from the development of speech in the child. This evidence again is of the greatest importance, but it is indirect, and so likely to be misleading. For children grow up in a social environment moulded by generations of speaking men. We may observe them as they gradually learn to speak the language of their group, but this is very different from observing the development of human speech *de novo.*

In addition to the lack of empirical data, a further cause of the ban upon the problem of origin is to be found in the realization of the intimate dependence of reason on speech. The acceptance of the dictum, "No speech without reason, and no reason without speech," has not been without important consequences. It has served to invest the problem of the development of speech with all the difficulties and dangers which are felt to surround the "naturalization" of reason. The whole gulf between reason and sense, between moral obligation and instinct, yawns between speaking man and speechless brute. Against this final bulwark of transcendentalism, the tide of evolutionary naturalism has now set too strongly to leave any doubt as to the final outcome. That, as a matter of historical fact, speaking and reasoning man did evolve by natural processes from anthropoid ancestors is not seriously disputed even by those whose deepest sympathies are opposed to such an admission. But so long as mystery surrounds the manner of that evolution, the refuge of ignorance remains. And the mystery is regarded by these transcendentalists as impenetrable. *"Die Causalität—ist selbst causal entstanden?"* reveals the essential futility of all attempts to account for the evolution of reason.

Possibility of a Tentative Theory.

IN spite of the difficulties and dangers of the enterprise, it is not to be believed that the attempt to reach an understanding of the evolution of speech from natural cries can be abandoned, or even indefinitely postponed. Some tentative theory of its genesis is essential to the development of an adequate psychology of language. With the attitude of transcendentalism just mentioned we need feel little sympathy. That we must perforce use our human intelligence, such as it is, to investigate the evolution of intelligence, is true, but can scarcely be taken as serious ground for refusing to make the attempt. The empirical difficulties in the way are on a different footing. But the lack of direct data, while it is a formidable obstacle, is not necessarily an insuperable one, provided sufficient indirect data are available. The hope of a successful theory of the evolutionary genesis of speech lies in casting the net widely enough, in bringing to bear upon the subject converging lines of evidence from widely different fields. And the test of any proposed theory must lie in the light it sheds upon the many closely related problems.

The building up of an adequate theory of the evolution of language—and of human intelligence, for the two are bound together—must be the work of many years and of many workers. Nothing definitive can be accomplished at present. Yet this does not mean that no tentative theory can profitably be advanced now. It may be the part of prudence, but it is not really the part of wisdom, to wait until all the data are accumulated and the evidence all in, before we try to theorize. The only danger in speculation lies in mistaking our formulations for established facts. Nor is tentative speculation a mere harmless diversion. Satisfactory theories do not spring full-fledged from a complete mass of empirical data as from the brow of Jove, but grow by gradual modifica-

8

tions and corrections of less satisfactory generalizations. Moreover, and this is the essential point, the real usefulness of theory lies in the fact that it sets specific problems to research, and directs attention to aspects and details which would otherwise remain unnoticed.

The Traditional Conception of Language: its Futility.

THE conviction that what is needed beyond everything else at the present time is precisely a reformulation of the problem of language in terms which will throw the whole subject into fresh and revealing relief and will set new and fruitful problems to research, has inspired the present undertaking. For what has stood in the way of formulating even a plausible theory of the origin of speech and has obscured the whole subject of the relation of speech to thought, has been first and foremost a certain metaphysical presupposition as to the sort of phenomenon language is. Language, we find it reiterated in one treatise and article after another, is the *means of expressing or communicating ideas.* Now this might seem to be an obvious enough statement, and as innocent as obvious. But it is not. The trouble does not lie in the fact that men have begun their investigations of the subject with a ready-made definition instead of waiting until the end to formulate one on the basis of their findings. One must inevitably begin an investigation with some preconception as to the sort of thing one is to investigate, if only for purposes of identification. The trouble in this case lies in the essential sterility of the preconception. It is doubtless true enough that language, at least in its highly evolved forms, does serve

9

to communicate ideas and thoughts. But to assume that this is its original and fundamental function is hopelessly to intellectualize it, and to divorce it, as something merely external, from the essential business of living and thinking. For why should ideas be expressed or communicated? Why, to go deeper, should the very having of ideas depend on the possibility of expressing them? Speech must be envisaged as effecting something vital in the practical life of men, as performing some objective and observable function, before one can hope to discern the factors which have led to its development, or even the source of its interdependence with thought. To state the problem of the evolution of speech and of its relation to thought in terms of the traditional preconception, is, whatever the ultimate metaphysical truth may be, to state it in essentially insoluble form. In the first place, language, as the means of expressing or communicating *ideas,* is contrasted with the inarticulate cries of animals, which, it is held, are expressions of mere *feelings,* or *emotions.* Thus any theory of the evolution of language from animal cries must first account for the evolution of ideas from mere feelings. In the second place, ideas are tacitly assumed to be prior to their means of expression. But the truth is, of course, that there exists no communicable content except in so far as its mode of expression is already developed.

Wundt's Treatment of Language.

THE inherent futility of the traditional conception shows itself very clearly in Wundt's lengthy treatment in the volume of his *Völkerpsychologie* entitled *Die Sprache*. Wundt's treatment is particularly instructive because he makes perfectly explicit what is involved in the conception of language as a means of expression. He states clearly the impossibility of supposing that thought could have come before language. The whole question of priority he dismisses as on a par with the controversy over the hen and the egg. The development of speech and the development of thought are related, he affirms, as two complementary aspects of a single process of evolution. But the relationship of speech and thought thus becomes in effect a typical *parallelism*, and as such an ultimate mystery. Thus, according to Wundt, it is a fundamental datum of psychology that every mental content, whether affective or ideational, is accompanied by bodily movements, which in their form are an adequate expression of the inner process. Language, whether vocal speech or gesture, is merely a specialized form of correlative bodily movement. "What holds in this respect for the psychical functions generally, holds also for the expressive movements which belong to them as their natural complements; and speech, accordingly, is nothing else than that form of expressive movements which is adequate for the stage of development of human consciousness."[1] The fact that speech and the capacity for conceptual thought have developed together sets no particular problem to Wundt's thought. It belongs to the character of a rational being such as man to express himself in the symbolic form of language, just as it belongs to

[1] W. Wundt, *Die Sprache*, Vol. II, p. 636.

the nature of a pig to grunt or of a bird to sing. Nothing short of explaining how man comes to be man can explain how man comes to speak. The special problem of language, in short, is not insoluble, but insignificant.

Just as it is natural for Wundt, as for all who hold his general psychological position, to classify speech as a form of bodily activity correlative to, but essentially independent of, the processes of the mind, so it is equally natural for him to relegate to a place of secondary importance the relation of speech to distinctively human social phenomena. The fact that without speech there could have been no division of labor, no government, no religion, no morality, in short, no civilization, is apparently not regarded by Wundt as significant for a psychology of speech. The part that speech has played in social evolution is merely a by-product of its development in the individual. It is recognized, to be sure, that individuals could not have developed the power of speech except in connection with one another, and that the history of language has been modified by the influence of the institutions of society. But these facts are not conceived to throw any light upon the problem how human speech arose from the cries of animals, or how it is related to conceptual thought. So long as feelings and thoughts are conceived as "inner" processes taking place in the individual and constituting his "mind," the only consistent mode of conceiving speech is as the expression of these inner processes in the form of bodily movements.

It is characteristic of Wundt's mode of thought to regard the *expression* of ideas as the fundamental function of speech. The communication of them to others is a merely secondary and almost accidental result. This view is clearly expressed in the following passage. "Psychophysical manifestations of life, among which speech is to be included as a special peculiarly developed form, we designate, according to their general concept, as 'movements of expression.' . . . If this is the definition which belongs to movements of expression in general, it is usual to regard the following characteristic as that which distinguishes speech from other similar movements—namely, that it can serve, through the expression of ideas, as the *communication of thought*. This characteristic, however, does not mark any absolute distinctiveness of speech, since other movements of expression are frequently accompanied by ideational indications, and since, on the other hand, speech is able to express feelings as well as ideas. The communication of thought is always, therefore, a merely possible end, which is not necessarily realized in every single utterance of speech. In addition, a particular thought may often take on verbal form in connections which exclude not only the purpose, but the possibility of communication."[1]

Wundt does not, of course, leave the problem here. But the working-out of his theory of the beginnings of speech is predetermined by his general metaphysical position. Oral speech has arisen, according to him, as a modification of more general expressive movements of the body which constituted a sort of primitive gesture-

---

[1] W. Wundt, *Die Sprache*, Vol. I, p. 37.

language. These early expressive movements and cries, such as we may observe among animals, express chiefly emotion and affection. But since affective and cognitive elements are both present in every conscious state, the expressive movements, even of animals, represent in some degree cognitive content. Later, as the ideational side of consciousness develops, it is inevitable that it should manifest itself in appropriate movements. The pointing of the little child at objects of interest, and the tentative movements of the hands in tracing the outlines of objects, are cases in point. The *communication* of content to others Wundt accounts for chiefly by the operation of sympathetic response and imitation. The movements expressive of emotionally tinged ideas arouse by sympathy similar emotional states and similar ideational content in others, and these mental processes are in turn expressed in the same or slightly different movements. Thus one has intercommunication established. Wundt adds that the transition to the peculiarly human stage of development, at which there is a real communication of *ideas* in speech proper, is doubtless facilitated by the simultaneous development of voluntary action and the intention to make oneself intelligible to others. Such is the machinery that he has at his disposal.

Wundt's account is particularly interesting, because he exploits so consistently the theoretical possibilities of his initial conception. He is probably the most self-consciously metaphysical of the modern writers on the psychology of language. The weakness of his treatment, however, does not lie chiefly in the fact that it is metaphysical, but rather in the sterility of his metaphysical preconceptions for the treatment of the problem. In its details the actual treatment is empirical enough. There are pages devoted to minute physiological investigation of the reactions of facial muscles to pleasant and unpleasant stimuli, for example, to say nothing of the lengthy treatment of philological material. Other writers, who have been less consciously metaphysical, have not been therefore more successful in dealing with the problem; nor have they, indeed, escaped the insidious influence of the same metaphysical dualism. In truth, there is no escaping the metaphysical preconceptions of one's age by shutting one's eyes to them and vainly endeavoring to proceed by purely empirical means.

Further Illustrations of the Traditional Conception.

In order that the reader may realize how widespread and persistent this mode of thinking about language is, the following passages have been selected almost at random from representative writers on the subject—philologists, psychologists, and anthropologists. Similar quotations might be multiplied almost indefinitely.

"Language may be defined as the expression of thought by means of speech-sounds."[1]

"Language may be briefly and comprehensively defined as the means of expression of human thought. In a wider and freer sense, everything that bodies forth thought and makes it apprehensible, in whatever way,

[1] Henry Sweet, The History of Language, Chap. I.

is called language. . . . But for scientific purposes the term needs restriction, since it would apply else to nearly all human action and product which discloses the thought that gave it birth. Language, then, signifies rather certain instrumentalities whereby men consciously and with intention represent their thought, to the end, chiefly, of making it known to other men: it is expression for the sake of communication."[1]

"In order to evoke in one mind a train of ideas corresponding to one which has taken its rise in another mind, the mind can do nothing but create by the action of the motor nerves a physical product, which on its side calls forth the corresponding ideas, correspondingly associated in the mind of the other individual by exciting his sensitive nerves. The most important of the physical products which serve this purpose are precisely the sounds of language. Besides these, there are the tones of other kinds, facial expressions, gestures, pictures, etc.

"The means by which these physical products are qualified to serve as a medium for transmitting ideas to another individual is either *an inner and direct reference* to the ideas in question (as for instance, a cry of pain, a gesture of passion), or *a connection depending on an association of ideas,* in which process the idea standing in direct relation to the physical instrument forms the connecting link between this and the idea imparted; this is the case with language."[2]

[1] W. D. Whitney, *Life and Growth of Language*, p. 1.
[2] Hermann Paul, *Principles of the History of Language*, translated by H. A. Strong, p. xxxviii.

"In studying the means of expression among men in stages of mental culture far below our own, one of our first needs is to clear our minds of the kind of superstitious veneration with which articulate speech has so commonly been treated, as though it were not merely the principal but the sole means of uttering thought. We must cease to measure the historical importance of emotional exclamations, of gesture signs, and of picture-writing, by their comparative insignificance in modern civilized life, but must bring ourselves to associate the articulate words of the dictionary in one group with cries and gestures and pictures, as being all of them means of manifesting outwardly the inward workings of the mind."[1]

"The essence of language lies, not in the use of this or that special means of communication, but in the employment of fixed associations (however these may have originated) in order that something now sensible—a spoken word, a picture, a gesture, or what not—may call up the 'idea' of something else. Whenever this is done, what is now sensible may be called a 'sign' or 'symbol,' and that of which it is intended to call up the 'idea' may be called its 'meaning.' "[2]

"What they [languages] do, may be expressed as conveying images and their relations to one another; or, in other words, what is sought, is to reproduce what is in the speaker's mind, within that of the hearer. Since, however, it is only ideas and relations between them

[1] E. B. Tylor, *Primitive Culture*, pp. 210 f.
[2] Bertrand Russell, *The Analysis of Mind*, p. 191.

that are experienced, all that is required of the mechanism in question is, that it is able to qualify each of these to the degree required by the situation."[1]

"The way is now cleared for a serviceable definition of language. Language is a purely human and non-instinctive method of communicating ideas, emotions, and desires by means of a system of voluntarily produced symbols."[2]

"I have already pointed out that the essence of language consists in the assigning of conventional, voluntarily articulated sounds, or their equivalents, to the diverse elements of experience."[3]

"The elements of language, the symbols that ticket off experience, must therefore be associated with whole groups, delimited classes, of experience rather than with the single experiences themselves. Only so is communication possible, for the single experience lodges in an individual consciousness and is, strictly speaking, incommunicable. To be communicated it needs to be referred to a class which is tacitly accepted by the community as an identity. . . . In other words, the speech element 'house' is the symbol, first and foremost, not of a single perception, nor even of the notion of a particular object, but of a 'concept,' in other words, of a convenient capsule of thought that embraces thousands of distinct experiences and that is ready to take in thousands more. If the single significant elements of speech are the symbols of concepts, the actual flow of speech

[1] C. Wissler, *Man and Culture*, p. 83.
[2] Edward Sapir, *Language*, pp. 6 f.
[3] *Op. cit.*, p. 10.

18

may be interpreted as a record of the setting of these concepts into mutual relations."[1]

The Objective Function of Speech.

WHAT is primarily needed for the successful study of the psychology of speech is a deliberate setting aside, if not an abandonment, of the metaphysical dualism which can conceive speech only as an external physical manifestation of inner psychical processes. What is needed is a fresh conception of speech as an essential activity of human life, fulfilling an indispensable function in the economy of life. It is in the light of this function that the causes and course of its development must be sought. And it must equally be in the light of this function that an insight into its relation to conceptual thought is to be hoped for; nay more, that a new and deeper insight into the nature and place of conceptual thought itself may be attained.

Once we deliberately ask the question:—*What does speech do? What objective function does it perform in human life?*—the answer is not far to seek. Speech is the great medium through which human coöperation is brought about. It is the means by which the diverse activities of men are coördinated and correlated with each other for the attainment of common and reciprocal ends. Men do not speak simply to relieve their feelings or to air their views, but to awaken a response in their fellows and to influence their attitudes and acts. It is further the means by which men are brought into a new

[1] *Op. cit.*, pp. 11 f.

19

and momentous relationship with the external world, the very relationship which makes the world for them an objective order.[1]

Human speech has become the most complex and highly specialized of all vital functions; but the clue to the labyrinth of its complex forms lies in the fundamental function of social coördination it continues to perform. That it has itself become one of the chief human activities which it serves to correlate and coördinate, does not affect its fundamental nature, although it vastly complicates it. It is indeed the outstanding peculiarity of the function of speech that it is capable of this quasi-independence and self-determination. It marks in the evolution of life and mind a development as critical as the appearance of the distance-receptors.

Relation of Speech to the Animal Cry.

FROM the vantage-point of the conception of speech as a means of social coördination, we may consider its relation to the cries of animals. These have commonly been regarded as expressions of emotions. But the question arises, Why should an emotional state find expression in just this form? What function do the cries uttered in rage or fear or tenderness perform in the life-economy of animals? In a general way we know that the mani-

[1] During the last few years there have been signs of a reawakened interest in language and of a new attitude toward the whole subject. A point of view similar to that just indicated has been adopted by a number of important writers. Among them are Pierre Janet in *Les médications psychologiques*, Malinowski in the supplementary essay appended to Ogden and Richards's *Meaning of Meaning*, John Dewey in *Experience and Nature*, and G. H. Mead in various articles in the philo-

THE PROBLEM OF ORIGIN

festation of strong feeling on the part of one animal tends to interest and excite other animals of the same species and to bring out more or less definite responses from them. The cries and the accompanying behavior of animals do serve, in varying manners and degrees, to stimulate and control the behavior of individuals with reference to each other, on the one hand, and with reference to the objective situation, on the other hand. The problem which we have before us, then, is to compare and differentiate the type of social control effected by the cries of animals with that effected by speech in human society.

sophical journals. All of these writers except the first mentioned have published their views since this chapter was originally written. Occasional passages to a similar effect are also found in much earlier writers.

But it is one thing to recognize the truth of a general principle, and a very different thing to apply the principle persistently and systematically, above all when this must be done in opposition to a firmly established tradition. So far as the present writer is aware, there has been no attempt to apply the conception of speech as a mode of action, and not merely of expression, to the problems presented by the evolution of language-structure, on the one hand, and of human intelligence, on the other.

CHAPTER II

The Restatement of the Problem

The Expression of the Emotions.

ALTHOUGH there have been, since the time of Darwin, various studies of the expression of the emotions, on the one hand, and of the cries of animals and calls of birds on the other, interest has for the most part been directed to aspects of these phenomena with which we are not here chiefly concerned. And this fact is not without significance. As regards the so-called expressions of the emotions, as distinguished from the larger total responses, these have been viewed chiefly from the physiological point of view. The functions which they have been conceived to perform have been physiological rather than social; and their survival value has been sought in their immediate serviceableness to the individual rather than in their utility to the group. They have been thought of primarily as "expressions" of the emotional state, as vents through which the surplus energy finds release. There have been exceptions to this. The snarl which bares the teeth is, it has often been pointed out, not only a preparation for biting, but an intimidating threat to the enemy. And other instances might be cited.[1]

---

[1] For a discussion and criticism of Darwin's work on the expression of the emotions, in which the social function of the expression is clearly brought out, see Wallace Craig, "A Note on Darwin's Work on the Expression of the Emotions in Men and Animals," *Journal of Abnormal Psychology and Social Psychology*, Vol. XVI, p. 356.

SPEECH: ITS FUNCTION AND DEVELOPMENT

The Animal Cry as a Means of Social Control.

As regards the cries of animals and the songs of birds, it has of course been recognized in a general way that these serve to stimulate and control the behavior of others of the group. The songs of birds in particular, being a secondary sex characteristic of the male, have been supposed to be a means of attracting the female, and to owe their development and specialization to this function. But, with only one noteworthy exception, so far as the present writer has been able to ascertain, no systematic study of the cries of either animals or birds has been made with a view to discovering (1) the specific external stimuli and conditions which excite the different cries of a species, (2) the other responses in connection with which the cries occur, and (3) the nature of the responses which they stimulate in other members of the group. The exception referred to is so important, however, that it will repay somewhat detailed consideration. It is the study of the behavior of pigeons made by C. O. Whitman and Wallace Craig, results of which have been published in various places.[1]

The social organization of the species particularly studied by Craig, the blond ringdove, is, he states, so flexible and adaptable that it cannot be accounted for in terms of simple instinctive machinery. Each dove is an

[1] For Whitman's work the reader is referred to the posthumous volume, *The Behavior of Pigeons*, edited by H. A. Carr. Craig's study was made on Whitman's collection of pigeons, and he acknowledges his debt to Whitman. We shall be chiefly concerned with a paper by Craig entitled "The Voices of Pigeons Regarded as a Means of Social Control," *American Journal of Sociology*, 1908.

individual free to change its relations to other members of the society. So long as the status of an individual does remain fixed and a dove remains constant to its mate, it does so as the result of mutual influences of social control, among which song is an important factor. The life of the adult pigeon is a succession of cycles of reproductive activity, beginning with courtship and ending with the abandonment of the independent young. In these activities both male and female take a constant part. After the elaborate ceremonial of courtship (which includes searching for a nesting-site, carrying straws, toying with straws, etc.) has terminated in successful copulation, both male and female coöperate in the final choice of a site and the building of a nest. Both take turns in brooding, and when the young are hatched, the male as well as the female plays his part in feeding them, secreting in his crop also the "pigeon's milk." Now it is evident that the successful accomplishment of this long and complicated cycle depends on the synchronizing of the physiological states and the behavior of the male and female. This synchronizing is effected, Craig shows, by the reciprocal stimulating of each bird by the behavior, and particularly by the calls, of the other. Of course the physiological state and the activities of one stage are themselves appropriate stimuli for the next stage; *e.g.*, nest-building and egg-laying for brooding. But if it were not for the influence of the behavior of one bird on the other, the stages of one might lag behind those of the other. A certain measure of coöperation must also be secured. For example, the couple must agree as to the choice of a nesting-site and coöperate in the work of building the nest. When one of the birds has finally hit upon a spot which pleases him, he sits down and utters the characteristic "nest-call." His mate then joins him and "both sit together in the chosen spot and call and caress one another for a long period. Then one bird, usually the female, remains in the nest to build and fashion it, while the other bird flies off in search of building material. Each time the male returns with a straw, the female welcomes him with a low, complacent cooing, and an affectionate flutter of the wings; which must serve to confirm still further the union of the birds and the choice of a nesting-site."[1]

Once the young are hatched, a new source of control is added. Their movements against the breast of the parent bird, the fluttering of their wings, and above all the urgent "food-call," act as powerful stimuli to the secretion of the "pigeon's milk" in the crops of the parents and to the act of feeding. Not less important is the reciprocal influence which the voices and behavior of the older birds have over the behavior of the young.

Outside the family, the voices of pigeons have also a function to perform in social control. Conflicts are frequent, especially between males, and these are rarely decided by mere physical strength and prowess, but rather through a duel of elaborate cooing and gesturing, in which the superior determination of one combatant usually serves to put the other to flight, without resort to physical combat. This determination, which finds expression in the gesturing and cooing of the birds,

[1] Wallace Craig, *op. cit.*, p. 93.

26

Use is necessarily ambiguous in respect to purpose.

So two serve, 34, things compulsion on the account is purposive.

is not dependent on physical superiority, but often to a large extent on the situation. Thus, a gentle female, protecting her own nest, will often rout a much larger and stronger bird. Similarly, attacks of birds on their own home grounds are comparatively rare, and are met with the expression of such determined resistance in the cries of the defender that they are very seldom carried out.

Craig's whole study is most interesting and valuable. Of particular interest to us are his general conclusions. Characteristic calls go with each stage of the pigeon's life and play an important social rôle. The uses of song, says Craig, are so numerous and so complexly interrelated that a complete list of them could not be made. A partial list of them, however, is given by him as follows:

"1. Personal control; as that of the male over his mate.

"2. Suggestion; as the nest-call coo quickly brings the mate, the challenge coo causes the enemy to flee.

"3. Stimulation; as working up both male and female to the point of pairing, inducing oviposition in the female.

"4. Inhibition; as inhibiting adultery, inhibiting the use of nesting-sites other than the one chosen, inhibiting copulation out of the normal time.

"5. Coördination in space; as leading male and female to use the same nest.

"6. Coördination in time; as leading male and female to go through the brooding activities synchronously.

"7. To proclaim: (a) the bird's species; (b) the bird's sex; (c) the bird's individual identity; (d) the bird's rights.

"8. Tradition; as when an experienced bird is mated with an inexperienced one, the former takes the lead."[1]

Unfortunately, we have no such investigation of the part played by the varied and characteristic cries of any species of gregarious mammals in their group life. The scanty observations which have been made of the chattering of anthropoid apes have, for the most part, like those of Garner, been uncritical in character. Even the few observations made by competent scientists have had no such object as have those of Craig. There would be great difficulties in the way of a systematic study of the vocal behavior of anthropoid apes with a view to discovering the part it plays in social control within the group. It obviously could not be carried on with an isolated individual or two, but would need a colony of apes living under natural conditions.[2] Yet the scientific

[1] *Op. cit.*, p. 99.

[2] An interesting beginning has been made in the study of two young chimpanzees by Robert M. Yerkes and Blanche W. Learned: *Chimpanzee Intelligence and its Vocal Expressions*. W. Köhler, in *The Mentality of Apes*, describes a few gestures, particularly various forms of greeting, but dismisses the subject of cries with only a few words. I quote the most significant passage. "It is difficult to describe the methods of intercommunication among these animals, apart from their greetings. It may be taken as positively proved that their gamut of *phonetics* is entirely 'subjective,' and can only express emotions, never designate or describe objects. But they have so many phonetic elements which are also common to human languages, that their lack of articulate speech cannot be ascribed to *secondary* (glosso-labial) limitations. Their gestures too, of face and body like their expression in sound, never designate or 'describe' objects (Bühler)" (p. 317).

28

value of such a study would be so great that we may hope it will be undertaken at no distant date. It would be easier, though of less value for purposes of comparison with human speech, to study the vocal behavior of packs of hunting dogs; but so far as the writer has been able to discover, no such study has ever been made. The peculiar value of such a study would be largely in the fact that the members of the group coöperate in attaining a common end, and that this coöperation is brought about in large measure by cries.

It is of course impossible to attempt, on the basis of such scanty data as are available, any detailed comparison of the social control effected by the cries of animals with that effected by human speech. But attention may be called to certain outstanding features of the type of control which animal cries exercise.

Characteristics of the Cry: (1) Its Physiological Conditions.

In the case of pigeons, a determining condition for the utterance of a characteristic call is, in most cases, a specific physiological state. Thus each of the stages of reproductive activity has its own characteristic call. But while a specific physiological state is a predetermining condition for the giving of a call, there is usually necessary an immediate stimulus to set off the total response. Thus the presence of the female, or of a particular female, is necessary to set off the complicated activities of the behavior of courtship with its characteristic coo; but if the mating period is past and the nest is in process of construction, or if the young are already hatched, the presence of the female no longer stimulates courtship. In short, two factors must usually coöperate to produce a specific call—a predetermining physiological state and the adequate external stimulus. There are partial exceptions, however, even in the case of pigeons. Some stimuli are relatively independent of specific physiological state. Thus aggressive behavior on the part of another male usually tends to bring out an answering response of hostile activity with its challenge coo whether the attacked bird is courting or nest-building or feeding its young. The vigor and determination of the defensive hostility evoked, as manifested in the vocal duet which ensues, will, however, vary considerably with circumstances. The alarm-call, too, is largely independent of the physiological condition. An adequate external stimulus (such as a large bird flying overhead) may excite the alarm-call in whatever stage of reproductive activity the bird may be.[1] The utterance of the call will undoubtedly vary with other external conditions making up the total situation. These may be such as to inhibit it entirely, or to cause it to be repeated more or less vigorously. Generally speaking, the situation in which the individual is placed, *i.e.*, his relative position with reference to other individuals and objects of his environment, plays a most important part in regulating the vocal behavior.

As a general thing, it may safely be said that the cries

[1] It is to be observed, however, that an incubating or brooding dove shows a remarkable tendency to keep still and quiet, and that when the alarm-call is given by the bird on the nest, it is generally in a subdued tone, while the accompanying behavior is also much modified. I am indebted to a personal letter from Dr. Craig for this note.

of the gregarious mammals are less closely bound up with specific physiological states than is the case with the pigeons. Hunger in the young, sexual excitement in the adult, especially in the male, the secretion of milk in the suckling mother, are indeed very general pre-determining conditions for the uttering of characteristic cries. But the cries of hunting dogs, for example, are determined rather by external circumstances than by physiological condition.

(2) *The Cry as a Stimulus.*

So far, we have considered only the causes which operate to produce the utterance of cries. We must now consider the effects different cries have on the behavior of other members of the group. Instead of regarding the cry as a response to a stimulus, we must now regard it as a stimulus to a response in others. The first thing to be noted is that just as each characteristic call of the pigeon tends to arise from a specific physiological state, so each call tends to bring out a specific type-response in others. Thus the hunger-call of the young is a powerful stimulus to the feeding-response on the part of the parents. Even after the older birds have begun to show indifference toward their offspring, the insistent repeated call of hunger will rouse them to their neglected duty. The coo of courtship from the male induces receptive response on the part of the female, and the coo of alarm excites the typical fear-response in those who hear it.

Examination shows that the responses evoked by different calls may be divided into two classes: those which, like the response of feeding to the hunger-call of the young, or the receptive attitude of the female to the male's coo of courtship, are *responses directed immediately to the individual uttering the call;* others, notably the fear-response, evoked by the coo of alarm, are directed not so much to the individual uttering the call, as *to the external stimulus of the call itself.* In pigeons, as universally among gregarious animals, the alarm-cry brings out the same type-response as does the perception of the danger itself. From the accounts of Whitman and Craig, the nest-call acts primarily as a stimulus to the bird to join its mate. It also seems, however, to play a part in stimulating the search for straws in building the nest, and also to induce one bird to relieve its mate in sitting on the eggs. Among mammals, other calls than the alarm signal excite responses appropriate to the presence of the objective conditions which evoke the cry. Certain cries, that is, *proclaim* to the other members of the group the presence of danger, or enemy, or prey.

The central distinguishing feature of animal cries is their direct connection with specific type-responses. Instead of saying that they express feelings or emotions, we may say that they occur as elements of such responses.[1] A characteristic cry accompanies, or forms an integral part of, a specific attitude or activity. Even when a given cry, like the call of alarm, is a response to a definite object or event, it occurs as an element in the total response to the external stimulus. Only such

---

[1] For a discussion of the psychological status of the type-response, see Part II, Chap. II.

A function is a doing, a performing. And perform (through G. ~~form~~ ~~form~~ pramjan (cf. O.?.penuman)) is Latin per + fram = form.

So to perform is to through-form.

RESTATEMENT OF THE PROBLEM

objects and events as stand in direct affective relationship to the individual (such as "danger" or "prey") call out characteristic cries. Thus while certain cries may be said to "proclaim" the presence of some object or event, there is usually no precise discrimination of the particular sort of object beyond its general property of "dangerousness," etc. It is indeed rather the situation as a whole than any particular element of it that is proclaimed by the animal cry.

(3) *The Social Function of the Cry.*

CONSIDERED as modes of response, cries, which, like the alarm-call, proclaim the presence of some interesting thing, present characteristics which are of great importance for our study. Usually a response initiated by a stimulus external to the organism has for its end some readjustment of the individual to his environment. Flight, for example, changes the position of the individual with reference to the source of danger; attack serves to destroy or otherwise to remove the source of offense, etc. But the utterance of the alarm-call has no such end. It does not, except in a very indirect way, bring about a readjustment of the animal uttering the call to the external condition which evoked it. It functions to stimulate an activity in *another* individual or individuals which shall serve to adjust *them* to the external condition. Conversely, too, the cry of alarm viewed as a stimulus is similarly peculiar, for it does not excite a response to *itself*, but to a third thing, to which the stimulating cry stands in the peculiar relation of sign to thing signified. The psychological im-

33

portance of this three-cornered relationship will be considered later.

There are cases where the cry of alarm, for example, does seem to proclaim something more specific than mere danger. Thus Darwin in *The Descent of Man* cites Houzeau as authority for the observation that fowls have distinctive calls of alarm for a danger which, like a bird of prey, threatens from the sky, and one which is approaching on the ground.[1] It is to be remarked that where such a discrimination occurs in alarm-calls, each distinctive call serves as a signal for a specifically different response on the part of those hearing the call.

The same direct connection of cry and specific type-response is to be observed in the way in which the cries are responded to by other members of the group. They stimulate or inhibit chiefly, if not exclusively, type-responses. They arouse hostility or sexual excitement, they summon or drive away, or they set off such responses as feeding or brooding. The specificity and uniformity of the responses they evoke are correlative to the content they may be said to proclaim. If the song of the pigeon, as Craig says, proclaims on occasion the bird's species or sex or individuality or rights, this is tantamount to saying that it tends to evoke in other pigeons the specific attitude and response appropriate to the occasion.

The type of social control effected by animal cries is correlated with the relative simplicity of behavior of which the species is capable. The cycle of activities which constitute the life of the pigeon is relatively fixed and

[1] *Op. cit.*, chap. III.

invariable. The objective situations which the pigeon has to meet are comparatively simple and few, and the repertoire of responses at his command, with which to meet the exigencies of life, is correspondingly limited. So also the relations he sustains to other members of the group fall within the limits of well-recognized types; the common ends in the attainment of which coöperation is possible are the immediate necessities for the propagation of the species and the preservation of the group. Nevertheless, as Craig observes, it is because the organization of pigeon society is too flexible and adaptable to be regulated by simple instinctive machinery, that the more varied control by song is needed.

Speech Compared with the Animal Cry: Its Relative Independence.

If now we compare speech with animals' cries, we find that it presents a sharp contrast to them on all the points we have just considered, but that it is, nevertheless, a mode of behavior which performs a similar function.

In the first place, speech does not, like the cry, occur as a mere element in a larger response. On the contrary, it is an independent form of behavior. A man may talk whether he is active or idle. Moreover, what he is doing bears no direct or necessary connection with what he is saying. Speech differs further from the cry in its independence of the emotional state of the speaker. While this is not true of such lower forms of speech as ejaculations and swearing, it is characteristic of the typical higher forms of speech.

35

Speech as a Response to Objects.

SECONDLY, speech offers a significant contrast to the cry in the relations it bears to the conditions which evoke it. Characteristic cries are called out, we have just seen, only by circumstances which have a direct affective value for the animal. Speech, on the contrary, is or may be evoked by things or events which have only the most indirect "interest" for the speaker, and to which he may remain affectively indifferent. Furthermore, the cry, so far as it "proclaims" at all, is able to announce only the general sort of situation—like "danger" or "prey"—while speech may *specify* and *analyze* the situation. The characteristic feature of human speech is that instead of being, like the cry, a response to a total situation having a direct affective value for the individual, it is a complex response, capable of discriminating the objective elements making up the situation, together with the relations these bear, both to the individuals concerned, and to each other. Instead of being limited, like the alarm cry, to the mere proclamation of "danger," speech may announce, *e.g.*, "There is a fire in the next block and the wind is blowing in this direction." So also, instead of proclaiming, like the animal cry, mere friendliness or triumph, speech may announce in advance the acts in which the speaker intends to show his friendliness, or it may relate the victorious deeds of the past. The correlation between the speech-response and its objective conditions is a correlation between independently variable elements of response and independently variable elements of the external situation, or of past or future events.

The Forms of Speech as Means of Social Control.

THAT speech is used to influence the behavior of others is, of course, evident. That this is its essential function, and that the characteristic structure of language has evolved from the animal cry in order to meet the needs of expanding group life, it is our purpose to show in the succeeding pages. Here we shall only point out certain significant points of contrast between the type of social control exercised by speech and that exercised by the cry. For this purpose it will be convenient to consider separately the three fundamental forms of speech-response—or of language structure—the *declaration*, the *command*, and the *question*.

The question is a specialized instrument for calling out a reciprocal *verbal* response. It ordinarily serves to elicit speech in others and not bodily action. The question belongs, as we shall show later, to that stage of language development where speech, in the form of *conversation*, is a sort of independent reciprocal behavior carried on by two or more individuals. The question has a suggestive prototype in those animal calls which tend to elicit answering calls rather than what we shall henceforth term "primary" behavior. The question does often lead to primary behavior, but it does so only indirectly, through the reply.

The declaration and the command are both, in their simplest form, instruments for the control of primary behavior, although in characteristically different ways.

Elicit from elicere, draw forth, from e - and lacere, entice, allure; cognate with laqueus, 'noose', deliciae, delight, charm. Cf. delicious and lace.

Entice, fr. enticier, prov. orig. meant 'set on fire'. Lat. titio, a burning brand.

They constitute differentiations of the simple type of control exercised by the cry. The cry of alarm, for example, serves at once and indiscriminately to "proclaim" danger and to "command" flight. It "proclaims" danger in that it serves to call attention to something dangerous in the objective situation. It "commands" flight or concealment in that it serves to elicit this response on the part of those to whom the cry is directed. It is precisely because the cry does play this double rôle that it is neither a true declaration nor a true command. And it is able and even obliged thus to proclaim and command indistinguishably because the animals which use it have so limited a range of appropriate behavior at their disposal. The proclamation of danger in language is a *declaration* and not a *cry*, just because, while like the cry it directs attention to the objective situation which evokes it, *it does not tend to elicit any single type of response.* Yet the language proclamation does serve to call out some sort of responsive behavior. The announcement by an Indian scout that he has found the ashes of a camp fire, or that he has sighted buffalo, is as truly to be regarded as the stimulus of the resulting behavior of the camp, as is the alarm-call of a bird which puts the flock to flight. The crucial difference between the two lies in the fact that the cry is a direct stimulus to a single, relatively invariable type of behavior, while the announcement is a conditional stimulus to a response which varies from occasion to occasion and from individual to individual in the group. The announcement by the Indian scout that he has sighted buffalo does not immediately and unconditionally lead to action on the part of the

RESTATEMENT OF THE PROBLEM

group. It may be ignored if circumstances are, for various reasons, unfavorable for undertaking a hunt. Moreover, when it does initiate a hunt, the particular behavior to which it leads differs widely from individual to individual and from class to class within the tribe. Custom plays its part in determining the particular form the response takes; so also do the particular circumstances in which the group finds itself—its position with reference to the game, the nature of the ground, etc. The proclamation, then, is a determinant of behavior, but it is *conditional* and *indirect*. Its very conditionality and indirectness, as we shall see later, measure the range and flexibility of the control which speech may exercise over behavior.

The declaration we may conceive, accordingly, as arising from a differentiation and specialization of the *proclamatory* aspect of the animal cry. The command, on the other hand, is a corresponding differentiation and specialization of the *imperative* aspect of the cry. Like the cry, the command serves to elicit a particular response on the part of the one to whom it is directed. But while the cry prompts only to a type-response bound up with an affective attitude, the command prompts to a determinate and particular *act*, which may form an element in a course of action, and which may be performed independently of the affective state of the actor. The cry, again, acts as a direct *stimulus* to the response, while the verbal command prompts to the act it designates only *conditionally*. The chick may, to be sure, disregard the summoning "cluck" of the mother hen, but it normally comes when called. The child, on the

39

contrary, is—or may be—almost as likely to disobey as to obey the "Come here" of his mother. The immediate urgency of the cluck is partly a matter of instinct, but it has been reinforced by a uniform experience; so that the "cluck" is not a bare and uninviting "come," but a promise as well of appetizing worm or brooding warmth. The "come," on the contrary, makes no instinctive appeal except through the tone in which it is uttered, and whether it holds promise or threat depends on a variable experience and the particular circumstances under which it is heard by the child.

Like most specializations of function, the declaration and the command are mutually dependent. They supplement each other. Because the declaration is so indirect in its influence on behavior, it needs the command with its direct connection of word and act, to supplement it. It is often, indeed, through the mediation of the command that the declaration functions in its control of behavior. That is, a declaration made by one individual evokes directly a speech-response from another individual, in the form of a command which in turn evokes primary action. The following trivial examples show how natural is the sequence of declaration and command in common life: "It is raining, Mother." "Very well, put on your rubbers." "The baking powder is all used up, ma'am." "Then make an apple pie instead of the cake." "Union Pacific has risen six points." "Sell out at once."

These two forms of language, the proclamation (or declaration) and the command, represent two complementary phases of the functioning of speech as a means

Belonging to the cross roads or common streets. Hence commonplace.

40

of social control. Both forms act as conditional determinants of response. The proclamation orients others for action by calling to their attention, in a representative way, the relevant factors of the objective situation—the setting in which action is to take place. The command stimulates, more or less effectively, to a definite act, simple or complex, or to a definite modification of acts already in progress. Both of these phases of control are made possible by the fact that speech is itself a form of complex behavior composed of variable elements of response which are permanently correlated with independently variable elements of the objective situation.

In this schematic analysis of the complex function of speech no account has been taken of many features which are to be treated later. In particular, no account has been taken of the relative independence of speech-behavior, as a result of which *conversation* is developed, in which the speech of one party is alternately stimulus and response to the speech of the other, and which may be carried on without reference to the immediate surroundings. This represents a late stage in the evolution of language, and to have considered it here would have been hopelessly to complicate the statement of our problem.

The Problem Restated.

If we are right, it is to the great superiority of speech over animal cries as a means of *social control* that we must look for the chief cause of its evolutionary origin and development. The primary function of speech is the coördination of the behavior of the individual members

SPEECH: ITS FUNCTION AND DEVELOPMENT

of the social group. It is undoubtedly true that in the performance of this function, as speech has become a distinctive mode of response to the objective world, it has likewise brought about an enormous development of individual intelligence. The development of speech has thus acquired an indirect survival value through the increased general capacity of the human individual which it has occasioned. The psychological transformation of the individual through the acquisition of this new and distinctive function will be considered later. But it is not through the performance of any merely individual function, however important, that the evolution of speech can be explained. Its fundamental and primary value, the value that has led to its conservation and evolution, lies in its social function of associating individuals in a new and vastly more effective type of group organization.

The problem of the evolution of human speech from animal cries is, then, ready for restatement. Instead of asking how the expression of inner ideas has developed from the expression of feelings, or how the natural cry has been transformed into a symbol, we may put the matters as follows. The animal cry (1) is an element in the total type-response of an individual to a situation having a direct affective value, and (2) calls out in one or more other members of the group an appropriate type-response. How, then, could it be transformed into speech, which (1) is a specific and independent response to a complex situation having only indirect value to the individual—a response made up of independently variable elements correlated with independently variable

42

elements of the situation—and which (2) acts as a conditional stimulus to a complex response appropriate to the occasion, or to a definite modification of behavior already in progress?

CHAPTER III

Some Primitive Utilities

Social and Individual Aspects of Speech.

THE investigation of speech is peculiarly difficult because it involves entering two distinct yet related fields of inquiry. On the one hand, language is a social phenomenon, transmitted from one generation to another through social contacts and not by heredity. The ability to speak a particular language is not a congenital trait of the human individual. It is not even the result of a simple and spontaneous exercise of instinctive tendencies, as is walking, for example. It is an acquired art in a sense in which walking is not. The child's learning a language is in many respects like his learning to play ball or marbles. Whether he learns to speak at all depends on his belonging to a social group, and what particular language he learns depends on the particular group to which he belongs. We cannot hope to find the conditions of the origin or development of language in causes directly affecting the welfare of the individual or his mode of life. We must look rather to the conditions affecting the maintenance and development of the group as a distinguishable entity.

On the other hand, speech is a mode of individual behavior. Its appearance in the history of the human animal has been conditioned by specific and important organic modifications in the individual, and has carried with it profound and extensive psychological transformations. Not only its genesis, but its character and position as a natural and social phenomenon must be treated with this in view. It is a feature and a factor in the evolution of the human individual no less than a product of social evolution and a function of organized society. Its psychological status, its relation to human intelligence—in particular to the capacity for conceptual thought—can be determined and appreciated only by viewing speech as a mode of response in its relation to other modes of response both animal and human.

The two lines of approach, then, are distinct although interdependent. To view speech exclusively as a mode of individual behavior, *i.e.*, as a psychological phenomenon, is to fail to understand it. Particularly is this true so far as its genesis is concerned. The conditions which determined its appearance were probably those arising from and accompanying the transition from an arboreal to a terrestrial mode of life. This change undoubtedly involved organic modifications of an important nature; but these alone, although, as we shall presently see, they were favorable to the development of articulate speech, were not in themselves capable of giving rise to it. It was, as we shall try to show, the change in the conditions of life so far as they affected the *group*, that were the primary determinants of the appearance of speech. It is of course true that conditions affecting group life and group activities must act through the individuals who make up the group, but this fact does not affect the point at issue. The maintenance of the group was an essential condition of the survival of the individuals who made up the group; and except for the protection and aid afforded by the group they could not have survived to leave offspring. Hence we must grant a certain priority to factors conditioning the group as an organized whole. The biological and psychological traits which fit the individual for the changed group life attain, then, a high survival value; and there is a pressure on the stock which tends to bring about evolutionary changes in the direction of greater sociality.

The Descent from the Trees.

IT is fairly evident that the differentiation of the common human stem from the stock ancestral to both the anthropoids and man was connected with the change to a terrestrial mode of life. The distinguishing traits of man—for example, the specialization of arm and hand and foot, the greater length of the leg as compared with the arm, the erect posture, and the forward-looking head—all mark off the ground-dwelling animal from the arboreal. When, or under the urgencies of what necessities or advantages, the safe trees were forsaken for the hazards of life on the ground, we cannot say with assurance. It is possible that the impulse came from the need, or the attractiveness, of a new food supply. The destruction of the forests by the increasing cold and drought of the latter half of the Tertiary period may have been the determining cause. We are not to suppose that the change came suddenly. Some modern anthropoids spend a considerable part of the day upon the ground, collecting fruit or other vegetable food. The gorilla is commonly met with on the ground, and even makes his nest there secure in his great strength. Smaller primates frequently make concerted raids in search of food. It may well be that man's arboreal ancestors shared to an even greater extent the habit of making excursions away from their homes in the trees, and that the critical change came as an extension of a practice of long standing.

It is in this epoch-making change from arboreal to terrestrial life that we find the conditions for the appearance of the distinctive human group with its two characteristic features, language and tools. Man's ancestors unquestionably led a group life long before they left the trees. His nearest relatives, the anthropoid apes, are all highly social animals; and his own whole affective and emotional nature is rooted in instinctive tendencies which could have developed only through ages of group association. There is evidence also that the proto-human group was a group guided and more or less dominated by a leader.[1] Man is by nature fitted for such group life as this. His instinctive attitudes of submission and domination, approval and disapproval, self-display and shyness, all indicate an ancient heritage. Yet the human group is at least as sharply distinguished from the animal group as is the human individual from his nearest animal relative. It is not simply that the ape group, like the graminivorous herd, is essentially a defensive group, while the human group is an offensive group as well, and in this respect offers comparison with the wolf pack. It differs radically from both. It carries on both

[1] Among apes, according to Brehm, the leader owes his position to physical prowess, and enforces complete submission to his will on all occasions. He himself acts as scout and gives the signal—a peculiar cry "full of terror"—for flight.

defensive and offensive activities with the aid of selected or manufactured implements—what we may term "artificial limbs." Now although the use of clubs and missiles has an instinctive basis, their successful employment is based on intelligence and is an acquired art. Moreover, the tool of man is not an individual but a social product. Its development as an "artificial limb" depends on a continuous group organization and a social heredity. Not only so, but the use of tools is largely a coöperative enterprise and depends on the coördination of the activities of individuals. This coördination is itself intelligent and not instinctive, and must be attained by other than merely instinctive means. A system of instinctive animal cries is adequate for the coördination of only an instinctively determined coöperative behavior. To coördinate the intelligent behavior involved in the use of tools, language is necessary. *Language is correlative to the tool.* It is scarcely possible that either could have developed very far without the other; and, as we shall attempt to show later, their psychological interdependence in the individual is no less fundamental.

We are now ready to approach our problem more nearly. How did the change from the conditions of arboreal life to those of permanent ground-dwelling favor, and even make indispensable, the development of speech? How was the transition effected from the animal cry—which in one breath proclaimed the existence of a situation of direct and immediate concern to the group and urged to the simple and specific response appropriate to this situation—to speech, with its independent alternatives of (1) proclaiming the presence of particular

49

kinds of objects in their particular states and relations, and (2) of commanding the performance of particular acts and combinations of acts relatively independent of the specific situation?[1] It is evident that this transition from cry to speech was part of a much larger development, in which the simpler instinctive responses of the animal, being no longer adequate, were gradually broken down and replaced by more complicated systems of response, into which elements of the simpler responses entered as independently variable elements. Our inquiry must seek to discover how the change from arboreal to terrestrial life fostered and made necessary this general development, and how speech in particular is related to other features of the evolution.

In general, the solution of our problem lies in the fact that the adoption of ground-dwelling necessitated meeting conditions of life to which arboreal instincts and habits had not adapted man. This is true, of course, of other changes of habitat which have occurred from time to time in the course of organic evolution, as, for example, what is perhaps the most radical change of all— that from marine to terrestrial life. But such changes have commonly been made possible by slow modifications in organic structure and the gradual evolution of instincts which adapted the animal to the new environment. What is peculiar in man's change from arboreal

---

[1] In what follows, our attention will be confined to the consideration of the proclamation as the announcement of a given objective state of affairs. There are other important aspects of the proclamation which will be taken up later, but their separate treatment at this point would be confusing. These are (1) the proclamation of intended behavior, (2) the proclamation of past behavior, and (3) implicit predication.

to terrestrial life is just the fact that it was not effected entirely or mainly by the slow acquisition of a new instinctive equipment. The characteristic psychological difference between man and the anthropoid apes is not a difference in instincts. There are of course some differences of this sort, but these are not determinative. What enabled arboreal man to adapt himself to the new environment was his possession of a nervous organization sufficiently complex and flexible to permit him to reassemble, on a higher level, the elements of simpler and now inadequate responses.

The demand which the exigencies of arboreal life made upon him did not exhaust the potentialities of his organic equipment. The latent capacity for manipulation may serve as an illustration. The hand of the arboreal animal has undoubtedly been developed primarily as a grasping organ to aid him in climbing. But the same structure which fitted it for this function endowed it as well with an extraordinary capacity for varied and complicated dealing with things. The domesticated chimpanzee today, for example, easily learns to use knife and fork at table, etc. So long as the animal continues to live in the trees his hands are chiefly occupied with their primitive task of climbing. But when he descends to the ground he has greater opportunity and more pressing need to put his hands to other uses. The human hand is of course better in certain respects (notably in the superior development of the opposed thumb) for varied and delicate adjustments; but the point is that the arboreal hand was inherently capable of much more extensive and varied use than arboreal life demanded. It was not necessary, in order to meet the exigencies of the new terrestrial environment, to develop new or highly specialized organs. The hand that could climb could also wield the club or the sharp stick and jagged stone.

What is true of man's latent capacity for dealing with things with his hands, is also true of his latent capacity for entering into social relationships. The conditions of arboreal life—its comparative safety, on the one hand, and the limited field it offered for active coöperation, on the other, did not exhaust the potentialities of his instinctive endowment for social behavior. But the new conditions of life could only be met successfully by concerted coöperation of the group both in defense and in aggressive action. Let us consider this more narrowly.

Speech as an Instrument of Human Coöperation.

THE group of arboreal men was in all probability chiefly defensive. This is true of the groups of anthropoid apes, and there is no reason to suppose that the proto-human group was essentially different in this respect. Life in the trees is comparatively simple and does not call for either very complex or specialized coöperative action.[1] The gathering of fruits and other vegetable foods is, like grazing, rather gregarious than coöperative. Even where there are frequent excursions on the ground, the coöperation is mostly confined to defense. A leader to guide them to a common spot, to warn them

[1] It is interesting in this connection to learn that Köhler found very little actual coöperation, in the sense of acting together for a common end, among the chimpanzees he studied, despite the fact that in so many ways these animals are profoundly social. See, for example, the supplement "Building in Common," in *The Mentality of Apes.*

of approaching danger, to lead in united action against aggressors, or in flight from enemies too dangerous to be withstood, would seem to be all that conditions required. Nor need the means of defense have involved highly concerted action. So long as the trees could be reached they were comparatively safe, for few enemies could follow them there.

For such a simple defensive group life, speech is not necessary. The forms of concerted action required obviously do not call for a highly developed instrument of coördination. The leader could keep his followers together, lead them on foraging expeditions, summon them to hasty flight or to a defensive stand, and generally lord it over them, without the use of speech. Instinctive cries and gesticulations, which simultaneously proclaimed the existence of a situation of direct concern to the group, and urged to the performance of the simple and habitual acts appropriate to the specific situation, would serve as an adequate means of social control.[1]

But with the gradual abandonment of the trees and the adoption of a permanent mode of ground-dwelling,

[1] It is possible that investigation of the cries of the anthropoids would show that they are more nearly allied to speech than we are here supposing. The evidence, however, does not seem to point in that direction. The cries and gestures of apes undoubtedly perform in a high degree the function which Malinowski terms "phatic communion," *i.e.*, it keeps them in emotional and affective *rapport* with one another. It would not be surprising if the cries of the anthropoids should be found to exhibit a type of specialization which differentiates them to some extent from the animal cry as we have described it. But if this should prove to be the case, it would not affect the position taken in these pages. For speech with its characteristic structure is certainly not used by apes, but has been developed to meet the needs of the organized human group.

conditions were very much altered. So far as defense is concerned, it is evident that the safety of the individual depended more than ever upon group solidarity. Moreover, in the new condition it commonly happened that the former simple alternatives of group action no longer sufficed. Many of them were no longer appropriate. A formidable enemy encountered far from the trees could no longer be escaped by climbing and fleeing from branch to branch. Nor could man—especially primitive man with his inferior feet and legs—hope to escape by fleetness of foot. What remained, then, to be done? The answer is that no single expedient was to be found appropriate to all such occasions. A method successful against one foe under one set of conditions would fail against another foe or under other conditions. If, for example, the ground afforded cover, the group might successfully scatter and hide; if not, a desperate stand might be made, especially if a plentiful supply of stones or other effective missiles were at hand. If the enemy were sighted before he had perceived the group, a silent and cautious retreat toward a remembered cover might avail; if the enemy were sharp of scent, it would be better for the group to work around to windward, or perhaps to cross a stream or to wade single-file along its course. Again, the simple direct defense against an immediate danger must be supplemented by precautionary measures, varying with the nature of the ground and the sort of danger to be anticipated, as well as with the season, the presence of young, etc. We cannot, of course, supply authentic detail of these changes; but whatever they may have been, the significant fact which stands out is that *distinctions* had to be made—distinctions not only between different kinds of enemies which before had been indiscriminately fled, but distinctions between different conditions and circumstances under which the enemy was encountered. If the group was to survive, it must learn to respond to these differences by appropriate distinctions of group behavior. As an instrument for effecting such distinctions and for controlling new and unfamiliar modes of coöperative activity, it is evident that the old system of animal cries would have been quite inadequate. The system of cries had itself to undergo differentiation commensurate with the necessary differentiation of group behavior.

Were the conditions of life sufficiently simple and sufficiently stable, the evolution of animal cries might have branched off in a direction contrary to that which leads to speech. The cry of alarm, for example, might have kept its double character of proclamation and command, and at the same time have split up into a number of specialized cries of alarm. Each specialized cry would then indicate the presence of a specific kind of foe and call for a specific kind of response on the part of the group. We might suppose this sort of specialization, which is to be found among certain animals and birds, to be highly developed; but it could never lead to speech. It could be useful only where the group had a fixed and inflexible mode of responding to a limited range of typical situations of danger. So long as the announcement that a certain kind of foe is at hand is tantamount to the command to act in a certain habitual way, there is no possibility of highly organized cooperation. Nor, on the other hand, is there any need for, or possibility of, speech. Between the development of such a system of specialized cries and the development of speech, there is the same sort of difference that exists between instinctive and intelligent behavior. It is a difference in type of organization.

The evolution of speech from animal cries lies in an entirely different direction. What is essential to the emergence of speech is precisely the differentiation of the proclamation as such from the command. The simple case of alarm-signals may still serve as illustration. The modification of the simple alarm-cry in the direction of speech is equally in this case a specialization. Each kind, or object, of danger comes to have its own distinctive vocal signal whose declaratory significance remains constant. But—and this is the fundamental difference—the constant vocal signal ceases to be the unambiguous command to a specific group activity. The group has more than one way to meet the particular kind of danger announced. It has a choice of indefinitely flexible and complicated ways of acting. The announcement, then, does not stimulate any single or immediate response in those who hear it. Rather it *prepares* the group for defensive action, leaving the precise form of such action to be further determined. It rouses a definite *expectation* on the part of those who hear it, an expectation which would be realized by the actual sense-perception of the foe in question, and which displays itself in attitudes of attention to the probable source of danger and to the leader. Just in so far as the primitive cry of alarm ceases to be a direct determinant of immediate group action, and comes instead to serve as the conditional determinant of varying group action, to arouse and concentrate attentive preparation for action, it has become a true proclamation. Its indirectness as a means of social control is commensurate with the degree of its independence of emotional expression, on the one hand, and its true symbolism, on the other.

Human Hunting: Its Connection with Tools and Speech.

So far we have confined ourselves to the use of illustrations from the defensive activity of the group, using the cry of alarm as our point of departure. But the primitive group of ground-dwelling men was far more than a defensive group. If coöperation among members of the group had been limited to defensive activities, it would surely never have attained so high a degree of organization. It might well have been carried on with some instrument much simpler than human speech. As we have seen, man's descent from the trees was not improbably connected with the need for seeking a new food supply. At any rate, at some early period man became a hunter. We know practically nothing of the beginnings of human hunting. We are ignorant as to what change in conditions first led man to seek animal food in place of the vegetable diet to which he had been accustomed. Nor do we know what kinds of game he hunted nor by what means he captured his prey. Yet there are certain features of human hunting which stand out and which have great significance of our inquiry.

In the first place, man is not a hunting animal by instinct. He has no such instinctive desire to chase other animals, or to crouch and spring upon them, as have carnivores. The female very rarely hunts. While man's hunting is, of course, like all his activities, based upon congenital tendencies, it rests upon few or no specialized instincts. Now this means a relatively great flexibility and variability in the way in which hunting was carried on from the beginning. There was no single natural way for men to hunt, as there is for wolves or dogs or lions. If there had been, it is altogether improbable that he would ever have learned to use weapons.

The second important fact about human hunting is that men must have resorted from the beginning to some sort of indirect means, some sort of simple strategy. For long generations during the period of transition to terrestrial life, man must have been slow-moving and clumsy on his feet. He was strong enough in arms and jaws to have been a formidable antagonist if he could have come within reach of his prey. But he must have been hopelessly outdistanced by most animals. This great natural disadvantage under which man labored was undoubtedly one of the important causes which led to the development of weapons, particularly the missile, which kills or maims from a distance. Did man's dependence upon a supply of animal food have to wait upon the slow development of effective weapons? Was the killing of animal prey for long a lucky chance and the eating of it a rare treat? Were weapons developed primarily for defense, and only later used to procure food? Was hunting carried on at first by lying in wait, by surprise attacks, by snares or pitfalls, before effective weapons were discovered? We cannot answer these questions. But what is clear is that man could not have come to rely on hunting for any considerable part of his food supply, except on condition of his discovering or inventing some indirect methods or instruments. Whatever these may have been, they probably differed from group to group, as well as from occasion to occasion, with the kind of game hunted.

The next point of importance is that the development of hunting must have involved active coöperation. The solitary human hunter must be the man equipped with an effective weapon. The need for defense alone would probably have prevented primitive man from wandering far apart from the group in search of prey. There may have been certain advantages in scattering in individual pursuit. A stealthy approach may be more feasible for a man alone than for a group, although the cautious surrounding of game, particularly of a flock or herd, by a group of hunters is very effective when it can be carried out. But even if primitive men did sometimes make their kill single-handed and armed only with a club or picked-up stone, hunting as a regular enterprise and business of life must have depended, directly or indirectly, on a group organization. The presumable gregarious habit of primitive men, and the advantage of coöperative strategy and attack, probably resulted in coöperative hunting from the beginning. In any case, it is only within the organized group that tradition can grow up, by which the results of experience—whether of methods of pursuit, or of the sort of weapons to choose and the manner of fashioning the stick or stone—

can be passed on from one generation to another. Such coöperation as this requires could only have been achieved through the use of an instrument of social control far more flexible and complex than any system of animal cries. The evolution of language, marked by the differentiation of the proclamation, which prepares but does not precipitate response, and of the supplementary command, with its power to initiate and control particular acts, is an essential condition for the complex and varied coöperation that is involved in human hunting.

An important feature of the hunting-group which we have to notice is the division of labor, the specialization of the activities of the individual. This exists to a certain extent, to be sure, in any group. In lower forms of organization it is based almost exclusively on some sort of biological status, sex, age, or physical prowess. But in the higher forms of social organization it becomes more variable and flexible. In hunting, where success may depend on a cautious approach to and surrounding of the game, just what each individual does on a given occasion will depend on his relative position with reference to the game and with reference to other individuals. His movements must be controlled and regulated by the movements of others. Moreover, the strategy of the group, and consequently the particular part played by the individual, will depend on the kind of game hunted, the nature of the ground, etc. The proclamation of the presence of a particular kind of game, accordingly, becomes freed from specific imperative significance in that the response it indirectly determines differs from individual to individual, and from occasion to occasion on the part of the same individual. Moreover, just because its power to determine the response of each individual is so indirect and so conditional upon the presence of other factors, the proclamation must be supplemented by subsidiary signals, incipient commands, vocal and gesticulatory, given not only by the leader, but by other individuals to their neighbors.[1]

The Reorganization of Human Life.

BUT it is not to be supposed that it was only in the active coöperation of the hunt that language proved to be indispensable to group-life. The whole manner of living had to be altered. There was, for example, the necessity of finding some way of passing the night in safety on the ground. While men slept in the trees they were comparatively safe. But spending the night within reach of nocturnal prowlers—and their most dreaded enemies were nocturnal—presented entirely new problems to the group. We may suppose that many expedients were tried with varying success, and that many groups perished, before adequate customs were established governing the behavior of the group at night. These customs may well have varied from group to group, for instinct prompted to no single course of action, nor did the circumstances make any single expe-

---

[1] For an admirable account of the use of language in controlling the coöperation of a group of Trobriand natives of New Guinea on a fishing expedition, see the supplementary essay on "Primitive Languages" by B. Malinowski, in *The Meaning of Meaning*, by Ogden and Richards, pp. 471 ff. This account serves to illustrate also points made later in Chap. V.

dient inevitable. Natural shelters such as caves vary greatly in their defensive possibilities. Men had to *learn* how to appreciate and to take advantage of these, for their arboreal instincts and habits were hopelessly inadequate to meet the new situation. Moreover, crowded together in caves and other shelters at night, they must have had to make all sorts of mutual adjustments. The difficulty of securing themselves against outside intrusion could not have been much greater than the difficulties of internal accommodation. If life was to be tolerable, an ordering of its ways had to be discovered and enforced.[1]

Other exigencies than those of night-time with its perils necessitated the growth of custom. Among the most important of these was the care of children. An arboreal baby was provided for by nature. It instinctively clung at first to its mother as she climbed among the trees, herself not seriously hampered by her burden. Later it clung to the branches no less instinctively, and could safely be trusted to climb among them from a very early age. But the primitive human baby on the ground was ill-equipped with instincts to cope with its new environment. He was a far greater burden to his mother as she walked about than he had been in the trees. When

[1] It has been suggested that the loss of man's body hair was a result of his crowding with his fellows in ground shelters. The increase of vermin under these conditions, it is said, became so serious a menace to health that a variation in the direction of hairlessness had a marked survival value. This theory may not be true. It is mentioned here because it brings so vividly before our minds the profound transformation in human relationships and ways of life that was wrought by living in shelters on the ground. What is of chief interest to us, is, of course, the part that these conditions played in the development of *custom*.

Consuetudine, fr: consuetudinem, suetus, suescere, Suus (*swe-wos) 'to follow one's own ways).

From the base *swe comes ethos (from *swedho-

he left her arms he was still worse off. Imagination fails us when we try to picture the cares and perplexities of the primitive human mother, deprived of that immemorial refuge. Infant mortality must have been appalling, and a ruthless selection must have taken place which facilitated the evolution of the distinctively human traits. For us the important aspect of the changed conditions lies in the fact that the activities of the child had to be controlled and regulated in a way hitherto undreamed of. He had to be prevented from doing countless things and taught to do many others for which instinct provided no adequate warning or prompting. The ability to understand and respond to the admonitions and warnings of his elders must have been a trait of the highest survival value. Without some sort of crude speech the new and imperative need of education could not have been met. In the daily intercourse with the young, language was at once conserved and extended.

CHAPTER IV

Imitation and Vocal Play

BEFORE proceeding with our analysis of language in the light of its social function, we shall pause to consider the part played in the development of speech by certain psychological traits which we find exhibited in the child.

The Utility of Vocal Play.

AMONG the organic modifications conditioning the development of spoken language are those changes in the structure of the head and neck, incident to the erect posture of man, which have facilitated the uttering of articulate sounds.[1] Structural changes in this direction must have had some survival value to the children who possessed them, and must have favored their selection in the critical period of transition. But it was not enough that the structure permitting a wide range of vocal utterance should be present; there had also to be developed an innate tendency to what we shall term vocal play. The pre-human baby must have been not only a crowing and cooing baby like ours, but he must also, like our babies, have spent his waking hours in practicing his

---

[1] The importance of these changes must not, however, be exaggerated. It has sometimes been supposed that Neanderthal man could not have spoken because the structure of his head and neck did not permit free articulation. It is scarcely possible, however, that he could have developed such culture as he evidently possessed without language. While he did not possess the articulatory capacity of modern man, it must have been sufficient to enable him to speak. See Köhler's remarks on the articulatory capacity of the chimpanzee, quoted on page 28, note 2.

changing vocal repertoire of *goo's* and *mm's* and *da's*. The importance of this is not simply that he is learning by practice the vocal elements which make systematic language, but that he is preparing himself at the same time to imitate the speech of others. Speaking a language, as we have already remarked, is an acquired art like playing a game. Languages are slowly built up in the course of generations, and their development depends on the passing down from one generation to the next of traditional and standardized forms. There has been much discussion as to the part imitation has played in the evolution of language and the wildest speculation has been indulged in. But so much, at least, is certain: that language can be transmitted from one generation to another only by means of imitation. It was once supposed that there is a special instinct of imitation, but this is doubtful. An instinct is conceived as an innate tendency to perform some specific act, while the imitation of one act which we see another perform is psychologically a very different thing from imitating another and different act. Generally speaking, we can imitate acts of others only if we are already able to perform the same kind of acts ourselves, or at least the elementary acts of which they are composed. But further, we can imitate others only in so far *as we have already learned to imitate ourselves*. Now human babies, and also the young of other animals, are constantly learning to imitate their own acts. That is to say, many acts, originally performed by chance, act as stimuli to their own repetition. Nothing is commoner than the repeating over and over again by the baby of some chance act. At first the stimulus to its repetition may be the "feel" of the activity itself, but when the outcome of the act is interesting and pleasant, the perception of it (by sight or sound) comes by a very simple psychological mechanism to serve as an independently sufficient stimulus to the act. Thus the baby, who in his aimless gurglings and cooings utters a *ga* or an *mm*, finds the performance pleasant and repeats it. Presently the sound of his own voice, as well as the kinaesthetic "feel" of it, comes to control his utterance. There is thus built up a control over the vocal production of articulate sounds which makes it possible for him to imitate the sounds made by others. In a similar way he learns, through manipulatory and other play, to "do" to and with objects what he sees others do.

But vocal play has an even wider significance than the preparation for imitating the speech of others, essential as this is to the development of language. The importance of play as a factor in mental and social evolution has been emphasized by many writers. Play is the free exercise of a function or the free performance of an activity which is, or may be, useful either as a part of a larger activity, or in a wider setting. The complexly organized behavior of the higher animals, and particularly of man, is only possible when the partial acts of which it is composed come to be performed for their own sakes, as pleasurable acts which are ends in themselves. Language is no exception. The vocal utterance, which in its origin as a mere cry is only an element in a larger total response, can acquire an independent function only in so far as it becomes freed from its context and performed as a "free" act, pleasurable in itself. But

67

it is not enough that the sheer utterance of sounds should become play; there must also be a playful *use* of these sounds, which prepares the child for the serious employment of them as real language. For learning a language is not merely learning how to make the standard vocal complexes of which the language is composed. It is learning the meaning, or uses, of these complexes as well. It is the building up of a complex functional activity. How does this take place in the child; and how far does the process as it takes place in him throw light on the evolution of speech in the race?

The Development of Speech in the Child.

THE fact that the beginnings of speech in the child are his initiation into the use of a highly developed form of language, prompted and fostered by the myriad unescapable influences of a speech-moulded society, makes the evidence obtainable from this source extremely difficult to sift and interpret. Moreover, although the evolution of language is chiefly a social evolution, it has been conditioned by a considerable degree of organic modification. The child of today is the product of a selection in which survival value was appreciably determined by adaptability for speech. He is therefore presumably different in certain respects from the child of perhaps a million years ago. Yet much is doubtless to be learned from the speech-behavior of children. We are tempted to think of the child as beginning with the use of separate words which he afterwards puts together in sentences. But this is only partially true. He does first learn to use those complexes of articulate sounds which in the mouths of adults constitute words; but for the little child these are not yet true words. Again, the child takes a delight in learning names of objects, which might well give color to the belief that primitive man began his speaking career, like Eve in Mark Twain's tale, by inventing naturally appropriate names for things. But if we observe closely we may see that what we have called the child's delight in learning the names of objects is not just this. It is in fact a special form of a more general kind of behavior which is highly characteristic of the child, *i.e.*, the repetition of an act performed on, or with reference to, an object. A very simple case is the grasping and later carrying to the mouth of practically every object within reach. Later on, it may be throwing an object on the floor as long as someone has the patience to restore it to the child. Opening and shutting boxes, and the persistent attempt to open other objects, the untying of shoes, and the thousand other familiar tricks of babyhood, are cases in point. The child enjoys learning and performing with almost endless repetition any new reaction to things. The vocal response is no exception, as we have just seen. The little baby of five or six months delights in practicing his repertoire of noises just as he delights in waving his legs and grasping his toes. Later, when he learns to attach specific vocal utterances to objects, he is not engaged in *naming* these objects in the true sense of the term. He is merely practicing a new kind of response in reference to the objects, which has the additional charm of being a social game in which others take part. An illustration will perhaps make this clearer.

Vocal Gesture and the Use of Names.

ONE of the writer's own children, when about eight months old, learned to point to objects which attracted her attention. Pointing in this way appears very commonly in children of about this age. In her case the tendency was deliberately fostered by her grandfather who carried her about the room, himself pointing to objects likely to prove interesting, and immediately approaching any object to which the child pointed. The clock was one of the objects most frequently visited on these excursions, and the grandfather was in the habit of saying "tick-tick," as he or the child pointed to it. Presently the child imitated this true vocal gesture, saying rather a whispered "ti-ti" than "tick-tick." The similarity between the vocal utterance and the tick of the clock entirely escaped the child's notice, for soon every object which called out the pointing-gesture called out the "ti-ti" as well. For some weeks this play of pointing and saying "ti-ti" was carried on with or without her grandfather's company. She had learned a new response to objects, and she practiced it with the same sort of pleasure she had earlier taken in throwing objects on the floor or in untying shoes. There was the difference, however, that this was a social game. The pointing and saying "ti-ti" was not complete unless it served to call someone's else attention to the object in question.

Now it is evident that the "ti-ti" was very far from being a name. It may, like the pointing, be described properly enough as an expression of the child's interest

70

in the object. But the fact that it served, like the pointing, to call the attention of a companion to the object of interest, acted powerfully to reinforce it. If no one ever responded to the pointings and vocal gestures of a child, the interest would soon become abortive and die out. The pointing and the "ti-ti" are at once the announcement that something interesting is at hand and the summons to look at or attend to it. It is by an extension and differentiation of this simple play-behavior that a sort of naming develops. What is necessary for this is that the vocal gesture be varied according to the kind of object which attracts the attention. Viewed as a game, this introduces a new and exciting feature. When the growing child finally realizes that there is a specific response to be learned for each object, he takes fresh delight in the exercise of his powers. This realization sometimes seems to come quite suddenly, and it then markedly facilitates the learning of language. This was notably the case with both Laura Bridgman and Helen Keller, in whom the normal speech development was deferred. In the case of the writer's own child, the beginning of the differentiation of vocal gesture came about in the following way. For some weeks the "ti-ti" proved so attractive that no other response was substituted, in spite of the continued efforts of the grandfather. At length, however, the child learned in pointing to the moon to substitute "Moon-moon." At first this new response was used only on the occasions when she was carried to the window and the moon was pointed out to her. Then one night, when she chanced to be carried along a street lit by large round lamps, she pointed to these one after another in great excitement, repeating "Moon-moon." From that time on she rapidly acquired a vocabulary.

But so long as the vocal response, however much it may vary with the stimulating object, is a mere play and is practiced only as a new and interesting activity, it is not speech, nor are the "names" true words. What further is needed to make them words, is that they be used in a systematic way to control the behavior of others with reference to the objects whose names they are. The calling of another's attention to an interesting object is, to be sure, a form of social control; but this form of the function is too simple to constitute speech. It is only when the child learns to use the names for wider purposes than this simple play, that they become words and enter as elements into the structure of language. When the hungry baby has learned to call: "Din-din now!" he has begun to speak in earnest. The play activity has become incorporated in the serious business of social living.

Without some capacity for disinterested social play of the sort just described, our ancestors would probably never have developed human speech. But it was the adaptation of the play-activity to the needs of social coordination that was the essential agency in the process. Apart from this social function, vocal responses, even if we suppose them differentiated to correspond to different kinds of objects, could never have become *standardized*. This is well exemplified by children's spontaneous use of newly learned "names." A "name" originally used to denote one object in a given situation will often be extended in the most fantastic way to all sorts of objects and situations having the most remote analogy or association with the original case. The classification of the objective world which language effects is a classification fundamentally, if indirectly, determined by the exigencies of coördinated action within the social group.

CHAPTER V

Predication

WE are now ready to proceed with our examination of the structure of language, guided by the conception of it as the instrument of social coördination. So far we have been especially concerned to show that what is fundamental to speech, in distinction from the animal cry, is the differentiation of the proclamation and the command. The cry, with its more direct and simple relation to behavior, serves at once to announce that something of moment is at hand, and to arouse the simple appropriate response on the part of those who hear it. It is implicitly both proclamation and command, while explicitly it is neither the one nor the other. It is through a specialization and differentiation of these two functions of the cry that speech arises.

The proclamation not only announces that something interesting is at hand, but *specifies what that something is*. It arouses definite expectation but does not precipitate action, since the definiteness of expectation is commensurate with the range of possible response which the human being has at his disposal. Moreover, it is the function of the proclamation to mediate coöperation; and since coöperation can occur only if there are diverse acts to be coördinated, the proclamation must be capable of calling out different specific responses from different individuals and on different occasions. Indeed, as we have been at some pains to show, it was probably the increase in the diversity and complexity of human behavior, engendered by the new conditions of life on the ground, that led to the evolution of speech. The proclamation, then, while it announces specifically, controls behavior conditionally and indirectly. Consequently it has been supplemented by the development of the command with its specialized capacity for direct and particular control.

Language has a definite and complex *structure*. It is this internal structure which we must consider in this chapter with the hope of tracing the connection of its development with the increased complexity of the social function which speech has had to perform. Now the characteristic structure of language is the structure of the proclamation. While the command and the question are essential features of language and necessary complements to the proclamation, it is the latter that is the fundamental and distinctive form. It is primarily in the form of the proclamation that conversation exists, the perfected and independent activity of speech. And it is in the form of the proclamation that propositions are formulated and knowledge embodied. It is undoubtedly due to the peculiar part it plays in the practical functioning of speech that the proclamation has undergone so extensive and momentous a development. This development of the proclamation, that is to say, has gone on *pari passu* with the increasing *indirectness* of its control of behavior.

Classification of Animal Cries.

BEFORE we enter upon this inquiry into the structure of the proclamation, it will be well to examine a little more carefully the proclamatory aspect of animal cries. Hitherto we have used intentionally general terms in describing this aspect; we have spoken of the cry, for example, as announcing that something of moment is at hand, and we have used the cry of alarm as our stock illustration. Now while what the cry can announce is, in the nature of the case, vague and indefinite, there are significant differences in this respect between different kinds of cries; and these it is important to distinguish.

We may roughly group cries in their proclamatory aspect as follows: (1) the proclamation of presence, or of existence, (2) the predicative proclamation, (3) the proclamation that one is about to act in a certain way, (4) the proclamation that one has just acted in a certain way. As examples of (1) we may mention many characteristic animal cries which serve to warn others that something of moment is present. The cry of alarm is, of course, commonly of this sort. Even more explicit, perhaps, are the distinctive bayings of a pack of hunting dogs, which announce in turn that a scent is picked up, that the quarry is viewed, etc. Differences in these "discovery" calls are commonly said to indicate something as to the kind of quarry scented or sighted.

The predicative proclamation merges into (1). The warning cry is usually given to announce the presence of a danger which has not been perceived by others; sometimes, however, the object is already perceived as present, but is not recognized as dangerous. In this latter case the cry is "predicative" in that it serves to call attention to a property of the object, rather than to the existence of the object itself. The primitive function of the predicative cry is perhaps rather to inhibit an act already incipient, or to encourage a response which is hesitating, than to initiate behavior. It is by means of warning calls of this sort that birds teach their young to fear and avoid men, for example. The use of admonitory calls is by no means limited to the lower animals. We ourselves make use of natural cries and ejaculations in dealing with little children who have not yet learned to talk; and the children themselves use them before they have any "words." If, for example, we see a child with a dangerous object such as a box of matches or an open knife, in his hand, we are apt to make an ejaculation of alarm as we hasten to take it away; and this tends to characterize vaguely the forbidden object in the child's eyes. If, again, we catch the child about to put a disgusting or ill-tasting thing into his mouth, we utter a characteristic ejaculation of disgust, very likely the familiar "ca-ca." This "ca-ca" is quickly learned by the child in vocal play; and it is freely applied by him to appropriate objects and to acts as well, in a way which is at once qualificatory and inhibitory. Another equally natural ejaculation is the "mm-mm" of satisfaction with something good to eat. This, of course, is the reverse of inhibitory; but it easily comes to qualify the morsel on which attention is already centered, and accordingly becomes predicative. There are many cries and expressions which tend to inhibit or encourage specific acts directed toward a given object, by calling attention to, or suggesting, some quality of the object not observed by the one to whom the cry is addressed. The importance of this type of cry, in which predication is implicit, is very great.

The third kind of cry, proclaiming that one is about to act in a certain way, is well exemplified by the characteristic cry of attack so widespread among animals. Another example is the perch-call of the blond ringdove, given just before it flies from the perch. On the other hand, many of the typical acts of animals are followed by characteristic vocal responses, which accordingly serve to announce the completion of the act. As the cry of attack exemplifies (3), the cry of triumph with its flaunting behavior exemplifies (4).

It may perhaps be objected that these last two cries are plainly and simply expressions of the emotion of the animal which utters them. It is true that they do express emotion, and that they occur as accompaniments of other expressive behavior. We have indeed already shown that this is characteristic of the cry as distinguished from the true proclamation of speech. Nevertheless the cry of attack, with the threatening behavior which accompanies it, serves to announce to its hearers the attack which is to follow.[1] It is in the potential effect that it has on the behavior of others that

[1] This statement is, perhaps, ambiguous. I do not of course mean to imply that the function of the cry of attack is to prepare one's adversary—an obvious disadvantage. The cry in question may, and often does, have just this effect; but the function which has controlled its development must be found elsewhere. This function is, as a matter of fact, complex. The cry of attack may obviate an actual encounter by warning off or intimidating the opponent. Craig states that among pigeons conflicts are often settled in this way, by a sort of substitute vocal and gesticulatory combat, in which the bird whose behavior exhibits greater determination and energy is the victor. In a similar way, many a fight between small boys is decided before it is begun. We shall see later that

its proclamatory significance is to be found. This is true not only of the cries we have just distinguished as announcements of acts impending or completed, but generally of cries in so far as they are proclamatory. The cry of fear or of distress is an immediate expression of feeling on the part of the one uttering it; but objectively it functions as an announcement, in that it orients the hearer with reference to the occasion which has called it out.

The Utility of Differentiation.

THE four kinds of cries which we have just distinguished tend to merge into each other. They do not form distinct and independent groups into which we can unhesitatingly sort out all the cries of animals and children. Many cries serve to proclaim, for example, both what the external situation is and what the animal that utters the cry is about to do, is doing, or has done. But it is obvious that a development and differentiation of these various forms of proclamation are of great social advantage, and indeed are necessary to a highly developed coöperation. The information as to the course of conduct one individual is to follow is of the greatest utility in regulating the conduct of others; while the information as to what has already been done is, or may be, of equal importance. Furthermore the ability to

not the least important aspect of speech is its capacity to act as an anticipatory and representative substitute for primary behavior.

Where a conflict is impending which involves a group, the cry of attack given by one member is a summons to the others to come to his aid. It is by means of the inspiriting battle-cry that the leader is able to carry his men forward to the charge or to rally them in defeat.

make proclamations giving this sort of information is essential to the successful functioning of the proclamation of presence when the external situation to be announced is complex. A concerted course of action must be adopted, and if it is to be carried out successfully, the behavior of each must be regulated with reference to it. In simple cases it might perhaps be sufficient for the leader himself to make a start in one direction or another; but if the case is not simple, his ability to announce to his followers the course which he is about to pursue becomes indispensable. It is evident, moreover, that the ability to command another to perform a specific act, and the ability to announce one's own intention of performing it, are very closely connected, and that any improvement in either must react upon the other. It has been said that intelligent behavior arises by a "cross-fertilization" of instincts. We may borrow the expression and say that speech has arisen through a "cross-fertilization" of instinctive cries. But what has at once stimulated and regulated this "cross-fertilization" has been the functioning of cries in the social control of behavior.

In our later treatment (in Part III) of the psychological significance of the development of speech, we shall see the critical importance which the ability to announce one's intended act and to recount one's past deeds has had in the evolution of human intelligence. If we are right, it is through the development of the ability to perform these distinctive verbal acts that man has acquired the capacity for foresight and planning, on the one hand, and for reliving the past in free memory,

81

on the other. What we have to notice here, however, are certain social forms which these two kinds of primitive proclamation take. Before a band of savage warriors sets out on an important expedition, they prepare themselves by rehearsing in advance the deeds they are to do. The ceremonial and dance, with their symbolic representation of the conflict and the hoped-for victory, while they have not the magical efficacy which the participants suppose, do serve the purpose of rousing them to the necessary pitch of emotional excitement and mobilizing the latent energy of the organism. But even more important than this preparation of the individual is the preparation of the group. The real function of the rehearsal is the consolidation of the group by uniting its members for the common enterprise. It is in such moments as these, charged with profound emotion, that the participant feels himself in mystic unity with his tribe and totem. Not less important for the corporate life of the group is the ceremonial celebration which follows the successful war expedition. Here again is the mimic dance of triumph, to which is added the recital of the more remote traditional past. Thus the felt unity of the group gains an extension in time, the importance of which for the continuity and solidarity of social life it would be hard to exaggerate.

The great difficulty of our task of tracing the evolution of language lies, as we recognized at the outset, in the almost complete lack of data bearing directly on the early transitional stages of that evolution. As a consequence of this dearth of material, any theory of the beginnings of language must remain largely speculative, supported only by indirect evidence. If the theory we have advanced is sound, there must have been a genetic stage in which the proclamation was not as yet fully differentiated from the command; when, that is, the declaratory significance of the proclamation was not entirely fixed and definite, varying with the situation in which it was made, but when, at the same time, it was much more than an animal cry, in that it was already a variable and conditional determinant of response. Now although no existing language presents any such phenomenon, we do find a similar state of affairs in the long-distance signalling of American Indians.

An Analogy: Indian Signals.

In his report to the Bureau of American Ethnology[1] James Mooney gives an interesting account of the long-distance signalling in familiar use among the Indians. Many of the signals are clearly adaptations of gestures. Others, however, like the smoke or fire signals, are independent. A simple alarm fire is used to announce an interesting event without definitely indicating its nature. It puts the tribe on the *qui vive*. If they are expecting danger, it is a signal to flee; if food, it is a signal for appropriate preparation. Another signal of similar significance is what Mooney calls the signal of "discovery." This consists in riding in a circle. Like the alarm fire it serves in itself merely to put the tribe on the *qui vive*. It differs in one important respect, however. When the bustle in camp shows that the signal has been observed, it is at once followed by supplementary

[1] Bureau American Ethnology, Bulletin No. 30, 1910.

signals of a more specific character, which, together with the "discovery" signal, constitute a true proclamation. Thus the presence of buffalo or other large game is indicated by holding the blanket at two corners, with arms outstretched above the head, and gracefully bringing it down toward the ground. An enemy is signalled by confused and rapid riding back and forth, or by waving the blanket above the head. These last examples, it will be observed, approach true language more closely. The situation in these last cases does not suffice to determine completely the meaning of the announcement. This is accordingly supplemented and completed by signals having a relatively fixed significance, *e.g.*, large game, or enemy. The effect of the signals on the watching camp is first to arouse attention and general expectancy which is preparatory to some sort of action; while the succeeding signals serve to make the expectation specific, and to prepare for correspondingly specific alternatives of action.

The evidence which these phenomena furnish is, of course, of only suggestive value. The whole system of distance-signalling is far from primitive. It exists as a relatively independent supplement to other means of communication, and among people possessing a social organization made possible by a highly developed spoken language. And yet, rightly viewed, the phenomena are very instructive. The distance-signalling performs the same function of coördinating action for a common end that our analysis has found language to perform. Since it performs it under unfavorable conditions, that is, when the parties are at too great a distance for finer means to be employed, the instrument is crude and rudimentary. It does in an imperfect way what the scout does more definitely and completely when he has returned. It anticipates the larger features of his verbal report.

Mooney mentions, without describing them, other social signals used in daily life—for example, between lovers or between children at play. Lovers' signals are classic and often constitute quite a code. They are interesting in that they are examples of a kind of proto-language, the significance of whose terms is not fixed and universal, but dependent on a particular sort of situation. Given the situation—the beginnings of courtship—the signals, or terms, have a comparatively definite significance, and invite or check reciprocal behavior. But the signs are not available for a wider or universal use, as are the *words* of language.

The Structure of the Proclamation.

THE developed proclamation of true language is distinguished from rudimentary forms like the Indian signals by its complex inner *structure*. It is a complete sentence—that is, it consists of distinct functional parts, the subject and the predicate, each playing its peculiar rôle. The sentence is, moreover, composed of *words*. Now words are not only "parts of speech," whose functional differentiation is essential to the sentence, but they are isolable elements, whose fixed significance enables them to pass unchanged, or nearly so, from sentence to sentence. It used to be supposed that language began with words—separate names of things and acts and qualities

—which were afterwards put together to form sentences. It is no wonder that with this intellectualistic atomism the problem of the origin of language seemed insoluble. No one now, whether philologist or psychologist, really supposes this to have been the course of development. It would be more nearly true to say that language began with sentences than with words. At least, as we have seen, predication is a fundamental character of human speech from its beginnings. It does not, however, become explicit until the relatively homogeneous proclamation becomes differentiated into distinct functional elements, which may enter individually into other proclamations and commands. We must not, of course, assume uncritically that the appearance of the sentence came about in Spencerian fashion, by an inner differentiation of an originally homogeneous structure. As far as we can be guided by the course of language development in the child—which we shall now consider—as well as by the structure of gesture language, the process by which predication became explicit must have been synthetic as well as analytic.

The Sentence-Word.

THE supposition that language had its beginnings in words would seem at first sight to be supported by reference to the speech of the little child. For does not the baby learn words first, and much later learn "to put them together"? It is true that for some months his speech is confined to the use of single "words," or at least to what in the mouths of his elders are single words. But a little closer observation reveals the fact, that while the articulate utterances of the little child bear a recognizable resemblance to the words of his elders—from whom he has indeed learned them—they are not, as he uses them, true words. It is not merely that "naming" things is often a verbal play-response, as we have shown before. We refer now to the linguistic *use* which the child makes of his early words. As the baby uses a word, it is what the French call a *mot-phrase*, a sentence-word. What the baby does from the beginning, when he is not indulging in pure vocal play, is to talk in complete, if rudimentary, sentences.[1]

Thus a proper name of some individual known to the child is not used by him simply and definitely to designate that individual, but to make many sorts of announcements about the person in question, or even about objects and events connected with him. O. Bloch gives

---

[1] It is important to distinguish this use of sentence-words from a more primitive sort of linguistic phenomenon. The child does often at a very early age learn to associate a specific word or phrase with a definite act. That is to say, he will respond with a definite act or vocal utterance to a command or question. Clara and William Stern in *Die Kindersprache* give lists of expressions "understood" in this way by their children at the age of 10-14 months. (P. 18 and p. 85.) Thus to the question "Where is Hilda?" the child would respond by putting her hands over her eyes and then taking them away. To the command, "Give a kiss," she replied by smacking her lips. If her mother asked "Where am I?" she answered "Mama." It is interesting to observe that animals also learn to "understand" words and phrases in the same way. The vocal utterance acts, that is, as a direct stimulus to a specific response. Even the names of objects are "understood" in a similar fashion. For example, if one said "ball" to a fox terrier belonging to the writer's children, he would run off after his ball and bring it up joyfully to be thrown, a game in which he took great delight. "Ball" did not denote for him simply the object, ball, but was a signal for a specific activity connected with the object.

some interesting instances of this use of proper names by his children.[1] He writes: "The names of persons themselves, which, as has been remarked above, are those whose meaning becomes fixed the earliest, exhibit equally this complex and active significance, which gives to isolated words the value of a true sentence. The following observations are taken from the language of Françoise, because my attention has only recently been drawn to these facts, but they are numerous and clear. What gives them additional value is the fact that they all date from a period when Françoise already frequently used words in groups. At the twenty-fifth month, sitting on my knees, she pointed with her finger to her brother's slippers, which happened to be on the mantel-piece, saying simply 'mon-mon' [Raymond]; the next day, pointing out to me with the same gesture the school satchel of her sister, she said 'ninin' [Jacqueline]; several days later she brought her mother's boots, and, showing them to me, she said 'maman'; another day she offered me the paper saying to me 'papa'; she wanted to have a box of marbles belonging to her brother, and, stretching out her hand, she said 'mon-mon.' In all these cases the object was indicated by a gesture. Proper names also contain at times the idea of action. This was the case with the last example cited. Here are others still clearer. She had thrown some picture cards on the floor; I said to her: 'And now what must I do?' and, pointing to me, she replied,

[1] "Les premiers stades du language de l'enfant." *Journal de psychologie XVIII année*, 8-9.

'papa.' But at this period she freely used 'âsé' [*ramasser*]. Every time her brother teased her and made her cry she would come to find me, saying 'mon-mon.' One day, when her mother had put her out of the kitchen, she came crying into my office, saying 'maman.'"

It has seemed worth while to quote M. Bloch's observations at length because of their great interest for our inquiry. Proper names are not, of course, the only ones that serve as sentence-words. A common noun like "shoe," for example, which for the adult is a substantive denoting an object, is used by the child imperatively to demand that his shoes be given him, or to announce that he has just taken them off, or that they are lying near; or, again, to call attention to the fact that he has on a new pair, or that he has got them muddy, etc. Almost any part of speech may be similarly used. Thus two of M. Bloch's children used "pa te" [*par terre*] to call attention to an object lying on the floor, as well as to announce that the child had thrown it there. One child also used "pa te" as a request to be put on the floor himself.

Dependence of the Sentence-Word upon Perceptual Context.

THERE are two respects in which the sentence-word of the child differs from the true words of adult language: first, in their capacity to function alone without the aid of other words; second, in the looseness and fluidity of their significance. M. Bloch writes,[1] "Besides

---

[1] *Op. cit.*, p. 710.

the wide range and mobility of the meaning of words, the most remarkable trait of the language of the child in its beginnings is the active value which all words are apt to receive. A substantive does not denote simply an object, but all the actions with which it is in relation in the experience of the child." These two features—independence of function and fluidity of meaning—indeed go together. It is precisely because the words of the child are so indefinite in meaning, that they can serve such a variety of uses; and it is also—although this sounds paradoxical—for the same reason, that they are fit to function as complete rudimentary sentences.[1] A child's word does not, as we have seen, designate an object *or* a property *or* an act; rather it signifies loosely

[1] We find well exemplified in the speech of little children the use of the predicative proclamation. It attaches itself very naturally to the sort of vocal-gesture play described above. A child who has repeatedly been prevented from touching a certain object, or the objects in a certain place, the act of prevention being accompanied by a warning "no, no!" will often check his own impulse to touch, repeating to himself "no, no!" It may be remarked that the substitution of the vocal gesture for the instinctive grasping is more apt to take place if some grown person is present to whom he may turn for appreciation. But if the temptation to touch be not too strong, he may take obvious delight in his performance, repeating the "no, no!" over and over when he sees the object in question. The vocal response serves at once to inhibit and replace the simple instinctive grasping, to elicit signs of interest and approval in another, and—what is our primary concern at the moment—to qualify vaguely the object as *forbidden*. Acts as well as things become thus qualified, and often it is difficult to distinguish whether it is the act or the object to which the qualification applies. It may be the act in relation to certain objects and occasions, or the object in relation to certain acts and occasions, that is qualified. The world of the child, like that of primitive men, is divided, as soon as its features emerge to his view, into the realm of permitted things and acts, on the one hand, and the realm of those which are forbidden, on the other.

and vaguely the object together with its interesting properties and the acts with which it is commonly associated in the life of the child. The emphasis may be now on one, now on another, of these aspects, according to the exigencies of the occasion on which it is used. Just because the terms of the child's language are in themselves so indefinite, it is left *to the particular setting and context to determine the specific meaning for each occasion.* In order to understand what the baby is saying you must see what the baby is doing. The simple sentence-word is a complete proclamation or command or question, because the speech in which it occurs is so closely bound up with the attitude of response to his immediate surroundings. The independence of the primitive word with respect to other words is paid for by its dependence on the practical situation.

Now this twofold character of infant speech is just what we should expect, if speech is, indeed, as we have urged, fundamentally and essentially a means of controlling the behavior of others with reference to the objective world. The names of objects are not clearly distinguished from the acts connected with the objects, precisely because it is in the control of behavior with reference to them that objects come to be named at all. Similarly, verbal terms do not denote acts as such, but acts performed on, or in connection with, specific concrete objects. Because saying is so closely connected with doing, and because in its beginnings speech is used to control immediate action only, with reference to the objects at hand, the meaning of the terms is dependent on their physical and active setting.

Evolution of the Complete Sentence.

WE are now ready to ask how the differentiation of language into elements playing distinct and complementary rôles in the sentence has been brought about. The same problem is raised if we ask, conversely, how the sentence as an ordered combination of separable elements has come into existence. Every language now existing, even the most nearly primitive, exhibits this developed structure. Even gesture-language and such rudimentary tongues as Beche de mer and Pidgin English are made up of separable word-elements which combine into full-fledged sentences having distinct subject and predicate. But we must suppose that a more primitive state of affairs once existed. This earlier stage in linguistic evolution corresponded, in all probability, in its fundamental features, to the period of infantile speech before the child has learned "to put words together." That is to say, *the primitive "words," like those of the little child, were probably sentence-words.* But since primitive men did not, like the child of today, learn to speak under the moulding influence of a language-environment which tends to fix and standardize his usage, the terms of primitive speech must have been, to an even greater extent than the child's, fluid and vaguely inclusive; owing their significance from occasion to occasion to the concrete situation in which they were used.

There is of course no direct evidence in favor of this hypothesis and the indirect evidence needs, like all indirect evidence, interpretation. It has, however, the support of well-known philologists. A. Meillet, for example, in discussing the structure and form of the single-word sentence,[1] writes: "The sentence of a single term is a normal thing, and it is undoubtedly from this that language takes its point of departure. Philologists who have reflected on the theory of the sentence have been aware of this for a long time. The fact has been made very evident recently in a series of four brief but fundamental articles by the great philologist, H. Schuchardt, entitled *Sprachursprung*, which appeared in the *Sittungsberichte* of the Berlin Academy, 1919 and 1920." Jespersen, in his recent work on *Language* attempts to show that the farther back we trace the history of known languages, the more the sentence appears "as one indissoluble whole, in which those elements which we are accustomed to think of as single words were not yet separated."[2] He thus sums up his view of the course of the evolution of language: "The evolution of language shows a progressive tendency from inseparable irregular conglomerations to freely and regularly combinable short elements."[3]

Assuming, then, that language had its beginnings in the single-term sentence, how did the evolution of the developed sentence structure take place? How did implicit predication become explicit, and how did differentiated terms of fixed significance arise? In general, we may be sure, by the same agencies and through the same processes which conditioned the evolution of the

[1] "Remarques sur la théorie de la phrase," *Journal de psychologie*, XVIII *année*, 8-9.

[2] *Op. cit.*, p. 439.

[3] *Ibid.*, p. 429.

sentence-word from the cry. *Speech which is limited to the sentence-word can mediate coöperative action only with reference to a situation which is perceptually present to both parties concerned.* If the concrete perceptual context is not given, the significance of what is said remains indeterminate and uncertain. Furthermore, it can serve to control only a simple sort of behavior, which does not depend on an analysis of the situation. A situation which is perceptually present to both parties may be so complex that the significance of the single-term utterance is indeterminate or ambiguous. What brought about the evolution of the sentence was, then, (1) the need for coördinated action beyond the limits of the common perceptually present situation, (2) the need for coördinating such complex and varied behavior as depends on analysis of the situation. Now it is evident that these two needs are closely related to each other. An instrument that is capable of analyzing a present situation by resolving it into recognizable elements, is just in so far able to control action with reference to similar elements which lie beyond the reach of present perception.

The Differentiation of Words.

BUT how do the vaguely inclusive terms of primitive speech acquire that definiteness of meaning which enables them to serve as instruments of analysis? How, to be more specific, does the *name* of an object come to denote the object in distinction from the qualities which it possesses, and, more importantly, from the *acts* which are centered in it? It is because the objects of human action come to figure in more than one situation, and because, as they appear in one situation and another, they play different rôles. As a result of this, different properties take on importance, and different behavior toward them is called out. Similarly, acts become distinguished from objects in so far as the same acts are performed with reference to different objects, or by different individuals, or under different circumstances and with different results.[1]

There is a constant tendency on the part of the child to extend the use of his "words"—often in a ludicrous way. A term which serves very well in one situation will be transferred to other situations analogous in some way to the original one, or having features in common with it. What puts a limit to this extension is the child's need for making himself understood. He must conform to the established usage. But usage becomes established, and terms become fixed, through the functioning of speech to control reciprocal action in a *common environment*.

What makes the extension of terms from one situation to another mutually intelligible, is the fact that there is a real objective continuity between the situations. What is merely individual and subjective in the use of terms gets weeded out. Now the continuity of situations is of different sorts. Two situations may be

[1] This would explain M. Bloch's observation that it is proper names whose meanings become fixed the earliest. The persons with whom the baby is earliest and best acquainted are not connected with any single sort of activity. They are centers around which cluster all sorts of interesting doings, and which are sources of a great variety of interesting experiences. Compare what is said on this subject in Part II, Chapters V and VI of the present work.

continuous because the same object or objects appear in both. Thus, for example, the individuals of the immediate social group appear over and over again as features of innumerable situations. Again, while the objects themselves may vary, important properties may remain constant which call for similar behavior. This is notably true of the formal properties, such as distance, shape, and size, which form a universal nexus connecting situation with situation. Differences in state and condition of other human beings, or of animals, are also important common properties. Friendly and hostile, asleep and awake, hungry and fed, are examples of properties whose discrimination was early a matter of concern under widely varying circumstances. Finally, there are human acts which appear and reappear in varying typical combinations, thus linking situation with situation: coming and going, giving and taking, attacking and fleeing, etc. The advantage of a specific and independent instrument for controlling such definite acts tends to single them out for distinctive verbal representation.

Thus the forms of speech originally developed to regulate behavior within the limits of a given situation and with reference to a given perceptual environment become transferred to a similar regulation of behavior in other situations, where the implicit reference of the terms to the perceptual environment no longer serves. There is always a pressure tending to the extension of speech as of any other instrument. Just so far as the language forms are extended to new situations, and continue to serve effectively in the regulation of behavior, do they become independent of their reference to the perceptual and affective setting of the occasions of their use. It is thus that *words*, the independently variable elements of language, are formed.

If the same objects of perception did not, as we have said, enter as elements into more than one social situation, there would be no occasion and no need for the development of distinctive and unambiguous "names" for objects. The cry or sign that proclaims, for example, the presence of a certain kind of game, approaches in character a true name in so far, first, as it tends to call out some more or less distinctive method of hunting that particular kind of animal; and, secondly, in so far as the details of that method will vary with the state, position, etc., of the game on the particular occasion. But if the animal in question is not merely an object to be hunted and killed, but something to be prepared by the women for eating, and, in addition, something to be prepared in a certain way, and divided into more or less desirable portions and distributed accordingly, then the term indicating its presence has become so much the more a true name. It functions as a conditional determinant of two distinct sets of social activities in two distinct situations. Hence it may enter as an independent variable into numerous assertions and commands.

The Development of Linguistic Structure.

BUT the emergence of the true word is only one side of the process of development. From the sentence-word is derived not only the word, but the complete sentence with its grammatical structure. As the terms of primitive language become fixed and definite in meaning, they become correspondingly incapable of functioning alone. As the "name" comes to denote the object as such, in distinction from the acts which center in it and the qualities which it possesses, its use must be supplemented by that of a term which is capable of specifying the particular *act* demanded by the occasion, *i.e.*, by a verb, or by the predicate adjective which specifies the particular *quality* of importance on the occasion. As a matter of fact, it is only in so far as the sentence itself undergoes internal differentiation into its functional parts, the subject and the predicate, that the distinction between the noun, which denotes the person or object, and the verb, which denotes the act, can be definitely fixed. The process of the extension and fixation of terms proceeds *pari passu* with the process by which the implicit predication of the undifferentiated sentence-word becomes the explicit predication of the differentiated sentence. How did the latter process take place?

It will be recalled that we found it possible to distinguish four kinds of the primitive proclamation: (1) the proclamation of presence, (2) the predicative proclamation, (3) the announcement of intention, (4) the announcement of accomplishment. Of these, the predicative proclamation is of peculiar importance. What is proclaimed in it always has reference to some object or event or general state of affairs whose existence is *presumed*. This presumption may take the form of pointing to the thing in question, or perhaps of intently regarding it. The predicative proclamation does not announce its presence or existence, but calls attention to some specific property having a bearing on the given situation. In such a case there is virtual or implicit predication; but the language form is rudimentary. The verbal utterance must be supplemented by some other form of bodily response, like pointing, which serves to indicate the object to which the verbal specification applies. But when so supplemented, it does serve to *analyze* the situation in a limited way, or to connect it with something which is not perceptually present. When the little French child pointed to her brother's slippers and said "mon-mon," she was calling attention to the connection of the perceived slippers with her absent brother, Raymond. Similarly, the child who stretches out his dirty hand for inspection and exclaims "ca-ca," is calling attention to a *condition* of his hands, which in the child's experience calls out interesting expressions of disgust on the part of others, and usually leads to his being washed as well.

What is needed to transform this rudimentary predication into the full-fledged sentence, is that the act of pointing or otherwise indicating the object be replaced by an act of speech, the utterance of a word. For the child this substitution is made easy and natural by the vocal play which has preceded it. The pointing at objects of interest, so characteristic of a certain stage of a child's development, is accompanied by the utterance of distinctive sounds—vocal gestures, as we have termed them. Under the influence of the persons surrounding the civilized child, this vocal gesture comes to be varied with the kind of object pointed at; becomes, indeed, as the habit is fixed, virtually a *naming* of the object. It is easy, then, for the child to pass to the substitution of the vocal response for the pointing and to make the vocal response alone when for some reason the pointing-gesture is not made. It is interesting in this connection to note that, in gesture-language, when the object referred to is present it is indicated by pointing. It is only when the object is out of sight that the symbolic gesture is used.

Of course, as we have repeatedly urged, the linguistic development of the child cannot be taken as evidence of a completely parallel development in the race, since it takes place in a very different environment. Yet it must be based upon substantially the same endowment of inherited capacities for behavior. The same "random activities"—to use J. B. Watson's term—which furnish the basis for the development of speech in the child of today, must have appeared in the primitive child before language could have reached the evolutionary stage of the complete sentence. We must suppose that the primitive child, too, pointed and indulged in vocal play. If the conditions for the development of that play in the direction of language were less favorable, nevertheless the essential condition for the formation of language obtained then no less than now—its usefulness in controlling the behavior of others with reference to objective features not directly present to perception. The same influences which operate now to control the evolution of the sentence-word into the complete sentence in each generation of children, originally operated to control that evolution in the race.

The Indian signals described a few pages back may

serve to illustrate a transitional stage in the development of predication. It will be remembered that smoke is used as a signal of "discovery." When the situation is already determined, *e.g.*, if hostilities are expected, the signal by itself serves to announce the presence of that which was expected—the enemy. But if the situation is not thus determinate, the smoke is merely the signal of the discovery of *something of interest*. When the bustle in camp shows that the signal has been seen, it is followed by other signals, *e.g.*, that for large game. The smoke signal is like the pointing finger; but since it points to something that remains invisible, it must be supplemented by a sign which specifies the nature of the announced object or event. The case is interesting because it may be interpreted in two ways. We may regard the specific signal, *e.g.*, of "buffalo," as an incipient *naming* of that to which the smoke points. In this case we may construe our sentence as having the specific buffalo signal as subject, with the predicate, "exists" or "is at hand," expressed by the pointing smoke. Or the smoke signal in its signification of "something interesting" may be taken as the subject, which is qualified by the predicative specification "buffalo." The indeterminateness of the language form, which makes possible these alternative interpretations, is, of course, characteristic of transitional evolutionary forms.

The ways in which, as a matter of historical fact, explicit predication developed must have been numerous. It was a transition toward which many influences tended. Among these we may note as of special importance the need for an instrument of *inhibition*. We have already spoken of the way in which the little child learns to substitute the "no-no!" or the "ca-ca!" for the forbidden response which the object in question has formerly called out. These inhibitory ejaculations come, as we have seen, to qualify vaguely the object or situation to which they are applied, and hence are *predicative* in a rudimentary fashion. It may not, however, be the act as a whole that needs to be checked. If the situation is complex and the required response is equally so, it may be only some one element which must be inhibited. In this case the inhibitory announcement must *specify* the feature of the situation or of the response to which the qualification attaches. Let us suppose, for example, that a simple proclamation of discovery has been made, say of the presence of the members of a hostile tribe, and that appropriate group action has been begun. A scout observes that the approaching party is making signs of friendly intention. It is important that the preparations for hostilities be suspended, but that the group, nevertheless, hold itself in readiness for possible treachery. Now this result can hardly be brought about without the use of some more complex form of language than the single-term signal. Amplification of the structure of the implicit predication is required. The original "discovery" signal may be repeated and followed by another signal indicating friendship. Here the repeated sign, like the pointing finger, indicates what is now *presumed, i.e.,* the presence of the ordinarily hostile tribesmen, and accordingly serves as subject; while the second sign, correcting the customary connotation of the first term by qualifying the subject in a certain way, becomes the predicate of the complete sentence.

Let us take still another imaginary case. A party is on the march along a customary route, and a scout discovers that a stream which is usually forded at a certain point, is so swollen that it cannot safely be crossed there. This must have been a common sort of occurrence among primitive men, and it is one with which the undifferentiated sentence-word is inadequate to deal. Such a situation could be roughly met, of course, by the scout's attempting to lead the party off in a different direction. If the scout were himself the leader of the group, this simple procedure might suffice. But if the social organization of the group is of a higher type—in short, if there is to be any developed *coöperation* among the members of the group—it is essential that the distant situation be *specified* so that intelligent common action can be taken. In this example, it is not simply a case of the inhibition of the group-response as a whole—except temporarily, while a new orientation is made. The mere announcement that the stream is swollen does not of itself suffice to determine what action the group will take. That depends on many other circumstances, and perhaps on further information to be obtained by sending out scouts up and down the stream. What it does is to inhibit the *advance of the party in the direction they were following*. It does this by *naming* a feature of the situation whose existence as a whole is already *presumed*, and predicating of this subject a *qualification* having a practical bearing on the behavior of the group.

Closely related to, and merging into, the explicit

predication which arises from the need of inhibiting some feature of the response under way, is the predication which *further specifies* a feature of the situation. Thus, for example, the announcement of the discovery of buffalo may be supplemented by the specification of the number, position, etc. In this case the predication does not inhibit any part of an already determined response, but serves to complete the determination of a course of action still unsettled in the details of its carrying-out.

As we have already pointed out, it is not only the distant features of the situation that need specification. A situation may well be indeterminate through its complexity. Its component elements may all be potentially present to perception, but may escape the observation of some of the group; or, even if they are noticed, they may be open to more than one interpretation. In a simple case, attention may be called to a relevant property of a present object by touching or pointing to the object and using a single qualificatory term. But further specification may be necessary. Suppose, for example, that it is the position of one object with relation to another that is in question; the undifferentiated predication of the sentence-word will not suffice. Or it may be the *absence* of some thing or property that needs specific indication; in which case the object must be named, and the predicate "gone," or a similar negative term, added.

It is not to be supposed that the differentiation of structure occurred only in the proclamation of presence and the predicative proclamation. In all probability a "cross-fertilization" of the rudimentary forms of sentence-word took place. The same complexity and variety of human behavior which we have been assuming would equally have necessitated an evolution in the announcement of intention and that of accomplishment. So long as the speaker is announcing his own future or past deeds, the subject of the rudimentary sentence remains the same and is in no need of specification. It is rather the *object* toward which, or by means of which, the act is performed, that needs to be specified. And any distinctive use of the name makes it so much the more available for other uses. Moreover, although in the announcement of past and future acts it may seem natural to regard the speaker as the implicit subject of the sentence, and the specific name as belonging rather to the predicate, yet this is not the only possible construction to put upon it, nor always the natural one. If what is announced is, for example, some experience which has been undergone, rather than some act performed—and this is just as primitive a case—then what is specified may well be regarded as the subject. M. Bloch's little daughter who came running to him in tears, saying "mon-mon," when her brother, Raymond, had been teasing her, may be regarded as announcing either "I have been made unhappy by Raymond," or "Raymond has made me unhappy." If this rudimentary announcement be expanded—as it must needs be when the experience undergone, as well as the object or the person concerned, is itself specified by speech, and not indicated merely by signs of general distress—we have still the same ambiguous construction; *i.e.*, "I have been teased by Raymond," or "Raymond has been teasing me." It is noteworthy that the distinction between active and passive voice is also implicit here, and that any further development of sentence structure which serves to distinguish clearly the subject of the sentence must at the same time in some way differentiate the "voice" relationship.

Along with the development of the structure of the proclamation as such—the declarative sentence—must go a parallel differentiation and development of the command and of the question. It is natural to think of the command as tending to emphasize the act, and hence the *verb*, from the beginning, just as the proclamation of presence emphasizes the substantive, and the predicative proclamation the adjective. This is no doubt justified to a certain extent; but the developed command must be able to specify not only the act, but the object toward or by means of which the act is to be performed, and the place and manner of its performance as well. We must emphasize again the importance for the development of structure, of the mutual interaction of the different forms of speech. Each step in the differentiation of one form, *e.g.*, the command, must react strongly upon the differentiation and development of the other forms. The fact that a given term has been used as the grammatical object in a command favors its substantive use as the subject of a predicative proclamation. Once a term has come to pass freely from one substantive use to another, it has acquired that verbal currency which makes it at once a definite representative, or symbol, of some feature of the objective world, and constitutes it an independent variable of true language.[1]

The Context of Speech.

THE evolution of language is characterized by a progressive freeing of speech from dependence on the perceived conditions under which it is uttered and heard, and from the behavior which accompanies it. The extreme limit of this freedom is reached in language which is written (or printed) and read. For example, it is quite indifferent to the reader of these words, under what physical conditions they have been written, and whether they have been penned or typed. This represents, we repeat, the extreme limit of the process by which language comes to be increasingly independent of the conditions of its use. The transition from the sentence-word with its rudimentary structure to the complete sentence with its differentiated functional parts, is the first and most momentous stage in this evolution. *It marks as important a phase in social and psychological evolution as did the appearance of distance-receptors of sight and hearing in the evolution of the individual organism.* It enormously increases the range and extent of coöperative action. Not only does it enable concerted action to be prepared and initiated with reference to objects and events distant in space, but, through its instrumentality in analyzing the perceptually present situation, it makes possible a vastly

---

[1] The treatment of the interrogative sentence and of *conversation*, which logically belongs here, we have found it convenient to postpone to Part III, Chapter XV, *The Complete Act of Speech.*

increased fineness and complexity of social adjustments. Coöperative action need no longer be directed simply to the situation as a whole, but may take advantage, in definitely discriminable ways, of particular variations in the properties and relations of things and events. Further, the range of human action is extended not only as regards space, but also as regards time. Long and complicated courses of action may be organized and regulated. Past and future events, as well as spatially distant features, may be brought into connection with the present situation. It is true that this is not achieved at once by the differentiation and combining of words to form sentences. But the appearance of the sentence marks a new type of language instrument inherently capable of controlling a new type of socially organized behavior. That this linguistic development, fundamentally social in function as it is, has had a tremendous repercussion on the psychological development of the individual, is also true, as we shall see later.

But while the evolution of its structure permits language to function in ever greater independence of the concrete conditions of its use, it is very important to recognize that language never completely loses its dependence on *context*. The sentence is indeed a complete unit, but it does not stand alone. What happens is that a *language* context comes more and more to take the place of the *perceptual* context. The essential thing that is to be said needs to be led up to by introductory remarks which give it a setting. Yet spoken language—and it is speech that remains the only living language—is never wholly freed from its perceived context and accompaniments. Conversation takes place within a concrete situation, and is never fully intelligible when transcribed. The attitude and demeanor of the speaker have their share in the significance of what is said; while the intonation and inflection of the voice are vital to all speech. Even written language, or the printed language of a book, while it is independent of all these accompaniments of speech, is not so wholly free from all context as we are sometimes inclined to assume. The most impersonal and abstract of disquisitions is written with a whole background of unexpressed "representations" (to use the neo-positivist term), and in a situation of *presumptions*. If this presumed background is not shared by the reader, what is written must remain relatively unintelligible to him. This is the principal source of the difficulty of interpreting the literature of antiquity. The world of the writer must be laboriously recreated and realized by the reader, before the full significance of what was written in an earlier epoch can be appreciated.

Language, then, so long as it continues to function as true language, and does not become a mere dead form, remains dependent upon a context of *presumptions*. Language singles out and specifies certain features relevant to the occasion of its use, but the features thus singled out remain in vital connection with what is not specified but only presumed. This fact has been pointed out by various writers on logic and epistemology.[1] What

---

[1] It is central to the theory of meaning advanced in the recent volume by Ogden and Richards, *The Meaning of Meaning*. The way in which speech among savages is dependent on the perceived context is admirably illustrated in an appendix to that work, "Primitive Languages," by Malinowski, to which reference has already been made.

we are now in a position to see is that it is the natural and inevitable outcome of the evolution of language as the instrument of social coöperation.

Types of Language Structure.

In the account we have just given of the evolution of language, we have tried to avoid making any assumption as to the type of grammatical structure possessed by primitive language. What has been said of the factors operative in linguistic evolution holds, we believe, whatever type, or types, may have been primitive. For all language, whatever its grammatical type, exhibits a structure the unit of which is the sentence with its functional parts, the subject and predicate. All languages also are resolvable into elements of some sort which enter into variable combinations, and which are functionally dependent upon one another. That all languages are made up of words is perhaps not quite so clear, although it was for long the common belief that words were invented first and put together to form phrases and sentences. We are apt to be misled in our ideas about language by our familiarity with the form it takes on the printed page. But written language is far from being the exact equivalent of its spoken prototype. As language is spoken there is no such fixed separation of parts, nor such invariability of form as the printed page exhibits. This is not to assert, of course, that we do not ordinarily use words in speaking, but only that we are apt to gain an exaggerated idea of the definiteness and fixity of the real words as they enter into living speech. Moreover, the term *word* does not mean just the same thing when applied to an isolating language, like Chinese, as when applied to an inflectional language, like Latin, or to an incorporating language, like some of the Indian tongues.

It was formerly supposed by philologists that all languages could be classified under a few distinct types, the isolating, the agglutinative, and the inflectional, and that these types represent definite stages in development. Thus the original and primitive form of all language was the isolating type, in which the words do not belong to fixed "parts of speech," but may serve indifferently as noun, verb, adjective, or adverb, without internal modification—like the word *round* in English. From this supposedly primitive form, it was believed, language passed to the agglutinative stage as some of the terms lost their original independence of form and meaning and became mere adjuncts to the more important words in the sentence. Thus Chinese, commonly cited as a typical example of an isolating language, has both "full" words, which serve, *e.g.*, as substantives or verbs, and "empty" words, which serve as prepositions, or to indicate the syntax of the "full" words. From the agglutinative stage, it was believed, language passed into the more perfect inflectional form, in which the "empty" words have become welded as inflectional particles to the only true words. But this theory, which belongs in spirit to the era of Comte and Hegel, is no longer held. There is no single natural order of language development, no "law of progress" which applies here, any more than elsewhere among social phenomena. Inflectional languages often lose their distinct inflectional

III

form and take on agglutinative features, as has French to some extent. *Je n'en ai plus* is a fairly typical agglutinative complex. English, again, has almost entirely lost its inflections and has reached what closely resembles an isolating type of structure. *May have been seen, could have been done,* etc., are composed of elements which not only pass unchanged from combination to combination, but are capable of independent verbal use. Moreover, Chinese gives evidence of having formerly possessed more distinct agglutinative features than it does today. As a matter of fact, philologists have come to recognize that the terms *isolating, agglutinative, incorporating,* and *inflectional* do not represent any hard and fast divisions into which all known languages can unequivocally be placed. Languages, as we have already indicated, overlap such boundary lines. If Chinese is isolating on the whole, it might nevertheless be classed as agglutinative, while inflectional languages may exhibit to almost any extent isolating or agglutinative features. Some philologists today, like Sapir in his recent work on *Language,* doubt even the relative validity of the traditional terms of classification, and alternative systems have been proposed. Until, however, some new system of classification has met with general acceptance by philologists, we must continue to use the unsatisfactory conventional terms.

Was there in reality any one and only "original" type of language? We may well doubt it. It is conceivable that language developed independently in many centers and that there was a divergence in the type of structure possessed by these embryo languages from the first, some evolving in one direction, some in another. There are, however, some considerations which point to a certain priority of a structure analogous to the isolating type, which are worth examination. There is, first, the fact that gesture-language has such a structure. The terms of gesture-language, its "words," seem to have been "put together." They are relatively fixed in form and pass unchanged from one combination to another, while the syntax is chiefly indicated by order, and not by the form of the elements nor by the addition of subsidiary gestures analogous to agglutinative particles. That gestures lend themselves less readily to modification than do articulate utterances, may possibly be true. We cannot, of course, assume gesture-language to be parallel to primitive speech in its form and course of development. It is worth noting, however, that when it is developed spontaneously by deaf-mutes it has the same structure that the gesture-language of Indians, for example, exhibits. The like is true of those rudimentary hybrid tongues such as Beche de mer, Pidgin English, and the Chinook lingo. In the first two of these the vocabulary is chiefly English, although the terms borrowed are largely modified in form and meaning. There is no inherent distinction in parts of speech—almost any word may serve any function in the sentence, according to its order and connections. Names of objects are freely formed by the juxtaposition of unmodified elements.

Jespersen gives some amusing instances of this. Thus a piano is called "big fellow bokus (box) you fight him he cry"; and a concertina has the even more picturesque appellation, "little fellow bokus you shove him he cry you pull him he cry." The idea of being bald is thus conveyed: "grass belong head belong him all he die finish," or, "cocoanut belong him grass no stop."[1] In Pidgin English the structure is of the same simple sort, although the vocabulary is drawn from wider sources. Much the same thing is true of the Chinook lingo, or the Jargon, as it sometimes called. This is, like the others, a rudimentary tongue, which arose along the Columbia River from the intercourse of the white traders with the Indians. It contains words from more than one Indian language, as well as from English and from the French of the Canadians. Although the Indians who helped "invent" it spoke a highly complex language of their own, yet the resulting structure of Chinook, like that of Beche de mer and Pidgin English, is of the simplest isolating type. What Jespersen, quoting Hale, says of the dependence of the Chinook on the use of gesture and other bodily expression is so interesting that we repeat it here: " 'The Indians in general,' says Hale, 'are very sparing of their gesticulations. No languages, probably, require less assistance from this source than theirs. . . . We frequently had occasion to observe the sudden change produced when a party of the natives, who had been conversing in their own tongue, were joined by a foreigner, with whom it was necessary to speak in the Jargon. The countenances, which had before been grave, stolid and inexpres-

---

[1] *Language*, pp. 217 f. These examples also illustrate the use of "belong" and "fellow," which are well on the way to being agglutinative particles.

sive, were instantly lighted up with animation; the low monotonous tone became lively and modulated; every feature was active; the head, the arms, and the whole body was in motion, and every look and gesture became instinct with meaning.' "[1] This is interesting because it points to the conclusion that the Chinook is really like a reversion to a simpler and more primitive type of language, in which the spoken utterance is still measurably dependent on the aid of other bodily activity.

The structure of the spontaneous "languages" which are sometimes invented by twins or other children more or less isolated would be more significant; but unfortunately there is very little trustworthy evidence available concerning them. What there is, however, points in the same direction. Jespersen has investigated reports concerning several such cases and is of the opinion that the vocabulary is usually drawn from the language of the group to which the children in question belong, although the words used are apt to be greatly modified. The one such language he was able to investigate personally (that of Danish boy twins who had been left practically uncared for until the age of four) had the same rudimentary isolating structure exhibited by the lingoes we have just considered. In the few sentences he cites from it: *"Bap ep dop"*—"Mandse has broken the hobby-horse"—literally "Mandse horse piece"; and *"Hos ia bov lhalh"*—"Brother's trousers are wet, Maria," literally, "Trousers Maria brother

[1] *Op. cit.*, p. 231.

water," we find no distinction between substantive and verb save that of order in the sentence.

While the evidence furnished by these cases cannot be regarded as conclusive, it is nevertheless very suggestive that, alike in gesture-language and wherever makeshift tongues have grown up, the same rudimentary structure has appeared, even where, as in the case of Beche de mer and Chinook, the individuals using it have been accustomed to a language of a very different and highly complex grammatical structure.

In the account we have given of the evolution of explicit predication, we have supposed it to take place through the combining in one utterance of two previously independent sentence-words. If this is true, it is more natural to think of the isolating structure as being primitive. But this must not be too hastily assumed. In all languages—the most highly inflectional or the most richly incorporating, as well as the purely isolating— sentences are ordinarily formed by the combination of separate terms performing distinct functions. It is not the fact that the subject and the predicate are separate and separable terms combined to form the sentence that characterizes a given language as isolating. What differentiates the isolating language is, first, the fact that the terms are not in themselves parts of speech; a given term may on occasion serve as substantive, verb, adjective, preposition, etc. Second, the terms pass *unmodified* in form from one combination to another. This involves, third, that all syntactical relationships must be indicated by the *order* of terms in the sentence—aided by intonation and pitch of voice. In inflectional and incorporating languages, on the contrary, the terms belong permanently to regular functional classes; a substantive cannot, for example, play the part of the verb. In inflectional languages the terms themselves undergo certain regular internal modifications to denote the syntactical relationships (*i.e.*, case), and certain conventionally limited changes in meaning (*i.e.*, number, gender, or mood). Incorporating languages differ from the inflectional type in that the syntactical changes are indicated by the addition, or inclusion, of comparatively independent particles, rather than by modifications of the stem itself or by prefixes and suffixes which become thoroughly fused with it. There is usually also a wider range of meanings denoted by these fixed and conventionalized particles than is possible through inflections alone. Thus in certain Indian languages the form of a substantive may denote not only gender and number, but also whether the object is animate or inanimate, standing or sitting, etc.; while a verb may denote by its form whether the action expressed was witnessed by the speaker himself, inferred from evidence, or known on hearsay. The inflectional and incorporating types of language, and, to a lesser degree, the agglutinative, represent a greater and more complex *conventionalization* of structure than does the isolating type. Yet there is, of course, convention present in the isolating language, else it would not be a language. If all explicit predication arose, as we have argued, from the combining of formerly independent terms, a completely developed isolating structure was not established until a regular and conventionally fixed *order* of combination grew up.

Doubtless there is a natural order in which the chief parts of the sentence tend to follow each other; but much of the necessary regularity of a language instrument fitted to meet growing social needs remains to be established by convention. In the initial stages of development, primitive languages must have leaned more heavily on the aid of such inarticulate features of vocal expression as intonation and pitch, as well as of attitude, facial expression, etc. The ambiguity of the unconventionalized and poorly regularized utterances was for long compensated by these instinctive means. Now it may well have been that, in many cases, before a conventional *order* of sentence structure became established, the beginnings of other modifications of the internal structure of terms according to their function and meaning had already been made. Changes in intonation, pitch, and accent tend to carry with them changes in the articulate form as well. Once these articulate modifications obtained a foothold, they would tend to replace the more instinctive, but less adequate, forms of expression, and also to obviate the necessity for a greater fixity of word order. Whether, or how far, the evolution of the primitively structureless sentence took this direction from the beginning, one can only speculate; and the question remains, after all, outside the scope of our present inquiry.

No attempt will be made to show how the further development of the structure of language—*e.g.*, the differentiation of gender, number, and case, or of voice, mood, and tense—has been influenced by the utility of language in social control. We have been concerned only with the essentials of explicit predication in the complete sentence, which are common to all languages whatever their morphological type. It is evident that the particular form taken by such further functional differentiations will depend on the general type of structure of the given language. The significant feature of language development is not, in all probability, the attainment of one type of structure rather than another. It consists rather in a true differentiation of function performed by the various elements, and the evolution of some sort of structural organization, either in the terms themselves or in their mode of combination in the sentence, to represent and make possible this functional differentiation. Our knowledge of the various families of languages and their histories would lead us to infer that no single type of structure has any marked superiority. If this be true, it would seem to follow that the evolutionary changes in form and structure which languages undergo are relatively independent of the fundamental function performed by all language. As in chess "All gambits are sound," so in language all types of structure are adequate. The factors which bring about the changes within a given language are doubtless exceedingly complex. To a considerable extent they are internal to the language itself and arise from the structure already existing, just as the particular moves in a chess game are determined by the opening chosen and the existing state of the game. But although the object of a chess game does not suffice to explain the varying course of the play, nevertheless without a knowledge of what that object is, we should seek in vain to make the moves intelligible. Even so, although the conception of language as the instrument of social coördination does not provide a theory of the complex changes in structure and form which languages undergo, still, if our contention is sound, that this is the essential function of all language, no theory can hope for success which does not keep this conception clearly in view.

PART II
Aspects of Mental Evolution

CHAPTER VI

Behaviorism and the Problem of Cognition

The Meaning of Behaviorism.

ALTHOUGH the foregoing treatment of the social character and evolutionary origin of language may be regarded as an independent empirical study to be judged on its own merits, it represents, nevertheless, a deliberate attempt to apply in this special field a very general psychological theory and method. In the remainder of our work it will be necessary for us to emphasize and keep distinctly in mind the fundamental assumptions on which we are proceeding. While it was possible to discuss the problem of the origin of language without direct reference to any general psychological theory, the consideration of the rôle that speech plays in the life-economy of the individual can be undertaken only from the standpoint of some such theory. However earnest we may be in our desire to conduct the investigation in a truly empirical spirit, and to face the facts without prejudice, we can never hope to succeed by turning our backs on general theoretical considerations. Our only safe recourse is to make our principles as explicit as possible, to bring them out into the open where they may be examined and seen for what they are.

We shall, accordingly, in the succeeding pages frankly adopt the method of behaviorism.[1] The results of our

---

[1] Behaviorism has interesting points of contact with the doctrines of the sociological school of Durkheim. The thinkers of that school

investigation, once they are reached, may be construed by the reader in terms of a dualism if he wishes to do so. There will be nothing in them, that is, to contradict the belief in the existence of distinct conscious processes revealed only in introspection. But such a construction, while it is compatible with the theory to be developed here, can add nothing to it, but must remain a merely external addition. Moreover, what is more significant, it

are, to be sure, indifferent to any theoretical considerations of individual psychology, since it is a corner stone of their system that social phenomena are the subject-matter of a wholly independent science. But they are one with the behaviorists in insisting on the necessity of a thoroughly objective treatment of the phenomena in question. Social phenomena are, they admit, psychical and not physical or biological; but this does not imply that they are mental states or processes taking place in "minds." So far as *"representations collectives"* are open to scientific study, it is as objectively observable rites and institutions and formulated beliefs. Hence our own claim that the successful treatment of language depends on envisaging it as an objective phenomenon and in the light of its own objective relationships, instead of as a manifestation of inner mental states, is as much in accord with the spirit of Durkheim's sociology as it is with behaviorism.

The influence of Durkheim's school on recent writers on linguistics is a significant symptom of a widespread trend of contemporary thought. The essentially social character of language is more and more acknowledged and even insisted on in recent contributions to philological and psychological journals. What is lacking so far is the conception of the social *function* of speech. Speech continues to be referred to as the communication of ideas, which are still implicitly regarded as inner processes in individual minds. It would be far more in accord with Durkheim's general theory to regard the *function* of speech equally with the structure of language, as an objective social phenomenon. It is not the least merit of behaviorism that it provides a new view of the phenomena both of society and of the individual and of their interrelations. This does not mean "reduction" of the one to the other, any more than the general program of behaviorism means a reduction of psychology to biology. It does mean, however, a closer interrelationship and interdependence of all three sciences; and this is, in so far, a sign of real scientific advance.

is only by definitely abandoning the assumption of a dualism that our present investigation is made possible.

Even though psychology has hitherto held that its proper subject-matter is a realm of mental states or processes, it has never been able to identify, describe, or explain these phenomena except with reference to the bodily organism and the outside world. The record of its scientific achievements from Berkeley's theory of vision to Binet's mental tests is a record of the progressive linking of psychological phenomena (essentially "mental," if you will) with the organism and its activities. Indeed, the history of psychological science could be written as a record of the varying ways in which such linkages have been systematically sought. Early sensationalism, for example, attempted to construe mind in terms of the action of external stimuli upon the sense organs, and of the concomitance and succession of such stimulation. Physiological psychology was more ambitious and attempted to base its identification and classification of mental phenomena upon a minute and elaborate analysis of the physiological apparatus, tracing the course of sensory stimulation from end-organ to higher center. Even the development of introspection as a method of experimental psychology was made possible only by the standardizing of the conditions of its use, *i.e.*, by making the introspective report a function of previously determined objective conditions. And the measure of its success as a psychological method has been the degree to which such dependence upon objective conditions has been secured.

The methodological significance of this fact is very

clear. Science, it is universally admitted, is possible only when the observations made by one investigator are verifiable by others. Consequently, if introspection is the observation of essentially inner and private states, open by definition to the view of but one person, it is evident that it can have, as such, no scientific validity. It must be capable of appearing in some other guise, if it is to make good its scientific pretensions. The famous "argument from analogy"—by which I am led to ascribe conscious processes similar to my own to other beings whose physical structure and behavior are similar to mine—serves only to obscure the issue. It still remains necessary to determine what shall constitute the essential similarity of objective conditions which justifies us in inferring the presence in other living beings of the mental content observed in ourselves. These introspective readings can pass current as scientific legal tender only if they bear the official stamp: *observed under objective conditions, A, B, C*. As a matter of fact, even this statement of the case of introspection is too generous. For the introspective report of the observer in rigorous experimental procedure is not taken as are the findings of an ordinary experimental observer in other fields. It yields, rather, *data*, to be recorded by the conductor of the experiment—who is himself the real scientific observer— and to be interpreted in the light of the conditions under which they occur. That the theoretical significance of this procedure on the part of experimental psychology has not been more generally recognized, is due to the metaphysical preconceptions of psychologists, which have constantly led them to interpret the phenomena in terms of an ontological dualism. But whether we accept or reject dualism as an ultimate metaphysical doctrine, it is an undeniable fact that the development of scientific psychology has been accompanied by an ever closer linking of mental phenomena with the objective conditions of their appearance. Treated at first as related in a partial and merely external way to these conditions, they have come more and more to be individuated and described as functions of them.

Behaviorism we may regard as the last stage in this development. It is a very interesting fact that behaviorism has simultaneously appeared both as a metaphysical theory and as an empirical scientific method. It is fresh evidence of a relation to which the history of thought already abundantly testified, namely the mutual dependence of metaphysics and scientific methodology. As a metaphysical theory, behaviorism replaces the dualism of mind and body with a monism, and endeavors to interpret consciousness in terms of the organism and its behavior. With behaviorism as a metaphysical theory we are not here concerned, except to note its relation to psychological method. We shall not ask whether ultimately there is or is not any distinctive "mental" existent, or whether the monism which behaviorism advocates is or is not "materialism." These questions are fundamental questions, and would merit the most careful consideration were our purpose less special. Our concern is with behaviorism as a theory of psychological method. As such a theory it stands for a complete and thoroughgoing description of mental phenomena in terms of objective conditions, including under these both the organism and the external surroundings in which it lives and acts. When we say "in terms of," this does not imply that psychological phenomena are to be identified with the objective conditions by which they are determined. Energy is not identical with mass, or time, or space; yet it is only in terms of its relation to these that it can be defined or dealt with by physics. It may be said that psychological phenomena are *functions* of their objective conditions, if the term *function* is used in a large enough sense to embrace qualitative as well as quantitative determinations. For psychological phenomena cannot be even identified for purposes of scientific discussion, except in so far as they are related to objective and publicly observable conditions. One may "know" what pain and hunger and rage and sweet are, in the sense of having felt or experienced them; but such "knowledge" of, or acquaintance with, these mental phenomena remains outside the reach of science. We cannot be sure we are talking about the same things when we use the words "hunger" and "sweet," unless we refer each to its appropriate objective condition—and this is by no means a simple matter. That hunger and sweet are "in themselves" something quite distinct, something immediately felt, may be true; but what they are thus immediately and "in themselves" does not enter into science. As immediately given, sweet and hunger may conceivably differ from individual to individual; but if they do, such differences are beyond the reach of discovery, and science is indifferent to them. It may be true that science, as "knowledge by description," would be impossible if there were no "knowledge by acquaintance"; but if so, this is no peculiar characteristic of psychology. Chemistry and physics, equally with the science of mind, depend in the last resort upon an observation into which an immediate recognition and discrimination enter. *What* is observed, however, becomes a datum for science, only in so far as it is publicly identifiable. One of the great advantages of the use of instruments lies in the fact that they provide an indirect means of observing the phenomena they record, through which the immediacy attaching to a direct observation is cancelled out. A thermometer, for example, not only records changes in temperature which escape direct observation, but by translating these into visual form cancels out the immediate qualities of warmth and cold. The process of "reading" the thermometer takes place through a recognition of the silvery sheen of the mercury and the black lines on the glass—visual data as immediate as warmth and cold—but *what is observed* is not these but the *relation* of the top of the column of mercury to the divisions of the scale. Scientific observation is always directed to relationships of some sort, since it is only as phenomena enter into relations that they are publicly observable and verifiable; and this is as true for psychology as for physics.

Behaviorism, we have said, is the last stage in the linking of mental phenomena to objective conditions. It does not regard the relation between them as merely external, as did the old physiological psychology, but treats it as essentially determinative. Now it is able to justify this claim—and thus to objectify mind—

precisely because it has reached a new and far more adequate conception of the nature of the objective conditions of which psychological phenomena are a function. Early sensationalism confined its attention to the stimulation of the sense organs. Physiological psychology contemplated the physiological changes of the nervous system, but regarded the processes by which the sensory centers of the cortex were stimulated as alone of direct importance for psychology. It was in the hidden processes going on in the cells of the cortex that mind and body were somehow related, although one could not tell how. The value of locating the connection lay in the fact that the neural processes and their relationships could be substituted to fill out gaps in the psychical order.[1] Although they were inherently and metaphysically different, neural processes and their antecedents and consequents could be taken as a clue to the order of psychical antecedents and consequents. As a matter of fact, this service of filling in gaps was more or less reciprocal, and a mythical chemistry of nerve-cells was not infrequently resorted to for the purpose of completing the physiological schema. In a general way it was believed that the most promising method of

[1] This statement applies literally only to the parallelistic interpretation of the matter. For interactionism, the gaps in both the physical and psychical orders are real, and the two must be taken together to make a continuous causal sequence. Nevertheless, the relation between the psychical process and the cerebral process remained external in a peculiar sense and marked an absolute limit to any possible scientific explanation. That the stimulation of one cell gave rise to a sensation of blue and that of another to a sensation of red, was accepted as fact, but as a fact that could be brought under no general principle, other than the providence of God.

getting more insight into the neural determination (or correlation) of psychical processes was to delve deeper into the molecular and atomic changes in nerve-cells. It became a scientific ideal to isolate the final element of mind and relate it to its corresponding element of neural process.

To this whole manner of thought behaviorism offers a clear contrast. Instead of attempting a microscopic examination of nerve-cells, it strives to get a comprehensive view which will embrace both the nervous system as a whole and the complete organism in its environmental setting. Psychological phenomena are conceived to be conditioned not by *processes* within nerve-cells, but by the *functioning* of the nervous system in its control of the actions of the organism with reference to the environment.

The Psychological Environment.

BEHAVIORISTIC psychology has thus formulated a new empirical problem; it has discovered a new field to be exploited. The richness of the material to be analyzed and systematized we have only just begun to appreciate. From whatever direction we approach the task, it becomes evident that we have to do with the subject-matter of a distinct science. The comparative method may be chosen, for example; and by studying different species of organisms, we are able to distinguish characteristically different types of behavior, related to each other through a common descent. Or an intensive study of the behavior of a single species may be made with a view to determining, for example, the conditions under which a given response is stimulated; what changes in environment are discriminated, and how; the interrelations of different responses to each other, etc. Under this last topic, a genetic study may be made of the developmental order of different modes of behavior, the processes by which responses become modified and by which changes in the coördination and interdependence of responses are effected. But whether the study of behavior is approached from one of these directions or another, what is studied is not physical changes in spatial position, nor movements of body and limbs, nor nervous discharges, but activities stimulated by, and directed toward, objective conditions—moments or phases in a functional system.

But behavioristic psychology is not only a study of behavior in its relation to objective conditions; it is equally a study of the environment as related to animal behavior. The whole world becomes subject to a new analysis and classification in the light of its relation to the life-economy of the animal. This analysis will vary according as it is made with reference to one organic species or another, just as the behavior-system of one species differs from that of another. We may consider any given behavior-system as a complex instrument of selection to which the world is subjected by the animal organism. The behavior-system is, as it were, projected upon the world. The features thus brought into relief are seen to take on new properties and to enter into new relationships with one another. They constitute the *psychological environment*. This is not identi-

cal with the physical environment or even with the biological environment.

The psychological environment of man contains, for
example, the secondary qualities and the whole array
of values, which are not present in the physical world. *cf. 127*
Let us take for consideration the temperature qualities,
warm, cold, and hot. These have a basis in the physical
world; that is to say, physical objects exhibit differences of temperature. But physical heat is continuous
and admits of only quantitative differences. Physically
speaking, there are not heat *and* cold, but only different
degrees of heat. Viewed in relation to the selective capacity of the human organism, however, the continuity
of temperatures disappears. At certain points in the
temperature scale a striking discontinuity shows itself,
and the homogeneous heat of the physical world becomes broken up into the opposed qualities of cold,
warm, and hot, which are closely connected with affective states of comfort and discomfort.

This case is typical of the transformation which the
physical world undergoes when the behavior-system is
projected upon it. Phenomena which, physically, are
distinct from each other, lose their differences and become indistinguishable as features of the psychological
environment; quantitative differences become qualitative; the nexus of physical relationships becomes obscured or disappears, and is replaced by a new and distinctive scheme of things. The psychological world is a
different world from that of physical science, but it is
related to the latter in a systematic way, albeit a way of
enormous complexity.

133

It is a fact of great moment that although this psychological world of man is in a way known to common sense, and is described in the vague and ambiguous terms of common sense, it has never been amenable to direct scientific treatment. Its phenomena, such as warmths, colors, odors, etc., do not fall into ordered classes and systematic interrelationships, as do the so-called primary qualities of the physical world. They are not measurable (except in very doubtful and indirect ways, on the basis of Weber's law). Some of the phenomena, notably those of color and sound, do admit of a sort of classification and systematization. But such order and regularity as they exhibit are wholly self-contained; that is to say, there are no interlocking sets of relationships between the different orders of secondary qualities. They are neither causes nor effects of each other, nor indeed of phenomena in the physical world. No instruments record their presence, or measure their increase or decrease—except the animal organism. For these reasons they have been regarded as mere "appearance" in contrast to the measurable regularity and fixity of interrelationship of the "real" world of primary qualities. Or else, because of their recognized relativity to the organism, they have been relegated to the "mind" as "mental entities," and held to be open only to introspective observation.

Behaviorism attempts to apply a sort of relativity-theory to psychological phenomena. Classical psychology operates with a physical stimulus *plus* a mental state, and regards each as an absolute existent independent of the other. Behaviorism would construe the physical stimulus in its relationship to the responsive behavior of the human organism and thus establish—or discover— its psychological status. Similarly it would construe the acts of the organism in their relation to the physical world, and in so doing establish their psychological status. The two constructions are reciprocal and must proceed *pari passu.*

The claim that the secondary qualities are attributes of things as related to the human—or animal—organism may seem open to certain objections. The color red and the odor of heliotrope are not, it is urged, reducible to terms of a mere relativity. They are absolute data of experience, positive and irreducible qualities. To this we must again reply what we have already said: that whether the color or the odor be absolute data of experience or not, they can become data for science only if they enter into determinate and systematic relations with the objective, *i.e.,* the public world. Furthermore, as we have already pointed out, they are not even identifiable except as functions of the objective conditions under which they are experienced. Whatever analysis and generalization they may be subject to, must be made with constant reference to this objective relationship. For example, even the fact that odors do not form an ordered series as do colors, but remain relatively isolated from and incomparable with each other, having at the same time an intensity of affective tone which colors do not possess, acquires a scientific interest for the first time when we correlate it with the different rôles which odors and colors play in regulating the behavior of men or animals with reference to the external world. For classical psychology, which was content to relate the differences in sensation-qualities to differences in end-organs and a hypothetical "specific energy" of nerves (or sensory-centers), this difference between odors and colors remained an unimportant circumstance without theoretic interest. A sensation was a sensation; and the profound differences between the different orders of sensation offered no problems to a theory which found the only linkage between mental processes and the outside world to lie in sensory stimulation.

The Problem of Cognition.

WE have hitherto written as if the psychological environment of man were made up exclusively of the so-called secondary qualities and affective values. A little reflection, however, shows that this is far from true. We perceive the "real" shapes and sizes of objects; we experience events as causes and effects; and we know, or may know, the inner structure of the world to an indefinite extent. Indeed, every discovery of science extends the bounds of the psychological environment of civilized man. This environment includes, then, the objective world so far as this is known to science; and if we recognize that there are vast stretches of it still beyond the reach of human knowledge, there is perhaps none that is absolutely unknowable.

But here we encounter a certain difficulty. If the psychological environment is the objective environment (physical, biological, etc.), *as relative to* man's organized capacity for responsive behavior, how is it that the objective world *as such, i.e.,* as independent of its relation to the human organism, can be included in the psychological environment? How, in other words, can man acquire a valid knowledge of an independent objective order, if he experiences it only as the correlate of his own human capacities for behavior? This seems to present a paradox, or even a contradiction in terms. But the contradiction is, after all, not a fundamental one. It admits of resolution.

The external and independent order of nature, whose existence behaviorism is bound to assume, becomes a psychological environment—or, to use a more familiar expression, becomes an object of possible experience— only in the measure and to the degree that it is subject to the selective discrimination of the human behavior-system. Man can be aware of only such features of the physical world, for example, as call for specifically discriminative behavior with reference to them. Now man, like other animals, is primarily and fundamentally concerned with things only in so far as they are actual or potential sources of advantage or disadvantage to him, either directly or indirectly. The fundamental problem of human knowledge, then, is to discover how the realities of the outer world *in their independent order of interrelationships* become, through the bearing they have on man's welfare, specifically discriminated by him in his behavior.

It has always been believed that in "conception" and "knowledge" man does in some way transcend the peculiar limitations of his organic structure, and enter upon an intercourse with objective realities which is determined rather by their universal relations with each other than by their specific relations to him. If the theory of behaviorism is sound, the capacity for conceptual thought and valid knowledge must be dependent upon the development of a new and distinctive level of behavior, *a new type of dealing with the objective world*. To understand knowledge as an empirical human phenomenon, it is necessary to distinguish this new type of behavior from simpler and more primitive types, and to analyze it in its genetic and structural relations to these.

We may be guided in this task by the fact, so often signalized, that conceptual thought is a peculiarly *human* characteristic. It is human reason, which, more profoundly than any other trait, separates man from the other animals. What we must look for, consequently, is some kind of behavior which man alone exhibits, and of which animals are incapable. One such kind of behavior is speech. In our previous treatment of speech we found it to perform the function of bringing individuals together in a distinctive type of social coöperation. We must now inquire whether, and in what way, it modifies human behavior with reference to things.

Closely connected with speech is a second peculiarly human characteristic—the use of tools. It has often been said that tools supply man with an indefinitely increased number of specialized limbs, which enormously extend the range and scope of his activities. It is equally true that they supply him with supplementary sense-organs. But their psychological importance is more profound than this. The transformation they have wrought in

man's power over nature is the measure of the transformation they have wrought in man himself.

That tools and speech are intimately connected in
human evolution, there is strong reason to believe. However they may have been related in their beginnings, it
is certain that it is only within the permanent organization of the social group, bound together by language,
that the use of tools could undergo any great development. The evolution of tools is essentially a social evolution. But the psychological connection of speech and
tools is, we believe, more direct and intimate than this
general consideration would indicate.

Our present concern is with speech; but we shall find
it profitable and even necessary to consider at some
length what is involved in the use and making of tools
as a distinctive type of behavior.

H

spondere : to promise

flex : bend back

CHAPTER VII

Some Features of Animal Behavior

The Response as a Functional Unit.

IT is customary to think of animal behavior as made up of responses to stimuli. While this view does not do justice to all the facts, as we shall see a little later, it does serve as a very convenient point of departure. There is, however, a certain ambiguity in the meaning of the term "response." As we shall use it here, a response is not a definite bodily movement regarded as a change in spatial position, but rather a movement, or series or complex of movements, taken in its objective relation to some more or less distinct end which it normally serves. It is a *functional* unit.

A very elementary sort of response, for example, is the avoiding-reaction. The form that this will take varies with the organic structure of the species concerned. But even within the limits of a single species, and a very low one, the avoiding-reaction is not one simple act. It usually involves several coördinated movements, the detail of which may vary from occasion to occasion. These movements are regarded as constituting a single response, because they occur together, either simultaneously or in close succession, and because they normally effect a single adjustment of the organism to something in its environment.[1]

[1] When a response consists of successive movements which occur in a fixed order, it is often found that the earlier movements act as im-

Very often a number of distinct responses become related so that they form a set of alternatives. This is illustrated in the familiar case of the stentor described by Jennings. If the stentor is irritated by the addition of carmine to the water, it first reacts merely by a slight change in position, continuing its normal activities. If the irritating stimulation continues, it next reverses the ciliary current; thirdly, it breaks off its normal activity completely by contracting strongly; and finally, when this fails, it resorts to the more radical expedient of detaching itself and swimming away. These four successive modes of acting with reference to the irritating stimulus are naturally regarded as four distinct responses; but the case is not always so simple. A cat, for example, in attacking an enemy will often bite *and* scratch at once or alternately; but it may do one without the other. Are these to be considered two distinct responses or parts of a single complex response?

In general, the simpler the behavior of the animal, the more clearly it may be resolved into distinct units. The movements, or simple acts, of which the lower organisms are capable, are organized into relatively fixed and stable groups, which must either occur as wholes or not at all. These unit-groups commonly are linked together in larger behavior-patterns. They may, like the four forms of the stentor's avoiding reaction, be *alternative* modes of response to the same stimulus. They may again, like these same responses, be on dif-

mediate stimuli of the succeeding movements. In this case we may continue to regard the total complex as a single response containing a number of elements.

ferent levels, the one occurring more often or as a first response, the others in general being called out when the first has failed. Or the evocation of one rather than another alternative may depend on the state of the organism, or on the strength of the stimulus. Response-units may also become grouped in *serial* order, so that while they may occur separately, they are also apt to occur in definite sequence so as to constitute a unitary course of conduct. Thus the stalking, the crouching, and the spring follow each other in this order in the cat's hunting. The cat may on occasion give any one of these responses without the others, but they normally occur as a series of acts.

Functionally Independent Acts.

But while the behavior of the simpler animals is largely resolvable into fixed functional units, there are acts performed by even the simplest which are not thus functionally distinct, and which therefore are not properly speaking *responses*. Movements of locomotion are a case in point. A simpler case still is the throwing out of pseudopodia by the amoeba. These acts are not responses in the same sense as the spring of the cat upon its prey, or the avoiding-reaction of the stentor. They are not functionally complete in themselves, but are rather elements which may enter into many different responses. The throwing out of pseudopodia by the amoeba serves no single end and performs no complete function. It may be a part of the process of surrounding and absorbing a food particle, or of swimming away from a danger; or it may occur aimlessly. Much the same thing is to be said of movements of locomotion, whether of swimming, flying, or walking on the ground. The act of walking, for example, is not simple, since it involves a coördination of movements, both simultaneous and successive; but it is not in itself a *response*, since taken by itself it serves no specific end. The change of position which it brings about is not itself an end, but rather a means to a great variety of ends, such as escape or capture. The fish often swims aimlessly about when he is not actively in pursuit of food or in flight from an enemy. So birds fly about, or hop from branch to branch, in a mere overflow of energy or in the sheer joy of living.

As we go higher up in the scale of animal organisms, we find that the number of such independently variable acts, or elements of response, increases. The more complex the animal, the greater is the range of his activity, *i.e.*, the greater is the number of distinct acts of which he is capable. He makes more kinds of movements with his limbs, for example, and these movements are capable of more kinds of coördination. The specialization of the different sense organs involves the development of coördinated acts of adjustment, such as looking, with its turning of the head toward the source of stimulation, the fixating by the eyes, etc., and listening, with its setting of the head and cocking of the ears, etc. Looking and listening may perhaps be regarded as distinct responses; but since their function is merely to secure fuller and better stimulation of the sense organ in question, they are more properly to be classed

144

with the movements of locomotion, as elements of response. They are also like the latter in the fact that
they occur constantly and aimlessly during waking life.
Animals go about smelling and listening and looking
with no further end than keeping themselves *en rapport* with the outside world. These activities perform
the generalized function of being conditional preparations for almost any sort of specifically purposive behavior.[1]

Types of Behavior Organization.

IF we compare the behavior of the lower organisms—
or of certain classes of them—with that of higher ones,
we observe a characteristic difference in the type of
organization. In the simplest organisms we find a very
few type-responses, fixed in character and entering very
slightly into complex groupings. The amoeba, to take
an extreme example, does nothing besides propelling
itself by its pseudopodia toward or away from stimulating sources, and surrounding and absorbing food-
particles, and ejecting non-assimilable particles. The
invertebrates with a specialized nervous system have a
vastly greater range of activity; but their behavior also
consists for the most part of type-responses, *i.e.*, more
or less complicated acts of relatively fixed pattern. The
unit-responses themselves are permanent complexes
which are performed as wholes; and the larger organi-

---

[1] Of course it is to be understood that such teleological terms as
"purposive," "aimless," and "end" are here used quite objectively, and
without reference to what is commonly called conscious purpose or
intention.

zations into which these units enter are comparatively inflexible. In the case of insects, there is often a high complexity of organization in the elaborate instincts; but these are as fixed as they are complicated.

In the higher vertebrates, particularly in the mammals, behavior shows a different type of organization. It is not so clearly resolvable into separate response-units. The flight of the dog with his tail between his legs, his cautious and stiff-legged approach to a strange dog and the exchange of sniffs are like type-responses; but they are far more flexible in form than the analogous actions of invertebrates. Each species of mammal is characterized by its typical responses, but there is more variation from individual to individual and from occasion to occasion in the performance of these than there is among invertebrate species. If a response is a complex of movements which performs a single and relatively complete function, we may say that such complexes are less fixed in their make-up. The ends which must be attained are less simple. The securing of food, for example, is a very complicated affair for carnivorous mammals. For the graminivorous mammals food-getting is often as simple, perhaps, as it is for the invertebrates; but the cropping and nibbling species make up for this simplicity of feeding by the elaborateness of their means of concealment, flight, or active defense.

Human Behavior.

WHEN we come to man we find this contrast in its extreme form. What is characteristic of man is not the

146

performance of any specific type-responses. It is very difficult to pick out specific responses—in the sense in which we are using the term—which are characteristic of the *genus homo*. The sucking of the infant is a unit-response, but it normally occurs as such only during the first months of infancy. Certain very simple acts, such as grasping an object touched and conveying it to the mouth, drawing away and turning the head aside, and pointing at a distant object with the forefinger, are common to all men and often occur as complete responses. But human behavior is not made up of such responses. There is a sense, indeed, in which human behavior is not made up of "responses" at all, but rather of what we shall later distinguish as "complete acts."

It is not merely that most of the acts that men perform have been acquired during their individual lives, and so are not "instinctive," but that what acts a given individual performs are determined in a large measure by the varying conditions of individual life. If we suppose an individual animal, even one so high in the scale as a dog, to be placed in given physical surroundings, we cannot predict, perhaps, the particular responses he will make in all their detail, but we can enumerate the different kinds of response which are open to him, and one of which he will make. But if we imagine a man to be placed in a similar situation, the number and variety of things he may do are so great that we could not hope to name them all.

The limbs or tails or horns or mouths of most animals are adapted to the performance of a comparatively few specific acts. The same is true of man's legs or feet. He can walk and run and hop and jump on land, and swim in various fashions in water. That is to say, he can support and propel his body in various ways. He can also kick and stamp. But man's hands are in a different category. They are generalized rather than specialized organs. The grasping of objects at a distance, which occupies so much of a baby's time and energy during his early months, is not ordinarily a complete manual response. It is preliminary to, or a part of, an indefinite number of complete acts which as an adult he may perform. The range and variety of possible coördinated movements of the two hands are unparalleled in any other species, the anthropoids not excepted.

There is one sort of human behavior, however, which resembles far more closely that of other animals. This is the behavior characteristic of the emotions. Fear, rage, and love, which are common to a large number of animal species, are characterized by an unusual degree of activity in the unstriped muscles which are controlled by the sympathetic nervous system. Reactions of this sort doubtless occur constantly in some degree; but in emotion they become greatly increased, and may easily be observed in blushing, trembling, stiffening, etc. These reactions are to be distinguished from what we have termed responses, in that they are not adaptive with respect to specific factors in the environment. We may rather say that they are concomitants of physiological changes which have an adaptive value. Along with these characteristic reactions of the autonomic system go acts which are true responses in that they normally show specific adaptation with respect to some external stimulus.[1] These responsive acts are generally regarded as instinctive. This seems to be true of them even in man, but to an extent as yet undetermined. In any case, the acts which are characteristic of the emotions in man approach more nearly the type-responses of animals than does most of human behavior. Striking, kicking, and biting are as typical of rage in man, for example, as in the lower animals. Yet even here it is to be remarked that this primitive type-response seldom occurs in complete form in the adult, although it appears normally in children. Man's superior organization enables him to inhibit this and other primitive emotional responses, and to substitute for them indefinitely complex and indirect acts which serve a similar end.

The Development of the Psychological Environment.

ALONG with the development of behavior, there goes a development of what we have called the "psychological environment"—a differentiation of sense qualities and, later, of objects and objective properties and relations.

We have seen that in the lowest organisms behavior consists chiefly in establishing contacts with nutritious substances and in avoiding contacts with deleterious ones. These two opposite functions are accomplished by means of movements which serve to propel the organism and to turn it, so that it may go either toward or away from the source of stimulation. In addition to

---

[1] We may note what is often overlooked in accounts of the emotions, namely, that it is largely the specific character of these *responses* which distinguish the various emotions from one another, since the autonomic reactions, so far as yet observed, are common to more than one emotion.

149

getting into contact with some things and away from others, the protozoön responds in characteristic ways to light, heat, and electrical stimulation. Its reactions to light and heat are selective, *i.e.*, they discriminate ranges of temperature and illumination which normally are favorable to the organism from those which are unfavorable. These adaptive reactions, however, are practically the same in form as those which the organism makes to favorable (*i.e.*, nutritious) substances, on the one hand, and to substances which act upon it unfavorably, either chemically or mechanically, on the other hand. There is this difference: that the presence of a nutritious particle causes the amoeba not only to establish contact with it, but to maintain the contact by surrounding the particle. The stimulus of light or warmth produces merely the response of swimming into the lighted or warmed area and staying there. But the two primitive and fundamental forms of animal behavior are (1) *going toward and establishing contact with*, and (2) *going away from and avoiding*. Accordingly the psychological environment in which the simplest organisms live falls into the two opposed qualities of *favorableness* and *unfavorableness*.

The mechanisms by which the two kinds of adaptive acts are brought about are comparatively simple. There is a relatively direct connection of the response with the stimulus. Certain specific agencies—which are alike in their common psychological quality of favorableness—act directly on the organism as a whole and bring about a positive response. Similarly, specific unfavorable agencies, acting directly on the organism, bring about

the negative (avoiding) reaction.[1] There is no inter-
vening nervous apparatus to discriminate different sorts
of favorableness or unfavorableness and to control specific adaptive responses.

With the differentiation of bodily structure into
specialized organs and an integrating nervous system,
there appears a very different type of behavior. Contacts, favorable and unfavorable, still remain the ultimate facts of life; but contact has come to include much
more than it does in the case of the free-swimming
protozoön. What may be termed "favorable contact"
varies with the differentiated parts of the body surface. For example, nutritious substances must be brought
into contact with the mouth, and for this, coördinated
movements of the body and limbs (or other locomotive
and prehensile apparatus) are necessary. To secure this
coördination, there must be differentiated discrimination of contacts and pressures by different parts of the
body.[2] Contacts are no longer simply and directly favorable and unfavorable. The character they possess is
conditional and indirect. It varies (a) with the part of
the body feeling the contact, and (b) with the contacts
simultaneously felt by other parts of the body. Accordingly, in animals with specialized organs and a nervous system, these two original psychological qualities
have become differentiated. The presence of food no

[1] From the chemist's standpoint what takes place may vary greatly
from case to case, and is probably in all cases very complex. But this
does not affect its psychological uniformity and simplicity.

[2] To a certain extent this must exist even in the one-celled organism
to provide for the turning and propelling movements of its pseudopodia
or filaments.

longer stimulates the whole body surface indiscriminately. It acts in a specific way upon one or more sense-organs and calls out a specific and variable response such that the food is brought into contact with the inside of the mouth.[1] Instead of a direct stimulus calling out a simple and direct response, the stimulus acts indirectly and calls out a complex and partly indirect response. The response is indirect since, to attain the end (*e.g.*, to get the food into the mouth), *coördinated*, and hence *specialized*, movements of the head, body, and limbs, controlled by many subsidiary stimuli of pressure, contact, etc., are necessary. The specific stimuli to such responses are still positive, but their psychological quality has become correspondingly differentiated; *e.g.*, into taste and warmth. Furthermore, the adequate stimulus to a specialized response like food-getting is rarely a simple excitation of end-organ. Usually it is a typical complex of sensory excitations, a stimulus-pattern, involving both simultaneous and successive elements.

The central feature of a stimulus-pattern may be, for example, an odor; but in order that the response may be directed toward the source of the odor, variations in intensity must accompany turnings of the head and sniffings, or varying pressures from the wind. Also, since the total response involves coördinated movements of different parts of the body, it can be completed only through the control exercised by many subsidiary stimuli

[1] It is worth noting that there is an anticipation of this differentiation in the protozoa. The paramoecium, for example, has on one side a sort of primitive mouth, and nutritious particles are conducted to this opening by water currents set in motion by movements of the cilia.

arising from the movements themselves, as well as from varying external contacts and pressures. The same thing is true in principle, if the central feature of the stimulus-pattern is visual or auditory rather than olfactory. In these cases it is evident that a very complex stimulus-pattern must be operative. We shall have more to say about the distance-receptors a little later. Here it is important for us to observe that not only is the simple positive quality differentiated into many specific qualities, but the affective quality as such comes to attach to the stimulus-pattern as a whole.

This development is accompanied, probably from a very early stage in the rise of the metazoa, by certain other changes. Of especial importance is the appearance of psychological qualities which are neither positive nor negative, but indifferent. The primitive contacts were all either favorable or unfavorable; but now we find such specifically favorable contacts as savory substances in the mouth, such specifically unfavorable ones as pain from directly injurious contacts, and in addition such indifferent ones as touch and kinaesthetic sensations. The favorable and unfavorable contacts still call out specific forms of the primitive positive and negative reactions; but—and this is the significant point—the indifferent stimuli *call for no specific response.* Yet they are stimuli in that they exercise a control over behavior. They are *conditional determinants* of response. They enter as subsidiary elements into many stimulus-patterns which serve to determine complete responses; but alone they are practically indeterminate. Their function seems to be to control the coördination of particular movements which enter as elements into many complete responses.

If we examine the behavior of a typical invertebrate, we find that it consists of a number of total responses, such as food-getting, escape from threatened danger, attack on enemies, and the sex response. Each of these is a complete functional whole, somewhat variable in its make-up, but varying in comparatively fixed ways. Any one of these characteristic responses, escape from danger, for example, shows generally some degree of adaptation to the particular occasion. The animal may carry out his escape in somewhat different ways; but these ways are limited in number and are alike for all members of the species. In addition to these total responses, there are a number of acts performed which are functionally incomplete in themselves, but which enter as elements into various larger responses. Coördinated movements of locomotion (such as swimming or flying) or movements of the antennae are examples. Such acts enter into food-getting, pursuit, or flight indifferently. They also occur aimlessly, without any specific end. They have no specific stimuli, but are occasioned by a great variety of stimuli, as well as directly by the organic state of the animal. They are *functionally independent elements of behavior*.

Thus at this stage of psychological evolution, we find various specific forms of the two primitive positive and negative reactions, involving coördinated movements occurring in characteristic patterns; and, along with these, functionally independent elements of total responses. On the side of stimulus, we find various specific positive and negative affective qualities instead of the primitive undifferentiated pair. Characteristic stimulus-patterns take the place of the primitive simple stimuli. Lastly, stimulus qualities appear which are in themselves not affective but indifferent, and which are only conditional determinants of response.

The Distance Receptors.

THERE are further features of this development which are of great significance for our inquiry, and which we must now consider. In the simplest animals, the stimulus to the avoiding-reaction is the contact itself, *i.e.*, *it is the actual beginning of the injurious action* that sets up the response of withdrawal. So also the stimulus to the positive reaction is the contact with the assimilable substance, and it is the actual beginnings of the assimilative process that stimulate the reaction whose end is to facilitate and maintain that process. The same thing holds of the positive reaction to warmth or to light. The great change that has come about with differentiation of structure is this: the specific adaptive response is set up by agencies other than the injurious or beneficial processes themselves, but which are related to these processes in determinate and regular ways. The organism, through its specialization of structure, has become responsive to properties of the environing objects which are not in themselves either favorable or unfavorable, but which occur in *definite connection with favorable and unfavorable properties*. The tasting of substances in the mouth, for example, is not the beginning of assimilation; but it permits the discrimination of assimilable from non-assimilable substances before they are taken into the digestive organs where they can do ultimate good or harm. Taste stimuli are to the normally adapted animal "warnings" of food or poison, *i.e.*, they call out the appropriate responses in advance. Smell performs the same function; but it has the advantage of anticipating by a greater interval the benefit or injury. Even taste is in a sense a distance-receptor, since it acts before the substance reaches the critical point of contact; but smell saves the animal the trouble and possible danger of near approach. Hence it has a very considerable advantage.

The true distance-receptors of sight and hearing represent a still further stage in the same development. Their primary importance lies in the fact that they enable the animal to anticipate by appropriate response the impending contact. But they do more than this. They cause a great increase in the psychological environment, and this not simply in its temporal and spatial extent, but in its complexity. Taste and smell stimuli differ from one another merely in quality or in intensive quantity. Accordingly they permit discrimination of substances, not simply as favorable or unfavorable, but as possessing distinctive qualities which are connected with specific favorableness or unfavorableness. But the correlation between the visual stimulus and the beneficial or injurious character of its source is too variable to be reduced to, or represented by, simple qualitative differences. The visual image of a given object will vary not only with the size and shape of the object, but also with its distance and position relative to the seeing organism.

Consequently it is necessary that the response be determined by a complex stimulus-pattern, the essential elements in which are not so much the distinctive color qualities (which are late in development), as spatial relations and determinate changes in these. The retina with its differentiated end-organs is a highly analytic instrument. It registers the sizes, shapes, and colors of things *relative to the seeing organism,* properties which are in themselves indifferent so far as the organism is concerned. In order that they may act as signs of impending benefit or injury, an elaborate integrating and mediating instrument is required in order to connect the appropriate response with each significant visual pattern. Moreover, the visual pattern must be coördinated with other sensory elements coming from contacts and pressures of moving muscles, and often with sensory excitations from other distance-receptors as well. The visual stimulus-pattern is in itself rarely, if ever, an adequate stimulus to a total response; but it is a determinate factor in the total stimulus-pattern to which many special senses contribute. The spatial position, for example, as registered in the visual stimulus-pattern, exercises a determinate control over response, but this control is *conditional.* If the object seen is prey to be pursued, the perceived position controls the direction of the approach *toward* the object; if it is an enemy to be avoided, the position controls the flight *away from* the object. As the behavior of the animal becomes more complicated, the position of a perceived object enters as a factor of control in an increasing variety of total responses. An object may be approached for other ends

157

than the seizure of food, *e.g.*, as a place of concealment from an enemy. Or it may be approached by a detour, so that its perceived position acts as a point of orientation for a complicated series of movements. However variously spatial position serves to control behavior, this control is characteristically conditional, and conditional in an increasingly determinate and systematic fashion.

A further feature connected with distance-receptors, which is of enormous importance for later psychological development, has already been referred to. This is the response of sniffing, or looking, or listening—the response by which the animal so adjusts itself that the distance-receptor concerned receives the fullest possible stimulation. Significant variations in stimulation with changes in position of the body or the sense organ are registered in this way. The partial response of adjustment to the stimulus serves as a preparation for the final total response. In the invertebrates, where the modes of possible response are limited and stereotyped, so that the alternatives are fixed in advance, the preparatory looking or listening seems to delay the final response and thus to facilitate the selection of the one appropriate to the stimulus as fully perceived. In the higher vertebrates the function of the perceptive adjustment is more important; for the response is not simply to be selected out of a number of already fixed alternatives, but must often be built up out of variously selected elements to suit the needs of the particular occasion.

We have already noted the fact that in this adjustment-reaction of the distance-receptors there appears a new type of functionally independent action, which enters as an element into many total responses, both positive and negative. Like the other functionally independent reactions (such as the movements of locomotion), it may also occur aimlessly, or without further end than the keeping *en rapport* with the environment. But in this very way all these independent partial responses acquire a certain completeness of their own and become *secondary positive responses*. It is of importance that movements of adjustment, as well as other complex coördinations of movements which are indispensable factors in securing the ends of life, should be perfected by practice. A nervous organization which permits and insures their independent exercise is of great advantage to the animal. The more complex the system of behavior becomes, the greater is the number of the functionally independent elements of response, and the greater is the extent to which they are performed for their own sake. They are often themselves stimuli to their own repetition, and are, so far, intrinsically pleasant. Often external stimuli, in themselves indifferent, acquire positive affective quality in that they independently call out reactions which serve to keep the animal adjusted to continued or repeated stimulation of the same sort. Thus we find the higher animals not only taking delight in moving about, running, flying, jumping, etc., but also in touching with mouth or limb, and in sniffing, listening, and looking.

CHAPTER VIII

The Complete Act and the Learning Process

The Modifiability of Response.

IT is not possible completely to separate the different stages in psychological development, nor would it be in keeping with our purpose to make the attempt to do so. We have considered the simpler behavior of the lowest animals, because there we can more clearly discern the fundamental traits from which the higher and more complex forms have evolved. Some of the features which must be emphasized, while they occur in the earlier stages, are peculiarly characteristic of the more complex behavior of the higher animals. This is notably the case with the modifiability of response, or, as it is commonly termed, the capacity to learn. It is present to some extent in all animal behavior. Even the protozoa show traces of it. But the extent to which responses are built up during the lifetime of the individual to meet its conditions of life, and the extent to which a specific mode of behavior once formed may be modified by later exigencies, increases enormously in the later stages of psychological evolution, especially among the vertebrates.

A typical insect performs many complicated acts. It is highly specialized, both as regards its bodily structure with its differentiated organs, and as regards its behavior. But while the behavior is composed of very complex functional units of response, these are practically invariable. All the individuals of a kind behave in very much the same way. The insect organism is sensitive to a set of very definite stimulus-patterns, and it reacts to these by equally definite type-responses. Within certain limits external conditions may vary and not bring about any corresponding variation in response. Variation beyond these limits brings about an effective change in the stimulus-pattern, such that it may cease to act as a stimulus at all or may call out an entirely different response. There may be more than one mode of response possible to meet a given situation. One may be tried, and if that fails, another may be resorted to. But such responses are strictly alternatives. One response is made or the other, and there is no synthesis or assimilation of a simpler response to a more complex one.

Now this type of behavior, loosely called "instinctive" as opposed to the more flexible "intelligent" behavior of the higher vertebrates, is advantageous so long as the environmental conditions are not subject to change. An animal of low intelligence may be adapted to a wide range of very complex conditions, provided these are permanent. He may be able to meet complicated changes in situation also, provided these changes occur in a regular and constant order. But he is unable to cope with a changing environment, or with variations in the usual and regular order of things. To meet a changing environment, a different type of behavior is necessary. It must be possible to meet a slight variation in external situation by a correspondingly slight variation in the response. The organism must be sensitive not merely to fixed patterns of sensory excitation, which, although complex physiologically, function as unanalyzable wholes. Both stimulus-pattern and total response must be composed of separable functional elements, which may be dropped out or recombined into differing wholes. There cannot be a highly developed capacity for learning—for that modifiability of response which we call "intelligent," unless the behavior-system falls, not into distinct units of response, functionally complete, but into independently variable factors, functionally incomplete, which may be performed independently. Similarly, the stimulus-patterns, which as functional wholes are affective in quality, must be resolvable into functionally independent factors, possessing what we shall henceforth term *cognitive*, as distinguished from *affective*, quality, in that they serve to stimulate and control, not functionally complete acts, but the factors of such acts.

The Function of Attention.

BEHAVIOR is intelligent in proportion as it is characterized by selective *attention*. There is a sense in which attention is present in even the simplest behavior. What is controlling behavior—that toward which the response is directed—is being attended to, in that sense of the term. But the selective attention which marks the higher forms of perception, for example, is a different matter. Perception involves a delaying of final action while all the available organs of sense are brought to bear on the source of stimulation with the end of gaining the fullest stimulus possible. Now this is necessary precisely

163

because a variety of final responses is possible. The holding up of action in attentive perception is not mere hesitation. It is the mobilization of an organized system of behavior in preparation for contingencies. As the system of possible responses becomes mobilized, the stimulus undergoes a reciprocal modification. It too becomes differentiated into determinate factors, correlative to the factors of the system of response.

Whatever in the environment demands attention of this sort does so because of its possible ambiguity for behavior. As we shall see, the kind of learning by which new adaptations of response are acquired is a process of discrimination between two situations or objects which previously were not distinguished. The doubtful or ambiguous situation must be attended to in order that the response proper to this occasion in its particularity may be called out. If the situation were very simple or very familiar, so that only one response was open, action would take place immediately, and no attentive scrutiny would be required. As John Dewey long ago pointed out, the process by which the response is selected and that by which the stimulus is discriminated—to use his own term, "constituted"—as the stimulus that it is, are one and the same process. What we have to remark here is the relation of attention to cognition. It is only the cognizable that is attended to. The pleasantness and unpleasantness of things, their fearfulness and charm, and all other affective qualities notoriously elude attentive scrutiny. Yet the objective features of the pleasant sound of rushing water, for example, or of the terrifying wild beast, may be attended to and discriminated. These features have functional independence. Each of them may occur in other situations having different affective quality. They are constant factors of the environment. Attention not only discriminates one thing *from* another, but it selects and analyzes identifiable features of the total situation. What is attentively discriminated is what is common, what is identifiable in other settings.[1]

The Learning-Process.

THE process by which responses become modified must be considered here in some detail. Let us suppose that a certain visual stimulus-pattern, *e.g.*, the sight of a moving insect, initiates the total response of seizing-and-eating, and that before the response is completed a stimulus from taste organs occurs which is *negative, i.e.,* inhibits the positive response which is in progress, and sets up the opposed total response of rejecting the offending morsel. If now the original stimulus be repeated, it may for a few times continue to act as before and to initiate the feeding-response, which is each time checked by the unpleasant taste. But after one or more repetitions, the response is inhibited at an earlier stage and before the second stimulus has a chance to act. Eventually the inhibition *reaches to the original stimulus*, changing its character, so that instead of calling out the positive response, it comes to call out a more or less pronounced avoiding-reaction. In the classic case of

---

[1] This topic was discussed by the author in an article entitled "Emotion and Perception from the Behaviorist Standpoint." *Psychological Review,* Vol. XXVI, No. 6 (November, 1919), pp. 409-427.

Lloyd Morgan's chick, a single experience of the bad-tasting Cinnabar caterpillar was sufficient to cause the chick to draw back when next presented with the caterpillar, and to wipe his bill.

The learning-process has a complementary aspect also, by which responses become confirmed. The chick in question not only avoided the bad-tasting Cinnabar caterpillar, but good-tasting worms of somewhat similar appearance. But when, at last, hunger and the repeated sight of the worms tempted him to peck, the secondary taste-stimulus, being positive, served to reinforce and complete the somewhat feeble feeding-response, and there was soon no more hesitation in seizing these worms.

There has been a great deal of speculation as to the *modus operandi* of the learning-process. In certain simple types of learning, such as learning a maze, what takes place seems to be the dropping out of useless movements. Watson has tried to account for this in terms of simple mechanical repetition, the successful movements being those which in a series of trials are performed most often. It is doubtful whether this is a satisfactory explanation of even this type of learning, and in more complicated cases, where the time-pattern is quite different, one must suppose other factors to be at work. It has generally been held that "pleasantness" and "unpleasantness," connected in some way with success and failure, are effective factors in learning. But just how "pleasantness" and "unpleasantness" contribute to the result has remained a mystery. The terms "stamping-in" and "stamping-out," used by Thorndike in referring to the matter, are obviously only metaphors. Indeed, there is no agreement as to what "pleasantness" and "unpleasantness" are themselves. The distinction is one that has been taken over from common sense and the terms appropriated by dualistic psychology as denoting ultimate aspects or elements of conscious processes. The search for a specific physiological substrate or correlate for them has so far proved unavailing, although it is evident that the autonomic system is somehow involved, as it is in emotion. What we need at present, however, is not so much explanatory principles as it is adequate descriptions and analyses of the phenomena in question. Our systematic preconceptions of a psycho-physical dualism, according to which each psychical process has its invariable physical or physiological correlate, has tended to blind us to the actually observable phenomena. Let us attempt a generalized description of the facts in question, leaving explanation temporarily aside.

As we have seen, the most primitive responses of animals are the so-called positive and negative reactions. In a general way the positive response involves a reaching out toward, or going toward and establishing contact, while the negative response involves movements of shrinking and withdrawal. Now the significant feature of the distinction is this: *the positive response is such that it leads to a continuation or enhancement of the stimulus which occasions it; and the negative response is such that it leads to a cessation or decrease of its stimulus.* In short, it is not its specific make-up of *movements toward* the source of stimulation that constitutes the one

167

type of response as positive, but it is the regulative function of continuance or enhancement of the stimulus. Similarly, what makes the negative response negative, is the fact that it normally leads to the cessation or decrease of the stimulus. However complex and specialized behavior becomes, these two opposed functional relationships remain characteristic of it. We may generalize, then, and state that in so far as any stimulus tends to set up activities which normally lead to its own continuance, it is positive, or pleasant; and that, contrariwise, any stimulus which sets up activities leading to its own discontinuance is negative or unpleasant. Similarly—and this is important—activities themselves are pleasant or unpleasant according as they tend to stimulate their own furtherance or repetition, on the one hand; or to inhibit themselves, on the other.

The Complete Act.

WITH this generalization in mind we may now proceed to our consideration of learning. In the simplest behavior, as we have already pointed out, it is the actual contacts with favorable or unfavorable objects—or media—which call out the positive and negative reactions. With the specialization of structure, and especially of distance-receptors, we find that the original stimulus of actual contact is supplemented by specific stimuli, which have a determinate relation to favorable and unfavorable contacts, and which initiate responses insuring the occurrence or avoidance of such contacts. That is to say, the specialized sensitivity of the distance-receptors has arisen genetically as a supplement

168

to the primitive sensitivity and continues to function as subsidiary to it. There is, then, a more or less definitely *predetermined functional relation* between stimuli acting on the distance-receptors and contact stimuli. Accordingly the total response initiated by the distance-receptor and reinforced by the contact stimulus (*e.g.*, reaching out toward, pecking at, and swallowing), forms a functional unit. The act is a *whole*, and is stimulated or inhibited as a whole. The initial visual stimulus-pattern and the supplementary taste-contact stimulus are not separate and distinct stimuli, the one to reaching-out-toward and seizing, and the other to swallowing, but they act together and constitute a single complex stimulus to the total response.

When the taste-contact of the substance in the mouth is pleasant,[1] *i.e.*, stimulates the swallowing of the morsel, which is the completion of the total response, it stimulates also *a repetition of reaching out and seizing*. When, as in the case of the chick which pecked at the Cinnabar caterpillar, the taste-contact stimulus is unpleasant, *i.e.*, inhibits the act of swallowing already prepared and initiates the opposed response of rejection and bill-wiping, it also tends to inhibit a repetition of the total response. A tension is thus created between the two connected stimuli of sight and taste. The visual stimulus-pattern, not being independent of the taste-contact,

[1] Whether a given taste is actually pleasant on any particular occasion will depend of course in part on the physiological state of the animal. If he is hungry a given morsel of food will taste pleasant; but if his hunger is satisfied, the pleasantness is apt to be replaced by unpleasantness. Indeed, it might well be said that in the last resort it is always the state of the organism which determines whether any stimulus or activity is pleasant or unpleasant.

is unable to elicit the former positive response; or, if it does so once more, the repeated and strengthened opposition of the correlative taste, in stimulating a total negative response, soon induces a transformation in the affective quality of the initial visual stimulus. As a result, the sight of the offending caterpillar not only ceases to be a stimulus to reaching-pecking-swallowing, but becomes a stimulus to drawing-back and even to bill-wiping. A similar thing occurs in human experience. The sight of luscious fruit not only stimulates us to preparations for eating, but causes the mouth to water in anticipation, while the very look of the spoonful of castor oil soon comes to start an incipient gagging.

Where behavior is more complex, we still find a similar relationship. Whether the total response be a single act or a coördinated series of acts, it still forms a functional whole, and the pleasantness or unpleasantness of the outcome does not attach simply to the final stage, but to the response as a whole. Indeed, we are not to suppose that the pleasantness or unpleasantness is something additional to the behavior in question, a further consequence—or cause—external to the activity in progress. The fact is that animal behavior does occur in the form of *complete acts,* some of which tend to be repeated at the time and to recur under similar conditions, while others tend to inhibit their own repetition and even to stimulate acts of an opposed character. The first sort of acts as completed wholes are pleasant, the second sort unpleasant. We may not know what the detailed mechanism of such acts is. It is indeed not unlikely that this may vary greatly from one pleasant act to another.

The pleasantness, that is, may not be correlated with any single physiological process or invariable physiological state at all.

What as psychologists we are primarily concerned with is not the physiological process as such, but the *identity of functional relationship* between varying processes. When we can discover and describe such a functional relationship, what we are describing is not a physical or physiological *correlate* of a psychological phenomenon, but the psychological phenomenon itself. Psychology must habitually conceive animal behavior as a system, or complex pattern, of adaptive acts by which the organism is brought into specific relations with the world in which it lives. Behavior is not a physical phenomenon analyzable into movements in space and time. The unit of behavior is the adaptive *act*. It is a functional unit—that is to say, it is individuated not by its mechanical or physical make-up, but by its place in the behavior-system. The same idea may be expressed by saying that psychology must adopt a consistent and thoroughgoing *relativism*. What is psychologically constant when viewed as a functional element of behavior, may be physically, and even physiologically, variable. Similarly, what is physiologically constant, may be psychologically variable, or even indeterminate. The attempt to use physiological elements as clues to the analysis of psychological phenomena has led to much barren speculation and futile experimental research. Psychological science, like every other science, must discover and formulate its own principles of individuation.

The Formation and Modification of Complete Acts.

LEARNING *always involves a modification or the formation of a complete act.* But it may take place in many ways. There are many types of learning. The type we have just considered, for example, consists in establishing a distinction between two stimuli at first not distinguished, as a result of which the affective quality of one is transformed. But learning does not always involve a transformation of the affective quality of the primary stimulus. It often consists in a modification of the response in its details. Thus in learning to run a maze or to open a box, the primary stimulus of food smelled or seen retains its original positive quality and continues to excite a total positive response. The learning consists in inhibiting certain elements of the total response and in establishing or reinforcing others so that a complete act is formed. If this result is sometimes brought about, as Watson believes, by mere frequency of repetition of some movements as compared with others, there are usually more complex factors at work. Even in maze-learning there are present some sort of secondary stimuli or "cues" which play a part in controlling the animal's turns and movements. These evidently vary greatly from one species to another.[1] Sometimes the secondary stimuli are visual, sometimes auditory, but more often the varying pressures from the floor and sides of the maze on parts of the moving animal's body serve as cues. Guided by some of these, the animal takes a wrong

---

[1] See Washburn, *The Animal Mind,* pp. 272-285, for an account of maze-learning and similar cases.

turn and finds his course unexpectedly blocked by a barrier against which perhaps he actually bumps. This contact is unpleasant, *i.e.*, it inhibits movements toward it and sets up avoiding movements. Now any secondary stimuli which had served to guide the animal into the *cul-de-sac*, being consequently in functional relation with the unpleasant contact of the obstructing wall, would tend to take on a negative affective quality. As a result of this induction of negative affective quality in the secondary stimuli in question, the earlier movements before controlled by them would be inhibited and the *cul-de-sac* avoided. If the movements of the animal in the maze were wholly at random, and no secondary stimuli whatever were at work, there could be no adaptive modification of the total response except through sheer mechanical habituation. Where there is true learning (of the type just mentioned) there is always an affective transformation of some secondary stimulus *which is in functional relation with the primary stimulus*. Often, indeed, as in learning a maze, there is a succession of such transformations. When a given maze is thoroughly learned, the secondary stimuli which come to control the course of the total response are evidently the *kinaesthetic stimuli* arising from the animal's own movements. These doubtless are operative in some degree from the start, and the learning is accomplished by the transfer to them of the affective quality of the secondary peripheral stimuli.

It is well known that the learning of "tricks" by the higher animals, as, for example, learning to lift a latch or to pull a string which opens a box where food is contained, is very greatly expedited if the animal's attention is once fixed on the critical part of the apparatus, *e.g.*, projecting latch or dangling string. Now the fixing of attention on a given stimulus means that this stimulus is playing a central rôle in determining behavior. But this is precisely the most favorable condition for a transformation of its affective quality. The hungry animal rushing about at random in the maze has his attention fixed so exclusively on the primary food-stimulus that the secondary stimuli exercise but little control over his movements and consequently acquire appropriate affective quality slowly. It is undoubtedly true that behavior which is controlled by attentive fixation of secondary stimuli is on a distinctly different psychological level. A stimulus which fixes the attention is presumably acting through the higher centers. Furthermore, the ability to attend to secondary stimuli is characteristic of a more complex psychological organization. Behavior of this sort falls into elementary acts which have a high degree of functional independence, and which accordingly may enter freely into more complex organizations of acts. But these are precisely the conditions which permit that modifiability of behavior which constitutes a high degree of learning capacity.

The Structure of the Complete Act.

THE recognition of the functionally complete act as the unit of behavior may serve to guide us further in our task of analysis. In simple behavior, as we have seen, the initial stimulus of sight, or other distance-receptor, and the final contact-stimulus are correlated as mutually dependent factors in a single whole. Not only do they vary together, but in a certain sense *they tend to occur together.* When the act that is in progress is relatively simple, as, for example, in the case of so-called sensori-motor action, the initial distance stimulus, *e.g.,* the sight of the tempting food, not only sets up the reaching-out and grasping reaction, but it also makes the mouth water and the digestive juices flow before the food is actually in the mouth. That is to say, it excites in anticipation the final stage of the complete act which is originally determined by the actual contact-stimulus of the food itself. It is as if the animal began eating the food from the moment he caught sight of it.

The advantage of this tendency to anticipate the final stage of an act is not merely to prepare the organism, but *to reinforce the course of action that has been initiated and to assure its being carried to completion.* The pleasantness attaches primarily to the act as a whole, and hence to the final stage which marks the completion of the act. It is only as completed that an act tends to repeat itself. In simple behavior, the direct contact in which the act terminates is a stimulus to the reaction that is producing it, or to a repetition of the act which has just led up to it. It is for this reason that the anticipation of the final stage—the actual setting-off of reactions such as mouth-watering, *as if* the final contact were actually being enjoyed—serves as a supplementary stimulus to the performance of the earlier stages of the complete act.

Where behavior is of a higher type than sensori-motor action, and the outcome of an act is less directly correlated with its initial stages, there is still an anticipation of the final stage, but in an *incomplete* and *representative* form. Where there are a number of stages to be gone through in a definite order before the act as a whole can be successfully finished, a too complete anticipation of the final stage might well get in the way of the preliminary movements and prevent their orderly performance. Anticipatory enjoyment might take the place of actual achievement, as sometimes happens with men when imagination is taken as a substitute for reality and a life of action is abandoned. But there is need for some sort of anticipation of the outcome of a course of conduct, either to keep the organism to its task and spur lagging efforts, or to warn of unpleasant consequences and thus avert them by inhibiting the action in progress. The anticipation has for its end the control of the course of behavior under way. It serves to bind together the constituent elements into a unitary whole.

An animal which goes to a distant spot where he was fed the day before does not have his mouth water at the outset of his trip and before the food is smelled. His action is commonly said to be controlled by a *memory* of his former experience. This statement may be accepted; but it needs analysis in order that we may see what is involved, and hence may be able to relate it in a systematic way to other analogous forms of behavior. In such a case as we have just mentioned, the act is not initiated by a perception of the object to be eaten. The state of hunger is the primary stimulus. But hunger alone would lead merely to restless undirected movements. Another factor is clearly at work, namely the anticipated enjoyment of the food in the familiar spot. It is this anticipated outcome of the act that helps to stimulate and control the movements of the animal. The anticipated eating of the food is less overt than the mouth-watering, but it is the same sort of phenomenon. It is a preparation for, and an implicit beginning of, the process of eating. It does not lead at once to the movements of chewing and swallowing, but, like the mouth-watering, acts as a stimulus to the complete act of food-getting in progress.

The Representative Image.

WHAT makes it possible for this partial and representative anticipation of the final stage of the act to occur is undoubtedly the development of a higher level of nervous organization. The more complex act is controlled by the higher centers, which, because of their more numerous motor connections, enable the anticipated eating to be *representative, i.e.*, to stimulate and control movements only indirectly connected with the ultimate movements of seizing, chewing, and swallowing.

M. F. Washburn's theory of the image and its place in the behavior system goes far toward making intelligible both how representative anticipation occurs and how it is able to perform the function here ascribed to it. According to this theory, an image arises when a sensory pathway is stimulated *via* a motor pathway through which it ordinarily discharges and from which it is separated by low synaptic resistance. When such a motor pathway is incompletely stimulated from another sensory center in such a way that its direct discharge is partly inhibited by action from some antagonistic center, it stimulates the sensory pathways more closely connected with it. The commonest source for the stimulation of imagery is kinaesthetic excitation due to "tentative movements," *i.e.*, actual slight movements.

The application of this theory to the complete act, as described in the preceding pages, is obvious. From the beginning of an organized course of behavior, such as constitutes a complete act, the later stages are anticipated in the form of tentative movements, *i.e.*, slight movements, which, if completed, would constitute the consummation of the act in progress. Being incomplete, they tend to stimulate the sensory centers in functional connection with them. This sensory excitation then acts through other functionally related motor centers to control movements which are earlier elements in the organized series making up the complete act. The tentative movements which play this important rôle are by no means confined to the muscles of the limbs or other external organs directly concerned in the consummation of the act. As Washburn points out, the tentative movements taking place in the internal organs, which determine in so large a measure the "attitude" of the organism—and, we may add, are so intimately related to the affective state—are of fundamental importance. (The part in the control of human purposive behavior played by the tentative movements of articulation, we shall discuss later.) It is suggested by Washburn, fol-

178

lowing Head's hypothesis of the distinction between the cortex and the optic thalamus, that it is the former which is concerned in the control of tentative movements. This would explain, she points out, the part the cortex plays in the higher mental processes.[1]

In its primitive form, memory is not distinguishable from imagination. The past experience of the individual plays a part in modifying later behavior, even in the simplest organisms. But even in the higher animals it is not so much a partial reinstatement of a past organic state which occurs, as it is a representative anticipation of an organic state which is being led up to by the activity going forward. Memory is not originally a distinct and independent function. *It occurs first as a moment in the complete act.* The distinct living over of past experience, memory proper, becomes only gradually freed from the control of the particular act and the particular occasion, and at the same time distinguished, as the *recall* of the past from the *imagination* of the possible future. We shall later try to show that this differentiation is dependent on the ability to speak.

In simpler behavior, what is anticipated is predominantly the affective quality of the consummatory stimulus—the enjoyment of the food in the mouth, or the unpleasantness of the castor oil, for example. But in proportion as behavior becomes constituted by functionally independent elements and controlled by affectively indifferent stimuli, the anticipation of the later stages of the act must include these as well. It is not enough for the animal searching for food to enjoy the

[1] M. F. Washburn, *Movement and Mental Imagery*, Chaps. III, IV.

pleasure of eating in advance. If he is to be guided to a certain spot, there must be some representative anticipation of the originally perceived features of the locality, with which the present perceptions may be connected. Moreover, when the complete act to be performed is complex, and consists of a series of relatively independent elementary acts, there must be some representative anticipation of the outcome of each stage. We have already seen the importance of the acquisition of secondary affective quality by subsidiary stimuli in learning. We also suggested, it will be remembered, that the ability to attend to secondary stimuli marked the capacity for a higher and more efficient learning. We can now see that this ability makes possible the representative anticipation of the outcome of each successive stage of the complete act.

As anticipation of the ends of action becomes representative, it becomes *selective*. It is not the consummation of the act in all its detail that is anticipated in the memory-image. Since the function of anticipation is the control of behavior in progress, what is represented in advance includes only those features of past experience which are relevant to the present occasion. This is not invariably the case, to be sure, but it is the rule. Now, a general condition for the recall of past experience is attention. We usually remember only what we have attended to. But what is attended to on any occasion is precisely what is controlling response at that time. Hence what is recalled in the anticipatory representation consists of those features which as a general thing are fitted to guide action on the given occasion.

That memory of the past ever occurs among animals lower than man (with the possible exception of the anthropoid apes), except as an immediate aid in the performance of a particular act—when, that is, it is indistinguishable from imagination—is very doubtful. It is speech, as we shall try to show, that has wrought this revolutionary advance by providing a specialized instrument of selective representation. What it is worth while to emphasize here is the fact that the reliving of the past as an end in itself without reference to an immediate future, is the same sort of phenomenon that we have already had occasion to remark; the differentiation, as a functionally independent act, of what is originally a subsidiary factor in a functional whole. Differentiation of this sort is a leading characteristic of psychological evolution. Reminiscence for its own sake, and also imagination for its own sake, give the same sort of advantage as does play of all sorts. Like play, they provide through exercise for the development of the function and thus for a more extended use.

Supplementary Note.

THE reader who is familiar with the writings of the school of *Gestalttheorie* will recognize that there is much in common between the psychological position taken in these pages and that of this German school. The general conception of behavior as psychologically analyzable into functional units and not into mechanical movements is in line with the theory of configurations—although it must be added that this conception is by no means peculiar to the *Gestalt* school. The importance ascribed by the present writer to the stimulus-pattern as the determinant of simple responses, and the treatment of the stimulus-pattern and the total response as correlative, is also in accord with the theory of configurations, although not peculiar to it. In the account of the learning process a more specific agreement is, I think, to be found. The view that simple learning at the level of perception depends upon a more or less predetermined functional relation between distance-stimulus and contact-stimulus might easily be stated in terms of configurations. The contention of the foregoing chapter—that learning always involves the modification or the formation of a *complete act*—is virtually complementary to the position taken by Koffka, that in learning a transformation of the perceptual configuration takes place.[1]

The treatment of learning and of the whole subject of cognition given in these pages differs from the *Gestalt* theory, however, quite markedly in the importance it ascribes to the principle of functional independence— or perhaps, rather, in the recognition and formulation of such a principle. In the view of the present writer what chiefly distinguishes "intelligent" learning (learning with insight) from the simpler "instinctive" learning is the greater degree of functional independence belonging to the factors of behavior, on the one hand, and to the members of the psychological environment, on the other. To speak in terms of the *Gestalt* theory,

[1] *The Growth of the Mind*, p. 191 ff.

one might say that "instinctive" learning occurs when the type of configuration is fixed and relatively incapable of resolution into factors. "Intelligent" learning is possible only when a different type of configuration exists, more complex and more plastic because resolvable into relatively distinct members. Now the writers of the *Gestalt* school have been so concerned to deny every sort of psychological atomism and to insist on the organic unity of the configuration, that they have failed to deal adequately with the problem of its analysis. Indeed, they seem sometimes to assume that the configuration is incapable of any kind of analysis. Yet in "intelligent" learning it does become transformed, sometimes by the admission of new members. It is true that an object must undergo internal modification on becoming a member of a new configuration, yet there is admittedly a certain continuity between the object in and out of the configuration. When one of Köhler's apes learned to use a stick to secure food beyond his reach outside the bars of his cage, what took place was that a new member, the stick, was introduced into the former configuration (fruit, his own grasping arm, and the hindering bars). Koffka remarks: "It is not merely a matter of seeing or noticing an object such as a stick, because before it is employed the object must cease to be an isolated neutral thing to the animal, and become a member of the situation in hand. The object must, in short, become a 'tool.' As a necessary condition for a correct type of behavior an *alteration must occur in the object of perception*. What at the beginning possessed only the character of 'indifference,' or 'something to bite upon,' etc., now obtains the character of a 'thing to fetch fruit with.' "[1]

If we raise the question how such a transformation is possible and under what conditions it takes place, we find many valuable and suggestive observations made, but, in the opinion of the present writer, no adequate theoretical analysis, and in particular no recognition of the general principle of what we have termed functional independence. One of the favorable conditions for the use of an object as a tool, which is most stressed by Köhler, is that the object in question be visible to the animal when gazing directly at the "objective," or that *vice versa* a direct look at the possible tool does not exclude the whole field of the objective. It helps greatly to see a stick as a "thing to fetch fruit with," for example, if it is perceived in visible proximity to the fruit. Conversely, "all objects, especially of a long or oval shape, or such as appear to be movable, become 'sticks' in the purely functional sense of 'grasping-tool' in these circumstances and tend in Koko's hands to wander to the critical spot."[2] Another condition mentioned as favorable to the employment of an object as a tool is its familiarity (provided, of course, that the object is at all suitable for the purpose in hand). Thus Köhler says of the blanket which one of the apes fetched from her sleeping den and used to beat the fruit toward her, ignoring the sticks on the opposite side of the cage, "the blanket is seen and used daily; and is thus *sui*

[1] *Op. cit.*, p. 191.
[2] Köhler, *The Mentality of Apes*, p. 36.

generis and in a different category to other objects."[1]
Our comment on this would be that the daily use of the
blanket has endowed it with greater functional independence, and that it is this functional independence of
an object that is the fundamental condition of its being
used as a tool or entering into any new configuration. If
the blanket, for example, had been used only as a
covering, it is not likely that the ape would have perceived it as a "thing to fetch fruit with." It was because the ape had, in all probability, played with the
blanket in a variety of ways, flapping it about, etc., that
she was able to adapt it to the use in question. Visible
proximity to the goal undoubtedly favors the use of an
object as a tool, even when it is unsuitable for the purpose. Thus the young ape, Koko, tried to use a piece
of stiff cardboard and even the brim of an old straw hat
which were lying near. But it is important to observe
that the more functional independence a given object,
like a stick, has acquired by employment in other situations, the less is its use on a given occasion determined
by visible proximity to the goal. Moreover, it is a mark
of intelligence in an animal to be able to free himself
from the dominating influence of visible proximity and
to take the remote stick, for example, in preference to
the hat brim or other unsuitable object lying near the
goal.

In particular instances, indeed, both Köhler and
Koffka seem to recognize that intelligent learning is
facilitated if objects are "detachable" from the configuration in which they occur. Köhler points out, for

[1] Köhler, *The Mentality of Apes*, p. 38, note.

example, that an object will more readily be used as a tool if it is not actually seen as a part of another object or as an integral member of another configuration. Thus it was only the cleverer of the apes which could see the branch of a tree as a "stick," and which accordingly broke it off to use. Another similar example is cited by Koffka. "For instance, one of the animals, Chica, strove with all her might to attain a goal suspended from the roof, without ever using a box which stood in the middle of the room, although she had already mastered the use of boxes in similar tests. It could not be said that the box was overlooked, for the animal repeatedly squatted upon it when she was out of breath, and yet she made not the slightest effort to bring the box under the goal. During the whole time, however, Tercera, another ape, was lying on the box; when at length Tercera chanced to fall off the box, Chica grasped it immediately, carried it under the goal, and mounting it snatched down the food. From this behavior it may be inferred that the box upon which Tercera was lying was not an 'object with which to fetch the goal,' but 'something upon which to lie.' Consequently the box simply did not come into connection with the goal so long as it possessed a definite configuration of its own that made it inappropriate as a tool in another situation. *To release a thing from one configuration, and transfer it by reconstruction into another configuration, would seem to be a relatively high-grade accomplishment.* Nor is this difficulty confined to chimpanzees; on the contrary, it plays an important part in human thought. For instance, when you have need of a shallow dish, it might never occur to you that you could use the cover to a pot, unless such a cover happened to be lying before you on the table, away from the pot, in which case you would probably make use of it at once."[1] But while there is this recognition of the importance of functional independence as applied to particular objects in specific cases, there is no recognition of it as a general principle.

It is of interest to compare Köhler's criterion of learning with insight to the position taken by the present writer. This criterion is "the appearance of a complete solution with reference to the whole lay-out of the field." Where learning of this sort occurs, there is a period of hesitation in which the animal makes a survey of the field, and then, suddenly, his demeanor changes, and he starts on his course of action which is carried through continuously, even when it is a "round-about" procedure. What Köhler emphasizes is the correspondence between the *unity* of the achieved act, on the one hand, and the *totality* of the complex situation, on the other. What is emphasized in these pages is the fact that both the intelligent behavior and the total situation to which it is a response, are composed of discriminable factors which may enter other configurations without thereby losing their identity. The survey of the field is useful precisely because it permits a discrimination of recognizable *objects* in determinate *relations* to each other. Otherwise the formation of a new configuration would be incomprehensible.

In the following chapters we try to show that levels in increasing objectivity are conditioned by stages in the

[1] *Op. cit.*, p. 196. Italics mine.

growth of precisely this capacity "to release a thing from one configuration and transfer it by reconstruction into another configuration."

CHAPTER IX

The Objectification of the Environment

Affective and Cognitive Aspects of Behavior.

WE have seen that the stimulus to a response is rarely a simple sensory excitation, but is almost always a stimulus-pattern of greater or less complexity. Sometimes, as in the case of the odor of food, a simple stimulus seems to be the determining factor; at least it is to the odor that the affective quality chiefly attaches, although where the food is seen as well as smelled, it looks as well as smells "good to eat." But while the smell may excite the appetite, the act of going toward and seizing the food is a *directed* response, which is oriented and controlled by a complex of factors. Where the sight of an approaching enemy causes the animal to flee or to put himself on the defensive, it is the stimulus-pattern as a whole to which the specific affective quality attaches. It is the sight of the *enemy approaching* together with the circumstances in which the animal is placed which rouses the *fear;* but it is the particular details which determine the *direction* of the flight, or the *form* of defensive preparations. Where the complete act—for example, pursuit and capture of prey—involves a long course of action, many subsidiary stimuli operate to determine and control the succeeding stages of the hunt. There are obstacles to be avoided, features of the ground to be taken advantage of, etc. Just how these features affect behavior on the given occasion will vary with the end of the act in progress, as well as with the other circumstances with which they occur. On another occasion these same features may be responded to differently.

In general, we may say of any act that is being performed that it is a certain specific sort of act. It has an end; the animal is engaged in doing *something*. The end may be more or less remote, and the behavior leading up to it more or less involved, but it is generally pertinent to ask the question, *What* is the animal doing? In addition to this specific character, behavior has a particular form. The animal is not only doing *something*, but he is doing it in a particular *way*. In so far as behavior can be characterized as even crudely intelligent, it involves a certain adaptation of means to end. These two aspects of behavior form the basis for the distinction between *affection* on the one hand, and *cognition* on the other. It is the affective properties of situations and things which determine the ends of action, and in the most general sense of the term it is the cognized properties and relations which determine the particular form which the action takes, the means by which the end is achieved. Affection and cognition then, in the sense in which the terms are here used, are aspects of all behavior.

In very simple behavior, where the organism has at its disposal a limited number of relatively invariable type-responses, so that in a given situation it is one specific response as a whole, *or* another that must be employed, cognition is at a minimum. Behavior becomes intelligent in proportion as the capacity to adapt means to end on the particular occasion, and to vary the response from one occasion to another, is increased. As we have already seen, this flexibility of response depends on the differentiation of behavior into functionally independent units of response, on the one hand, and on the differentiation of stimulus-patterns into functionally independent stimulus-units, on the other. In so far as the complete stimulus-pattern which is controlling behavior at a given time is resolvable into units, each of which is capable of acting as a conditional determinant of response in a definite manner, cognition is potentially present. A stimulus-unit has cognitive status in so far as it is a conditional determinant of response in a regular and systematic way. It has affective status in so far as it tends to call out a complete act.

Cognition and Objectification.

As we have already said, it is the situation as a whole which is the determinant of the complete act. But in proportion as the behavior of an animal falls not only into different *kinds* of acts, *e.g.*, food-getting, or defense, but shows adaptive variation from occasion to occasion, the situation as a whole becomes resolvable into more and more clearly discriminated factors. *The development of the function of cognition in the organism proceeds* pari passu *with the objectification of the environment*. The perception of a situation as made up of discriminable factors depends on the fact that such factors have a constant, although conditional, significance for behavior. Now it is evident that this may obtain in very different degrees. Let us consider the more important of these.

Probably one of the earliest discriminations made is that of things which serve as food. But to what extent these things are perceived as what we may properly term "objects," it is very difficult to say. The grass which a cow crops in the pasture is not objectified in a very high degree. The problem which the presence of grass presents is not a very complicated one. The two alternatives, to crop or not to crop, are simple, and the choice between them does not seem to be dependent on many other circumstances. Nor is the act of cropping one that calls for much variation of procedure. Still, grass must be discriminated from unpleasant weeds, and, what is probably more important from the standpoint of cognition, the particular patch or clump to be cropped must be located, and its distance and direction gauged as well as the size and shape of different clumps discriminated by appropriate movements of head, neck, mouth, and tongue. Perhaps, also, different kinds of grass have different degrees of toughness, and demand tugs of varying strengths. The technique of cropping may not be, after all, quite so simple a matter to a really efficient cow as we are inclined to suppose. If we reflect a moment on the actual complexity of sensory stimuli which is involved in even such simple behavior as we have just described—the bewildering variety of the visual images of a particular kind of grass, for instance, according to the illumination, the distance, and position of a clump relative to the movements of the cow; to say nothing of the objective differences in color and form due to advancement in growth, etc., we see the regular preferential discrimination of a given kind of grass, and the adjusted movements of walking about and cropping it, involve an unimaginably complicated differentiation and integration of the sensory excitations of the grass-cropping situation. The point is that grass, or a particular kind of grass, is objectified as a discriminable factor just in proportion as it calls for systematic and constant variations in behavior.

A living animal that is hunted as prey or shunned as an enemy is indubitably an object in a completer sense than is the cow's grass. Hunting is a far more complicated act than is grazing. It involves a long series of acts, *e.g.*, stalking, crouching, and the final dash; and each of these to be successful must depend not only on the distance and position of the prey, but the nature of the ground, the direction of the wind, etc. Moreover, different kinds of prey call for different methods of hunting. For one kind it is perhaps necessary to stalk up very close before the final dash; another kind of prey may be less swift, but quicker to smell or hear danger. Furthermore, an animal offers a kaleidoscopic variety of appearances because of his own movements and changes of attitude; and each of these must be countered by distinctive modifications of response. Of even greater importance is the fact that different movements and attitudes of the prey are often not to be responded to directly; they are signs of further conditions about to be realized, which must be anticipated on the part of the pursuer. Again, after the prey is captured and killed, it may not be eaten immediately. It may become virtually a new object, in the sense that it is now the center of another set of activities, *e.g.*, burying, defending against marauders, or carrying to mate or young. The existence of an "object" of this sort in the psychological environment is determined by the existence of an interlacing system of conditional responses in the repertoire of animal behavior. The complex behavior of a dog toward a rabbit, for example, is made up of a great many units of response, each one itself a complex of coördinated movements having functional independence. Each unit may enter as a constituent into many other systems which attach to other kinds of animals, or it may enter into other complete acts than that of hunting.

On the side of stimulus, it is important to observe that an "object" is never a single stimulus-pattern. The identity of the object rests on the fact that various stimulus-patterns, *i.e.*, typical complexes of sensory excitation (such as retinal images) which the object affords, have a determinate functional continuity and interdependence. If we consider the complex stimulus-pattern roused by a definite object at a given moment, we see that the particular response, or modification of response, that it stimulates is affected both by the succession of stimuli which has just been experienced, and by those which in the normal course of affairs *are about to occur*. We pointed out earlier the part played by the anticipatory image in the consolidation of the complete act. We can now see its importance in the objectification of perceptual content. The anticipation, through representative imagery, of stimulus-pattern units before they occur is necessary to the preparation of the appropriately modified response, and serves at the same time to weld together successive stimulus-units into a whole, thus making the perception of an object possible. The complex group of sensory excitations roused at any moment by the object *acts as a member of a specific functional system*. This accounts for the fact that although the actual excitations aroused differ very greatly from moment to moment, or from one occasion to another, they may stimulate the same total response. They are, in other words, perceived as the same object.

An object which, like the grass of the cow, or the prey of a hunting animal, is individuated merely by being the center of a single specific life-activity, like feeding or hunting, marks a certain level of objectivity. Its being differentiated from its background and thrown into relief as an object, depends on the fact that the specific activity to which it is correlative is variable and takes on different particular forms according to the situation in which the object is placed. The object detaches itself as a determining factor in a variety of situations and has a constant value from one to another. It is this systematic constancy which gives it identity despite the multiplicity and variety of the sensory excitations it arouses. But its clearness and distinctness as an object depend on the definiteness with which it is thrown into relief against its background. One background is not like another. On the contrary, they have distinctive differences which must be discriminated *in their bearing on the central object*. Determinate variations in the total response must be correlated with determinate features of the relevant situation. The object becomes objectified to the degree to which it comes to bear *systematic relationships* to other objective features of the situation. Thus the stalking of prey to be successful must be modified with reference to the nature of the ground in which the prey is sighted. Clumps of bushes, or other suitable cover near the prey, will determine the direction of the stalk; the distance between the prey and the last bit of cover may determine the final rush. Or it may be that the presence of the mate of the prey may call for a period of waiting, or a different procedure.

Now it is evident that the objectification of what we shall call a *primary* object, *i.e.*, an object which is the center of a specific activity, is limited by the degree to which secondary features of situations in which the primary object appears, are themselves differentiated and objectified. In other words, *secondary* objects, *i.e.*, objects with which the primary objects enter into determinate and constant relationships, must also be differentiated. Things indifferent in themselves, but which are, on occasion, obstacles or aids to be taken account of, become thus individuated. Among secondary objects may also be counted such things as bear more than a single specific relation to behavior. A stream of water, for instance, may be a drinking-place, a spot where prey may be found or where enemies congregate, an obstacle to be waded or swum, a refuge where scent is lost, etc. Secondary objects occupy a psychological status distinctly different from that of primary objects, and their appearance as features of the psychological environment marks an important stage in the evolution of cognition. Their importance lies in this. Just because they do not stand in a single specific relation to the organism —just because they are not *ends* to which affective values attach, but rather possible *means*—what determines behavior in respect to them is their *relations to other objects* and the properties they exhibit in these relations, rather than their direct relation to the responding organism itself.

The objective world as known by science is a world of objects in systematic interrelation, a world independent of and indifferent to the needs of the knower. The central problem of our investigation is to show how such a world is generated, or revealed, in the course of psychological evolution. The first step we find precisely here—in the discrimination of objects which in themselves have no specific interest or value, but which, because of their status as potential means or obstacles, must be attended to and definitely taken account of.

The Spatial Order.

THE objectification of the psychological environment, which keeps pace with the evolving function of cognition, is not merely the differentiation and integration of *objects*. Or rather, let us say, the differentiation of objects involves the appearance of other objective factors than the objects themselves. To be an object is, as Kant long ago showed, to possess points of likeness and difference in relation to other objects; it is to be in some sense a member of a more or less systematic *order*. Objects are characterized by the possession of properties. We are not to suppose, of course, that in the pre-conceptual world of the lower animals, properties are distinguished from the particular objects which they qualify. The attention of the animal is always in the service of a particular specific act, and it is directed to the correlate of the specific act, *i.e.*, the concrete object in its particular setting. A dog, for example, is incapable of attending to and discriminating the *shape* of the stick he plays with, or its *size*, or its momentary *distance* from him. Yet the dog adapts his behavior to the particular stick having a definite shape and size, at a particular distance from himself, and moving at a particular rate and in a particular direction. If the stick is brought nearer and moved farther away, he will not only follow it with his eyes, but will gauge his pounce correctly for any distance within his reach. Moreover, the distance of an object from himself exercises a constant though conditional control over his behavior. So also does size, shape, and the rate and direction of moving objects. In other words, the objects of the dog's environment are *spatialized;* they are qualified by constant and distinctive spatial properties. Otherwise, indeed, as we must again recognize with Kant, there would be no objects.

We have already shown that locomotion is the earliest form of functionally independent activity, and that in general the capacity for adaptive movement depends on the existence of independently variable units of response. The spatialization of the world is the correlative aspect of this fact. Consider, for example, the case of the distance of an object from the organism. It is a typically cognitive property; *i.e.*, it calls for no specific response, yet it acts as a conditional determinant of response in a highly systematic way. If the object is to be reached, the distance determines the length and direction of the spring, or the run, or the gradual approach. If it is to be avoided, the distance is equally definite in its determination of the avoiding-act. In more complicated behavior, it may determine in a great variety of ways the preparatory action to be taken.

Although the spatialization of the world has its beginnings in the necessity for coördinated movements of locomotion, and hence is a primitive and fundamental character, it obtains in very different degrees for different animal species. Generally speaking, the more complex and varied the coördinated movements of an animal, not only in getting about in the world, but in dealing with things, the higher is the degree of spatialization. The possession of distance-receptors—particularly of the eye, which registers and reacts to differences in size, distance, position, and direction of movement, and thus makes possible anticipatory tentative movements—marks a critical stage in the evolution of the perception of a spatialized world. But even more important is the development of specialized "manipulatory" organs. The movements an animal makes in locomotion, in moving about among things, approaching and avoiding, do not call for much discrimination of shapes and sizes of objects. But for seizing and grasping and dragging about, these properties become of great importance.

The fundamental importance of the spatial properties of the perceived and known world is too well recognized to call for further comment here. What marks them off as preëminent among the cognizable features of the environment, is not only the fact that some degree of differentiation of them is fundamental to any coördinated movements, but also the further fact that they are capable of such great systematization and organization among themselves. In perception, the interdependence of "apparent" size and distance, shape and position, is very great. These features enter as units into the most highly complex and systematic stimulus-patterns; and these in turn are correlates of the highly organized units of response which form the elements for all direct dealing with the physical world.

Evolution is continuous everywhere; in the progressive objectification of the psychological environment as well as in the origination of species. Yet its course is marked by sudden turnings and rapid advances, during which changes of incalculable importance are brought about. Such a transformation occurs in the evolution of cognition from the higher animals to man.

The spatial properties which the animal has occasion to discriminate are for the most part *relative to himself*. Thus the distance that concerns him is almost always the distance of an object *from himself*. So also of direction. The perceptual localization of objects with reference to himself is often very accurate, far exceeding in some respects that of man. The migrations of hibernating animals from one locality to another, and the homing of pigeons, are notorious examples of this. But this capacity, remarkable as it is, serves the simple purpose of enabling the animal *to move himself* to the spot in question. The spatial relations which the given spot bears to surrounding objects and places do not exist for the animal *except as they determine his own movements toward it,* and then only occasionally. The animal has no problems of position to solve except such as directly concern the distance and direction of things with reference to the position and attitude of his own body. What he needs he secures with his own mouth and limbs; what he moves he moves by direct pulling and pushing, and almost never by the intermediation of a second thing.

What is true of the discrimination of distance and direction, holds also of shape and size. Differences in the shape of things are commonly discriminated by animals only so far as they demand different adjustments of mouth or limbs in seizing them or pulling them about. Projections on a piece of wood offer advantages in seizing, unless they are too sharp, when they must be avoided. A long stick is more easily pulled along if it is held in the mouth near one end; it is more easily balanced and carried if it is held near the middle, etc. But such adjustments as these do not demand any clear-cut or systematic individuation of shapes as constant properties of physical objects in their relations to each other.

Lloyd Morgan recounts some experimentation with a dog which illustrates this point very clearly.[1] The dog in question was a young fox terrier which, like others of the breed, took delight in fetching sticks thrown for him. The experiment consisted in throwing a stick into a field along one side of which ran a picket fence in

[1] C. Lloyd Morgan, *Introduction to Comparative Psychology*, pp. 253 ff.

which there was an opening wide enough to permit the dog to pass through. The dog got the stick and tried to bring it through the fence, holding it by the middle in his usual fashion. When the stick caught, Morgan whistled and the dog pushed and struggled vigorously. After some time he dropped the stick, came through the fence, and seized the stick from the other side, but, as before, by the middle. A short stick he learned to bring through by turning his head to one side; but one too long to be dealt with in this way, he never learned to manage in the only possible way, *i.e.*, by taking hold of it near one end. Other dogs with which Morgan experimented equally failed to make the necessary discrimination. The significance of the experiment lies in this: that the dog showed no perception whatever of the shape and size either of the stick or of the aperture in the fence. Even when his failure to pull the stick through broadside would naturally have called his attention to the great discrepancy between the long stick and the narrow aperture, had he possessed the mental capacity to pay such attention, he remained wholly oblivious to the source of his difficulty. "Long" and "short" as objective properties of sticks and openings apparently do not exist for the dog.

While it is clear from experiments with chimpanzees that the anthropoids have a limited power for discriminating objective spatial properties, it belongs to man in a peculiar sense to perceive the spatial properties of things as features of an objective order. But even with his distinctive congenital capacity for such perception, it must be developed at the cost of great pains by each growing child. The writer has observed one of her own children not quite two years old try repeatedly, when playing with a nest of blocks, to put a larger block inside a smaller one, even to put the very largest inside the very smallest. To one who has not watched the manipulatory play of a little child, which occupies so many strenuous hours, the utter lack of spatialization shown is incredible. To us adults it seems so simple and inevitable a matter to see that one object is larger than another, and that it cannot possibly go inside the smaller, that the inability to perceive this is almost unimaginable. But the truth is that if the cleverest child did not spend his days playing with objects, piling and rearranging them, and trying the thousand combinations that he does, he would not enter the human world of real shapes and sizes and distances and weights, but would remain, like the animal, oblivious to these physical relationships.

CHAPTER X

The Social Factor

Social Determination of Human Cognition.

IT is widely recognized today that the most characteristic features of human life—religion, art, morality,
science—are in a general way social products, owing
their existence and their varying forms to the organization of men in society. But the extent to which the under-
lying modes of human thought and sentiment, and even
the forms of men's perception of the sensible world, are
moulded and determined by their social life, we are only
now beginning to appreciate. While the fact of the social
determination of thought and sentiment is being more
clearly exhibited each year, the manner of this determination remains to be investigated. Particularly is this
true as regards cognition. The part played by the social
instincts and emotions has attracted far more attention
from psychologists than has that of the socially determined perceptions and ideas. Indeed, the suggestion that
perception owes anything to the influence of group association may very likely be dismissed by the reader as
fanciful, so accustomed have we been, since the days of
Heraclitus, to think of sense-perception as the very type
of individual consciousness, the world in which, as in a
dream, we wander solitary.

While the recognition of the conceptual world as a
common world, in which alone men can meet and come
to a mutual understanding, is as old as science, it has

played singularly little part in epistemological speculation. The rational animal of the 17th century thinkers
was a being independent and solitary in a world of
immutable realities. The categories of the understanding and the principles of pure reason celebrated in the
Critical Philosophy were indeed common to all men;
but they owed none of their determining power over
human experience to the purely contingent fact that
men lived together in society. Even so recent and in-
fluential a thinker as Bergson is content to treat con-
ceptualizing man as *par excellence* a tool-maker, dis-
missing his dealings with his fellow men, and even his
unique faculty of speech, as of no practical importance
in determining his conceptual order. Had Bergson not
failed so conspicuously to take account of these aspects
of human life, he never could have rested content with
his evaluation of conceptual thought, nor opposed to it
so completely an equally non-social intuition.

The time is happily almost past when theories of
cognition can be merely metaphysical. If we are to
understand man as a knower, no less than man as a
doer, we must consider him as a natural being. His
sublimest faith and his most abstract reasoning have
their roots in, and receive constant nourishment from,
the natural world of things and fellow beings with
which he is in constant and varied contact. If his powers
and achievements set him off as unique in the organic
realm, we must patiently seek to analyze the marks of
his distinctiveness, and to trace their evolutionary development from their animal source. By so doing we

may hope in time to replace epistemology by a scientific psychology of cognition.

Group association means the appearance of a whole new set of affective qualities. Although we may think of living together in groups as primitively a means of securing the ends of individual life, it has involved so great a psychological modification of the individual that it would be utterly misleading to think of the relations of a social animal to other members of the group as means to individual ends. The presence of the group, the acts and attitudes of other members toward himself, toward other members, and toward natural objects, and the relation of other kinds of animals and objects toward the group—all become matters of primary importance to the social animal, to be passionately sought after and avoided for their own sake. His instinctive emotional reactions are in large measure responses to specific *social* situations. Even those activities which most purely concern his merely individual welfare, such as the getting of food, are often not undertaken individually, but are coöperative affairs. How the socializing of life affects the objectification of the environment and the correlative evolution of cognition, we must consider at length.

The Cognition of Other Individuals.

An object which, like the cow's grass or the dog's rabbit, is the chief determining element in a situation calling out a specific response, we have referred to as a *primary object;* while the constant elements of the setting which serve to determine in a more or less regular and systematic way the form of the specific activity, we have called *secondary objects*. Now it is evident that another member of the group is, or may be, an object in both of these senses. Not only are mate and offspring the objects of specific acts—this is true for solitary as well as gregarious animals—but a member of the group is treated in distinctive fashion. Domestic dogs, when they meet each other, for example, go through a typical procedure, almost ceremonial in character, which serves to establish their status with respect to each other. Members of the group do not call for any single specific response, of course, as does an article of food. Rather they are the centers of many varying and complicated responses. They are followed, fought with and over, caressed, etc. Individuals of the same species but belonging to a different group are treated differently. They are not followed, their company is not sought so constantly and regularly, and they are apt to be met with hostility. A member of the group, therefore, being the center of not one but many specific responses, acquires a greater degree of objectivity even as a primary object, than does the prey or enemy which is only hunted or avoided.

But there are important distinctions made between members of the same group. There is the leader, first of all, who calls for quite special behavior. To him attaches a complex affective attitude, a sentiment of a peculiar sort. His acts and attitudes are attended to with marked interest, and are peculiarly liable to rouse emotional responses. Besides the leader, other individuals are singled out as particular friends or enemies, or as

208

calling for some sort of indirect preferential treatment. The females of the group, the males, and the young are all distinguished by appropriate differences in behavior on the part of the other members. It is within the group that the distinction is first and most clearly made between the individual object and the class to which it belongs.

The Cognition of Objects.

THE great significance which the appearance of group life has for the evolution of cognition, does not lie simply or chiefly in the fact that the members of the group become the direct objects of a new set of specific responses. It is rather to their character as secondary objects that their chief cognitive importance attaches. The transformation which group organization has wrought in the ends of life is paralleled by the transformation which has taken place at the same time in the means of attaining those ends.

The presence and attitude of other members of the group make many ends desirable which would otherwise be indifferent. The bone which the dog has left because he was tired of gnawing it, takes on a fresh attractiveness at the approach of another dog. For the human being, to have possession of a coveted thing is to enjoy it not merely for its own sake, but as a means of asserting one's superiority over one's less fortunate neighbor, and of making him envious. Again, there is the pleasure shared, which thereby is increased. Many occupations which are unattractive if one is alone, become very desirable if one has company. On the other hand, an attitude of indifference or contempt or disapproval on the part of others may rob an otherwise desired end of all its charm. The presence and attitude of another may make one afraid to do a desired thing; or it may, particularly among human beings, altogether change its character in one's eyes. The group member becomes accordingly a *conditional determinant of ends* in a highly complex and systematic way. Now this involves not merely a development of the affective nature of the social being, but a corresponding development of his cognitive capacity.

Just how the presence of another member will affect the values of things depends on his attitude toward oneself and toward the objects in question. His different attitudes must not only be discriminated directly, but they must be discriminated in their bearing on the objects and acts which call them out. Above all they must be anticipated. A very complex situation thus arises, in which behavior must be determined by the varying relation of two objects to each other. Suppose, for example, that one wants to get possession of a desired object but fears the resentment of another member of the group. If the case is very simple and the animal's intelligence is low, either the attempt is made regardless of the other's presence, or the impulse is inhibited. But if the animal is more intelligent, he will so act as to get the desired object *without rousing the resentment* of the other. He may employ stealth and go about his task with a wary eye on the other's movements; or he may perhaps try in some way to placate the other in advance, or to distract his attention. We may say of such a case that the end is unaffected, and that it is the means of attaining it which are modified by the presence and attitude of the other; or we may say that the end is double —to get the desired object *and* to avoid the resentment of the other. But however we describe it, it is evident that a high degree of cognition is involved. The other member is apprehended as an object having distinctive and recognizable attitudes and modes of action *toward other objects*, and not simply toward oneself. So also the other objects lose their simple subjective character as objects-for-oneself, and become in a sense objects-for-others.

The ways in which the presence and attitude of others determine and modify behavior are many, but they are regular and systematic and fall into recognizable types. Friendliness and hostility, favor and disfavor toward oneself are not only pleasant in themselves, but come to be sought after or avoided as general conditions for success or failure in the attainment of other ends. Friendliness or hostility to a third member are likewise discriminated, and are determining factors in controlling one's conduct both to that third member, and to still other members and objects. Again it may not be the affective attitudes of others, but the relations of other objects and animals to the group as a whole or to certain individuals, which must be discriminated and taken account of. A simple and obvious case is the approach of a danger to offspring. The response may be merely instinctive and invariable in form. In such cases it is the situation as an unanalyzed whole that is responded to. But in the more intelligent animals, and particularly among men, a higher type of cognition comes into play, and the response of the parent is adapted to the particular nature of the threatened danger. The very recognition that a danger is present comes to depend on an analytic discrimination of the factors of the situation *in their relation to each other*.

In all these social situations, then, we find a new and higher level of behavior. What is significant in it is that behavior is controlled by two (or more) distinct stimulus-centers, each of which is a functionally independent determinant of response, but which act correlatively and reciprocally in their control over response. What determines behavior in such a case is *two distinct objects in their relation to each other*.

The Influence of Coöperation.

IT is in coöperative activity that this new type of behavior reaches its highest development. So far as there is coöperation within the group, this means that the behavior of a given member must be controlled both by the acts and attitudes of the other coöperating individuals and also by the object to which the coöperative activity is directed. Of course, where the coöperative activity is instinctive and fixed in type, the response is to the unanalyzed type-situation in which the factors are not discriminated. Such coöperation makes no especial demands upon intelligence. In the case of the social insects, indeed, we find a highly specialized coöperation and a marked lack of intelligence. But where the coöperation is free, and determined rather by social than biological conditions—where, that is, functionally independent acts are involved, making the manner and degree of coöperation adaptable to changing conditions —new and great demands on intelligence are made. According to circumstances, what is being responded to may be now the common object itself, and now one or more of the coöperating group. It may be the object in its relation to the group as a whole or to certain of its members, the group or members in their relations to the object and oneself, or, lastly, the members in their relations to one another.

Where there are a leader and followers, especially in organized coöperation, such as we find among human beings, behavior is further complicated and diversified. For the follower, let us say, it is a matter of responding now to the leader and now to the object, *e.g.*, the quarry being hunted. He not only follows the leader, but the leader's movements and cries are signals to him for determinate variations in his behavior toward the quarry. For the leader, on the other hand, it is a matter of responding himself to the perceived signs of the quarry's presence and movements, and of so acting toward or on the rest of the group as to induce a determinate response on their part either to himself or to the quarry, or even to each other. This direct response to others in such a way as to control action on their part is a type of behavior of the greatest importance. It is not, to be sure, confined to group action. The young, particularly the child, accustomed to dependence on mother and other adults for the major satisfactions, learns early to act toward the mother with the definite expectation of specific satisfaction. The step from expectation to intention is easily taken by animals having a sufficiently high psychological organization, and one's behavior toward another for the sake of some desired action on his part, becomes varied and adapted to the particular occasion. But it is in common and coöperative action, rather than in reciprocal action (such as that between mother and child), that behavior toward another to elicit determinate response on his part becomes most important. For here the response which is sought, is not toward oneself, but *toward a common object*. The complex and ordered control of group action depends for its development upon the possibility of direct and specific action by one member on others with reference to the common end. This is provided for by the appearance of a new and highly specific type of response, namely signal cries and speech.

The Personal Order and the Impersonal Order.

BEFORE we leave the general topic of the social group, we must pause to point out that it is in social action even before the appearance of speech that the source of the so-called *"représentation collective"* is to be found. Any object, response to which is determined by its relation to the group and not simply by its relation to the individual, is necessarily perceived in the light of this determining relationship. It is so far, then, a "collective representation," a truly social object. Similarly other members of the group, since they also determine response through their objective relations to each other, are also "collective representations." It is at first chiefly in their affective values, as charged with complex and

214

conditional urgencies and restraints, temptations and compulsions, that the communal character of things appears. But along with these there also emerge to view properties and relations which things and beings have as reciprocal means and conditions of the realization of these values. It is thus that what we shall term the "personal order" emerges, that is, the order of the world as seen in the perspective of the attitudes and possible acts of others—a world characterized by favor and disfavor, help and hindrance, benefit and injury, intention and purpose, good and evil, and the whole system of properties of living beings in their relations to each other. The "impersonal order," which from the earliest times developed alongside of the personal, and which for long was largely obscured by the latter, owes its origin to a different source. To an examination of this we now turn.

CHAPTER XI

The Use of Tools

No trait of man is more characteristic of him, or more clearly manifests his distinctive intellectual powers, than the use and making of tools. It is true that the anthropoids use sticks and other natural implements, and even show some capacity for "improving" these tools. But the permanent dependence on tools for the essential business of life, the regular supplementation of natural limbs by artificial ones, adapted to a variety of special uses; and, above all, the making of tools by means of other tools, is peculiar to man. It marks the transition from the condition in which life is carried on by means of adaptations of the organism to the environment—the condition which prevails generally throughout the organic world below man—to the condition in which the activities of life are directed to bringing about changes in the environment which adapt it to the organism.

The development of the use of tools roughly coincides, as we pointed out earlier, with the appearance of the other distinctive characteristics of man. While we find a simple sort of tool-using among the anthropoids, which is evidently independent of the ability to use language, it is certain that no very extensive development of tools could have taken place except under the conditions of organized and stable group life. Not only must there have been intelligent imitation such as we find chimpanzees displaying, but an enduring social tradition also was necessary to pass down slowly acquired methods from one generation to another. It is scarcely credible, even aside from the more theoretical psychological considerations, that the art of chipping stone implements could have been developed by men who had not yet learned to speak. The belief that the two great human functions are somehow causally interdependent is probably held quite widely at the present time. Just what the nature of their relationship is it will shortly be our task to consider, although no final solution of this problem can be hoped for until more data are available. Here we shall discuss the use of tools with the hope of discovering what is psychologically involved, first, in the use of a simple natural implement, like the club or stick; and, second, what is involved in the act of shaping an implement to adapt it to a specific use.

Indirect Manipulation and Primary Qualities.

So long as behavior is limited to a direct dealing with objects, the spatial properties of things are discriminated by the animal *only as relative to himself*. In order that the objective properties of things may be perceived—*i.e.*, the properties which they have in relation to each other independently of their relation to the perceiving organism, and which constitute the physical order of the external world—it is necessary that these objective qualities and relations should act as functionally independent elements in the control of behavior. Now this condition is most fully realized when the animal acts on one thing by means of another thing, when, that is, he uses implements, or tools.

The club or stick that is used to strike or poke things is in certain respects like a supplementary limb. It enables the ape or man who uses it to act at a greater distance and perhaps out of the reach of an antagonist. It increases the range of distances which he can discriminate. But if he used always the same stick, and so always had to aim a successful stroke from a constant distance from the object he wished to strike, he would still need to discriminate only distances of things *from himself*. He would come to use the stick virtually as a part of himself, as the blind man uses his cane, and nothing psychologically new would be involved.

But sticks are not all of the same length. Some are too long to be wielded, and some too short. He must learn to choose those of usable length, and to adapt his movements in wielding them to their differing sizes. A long stick must be handled differently from a shorter one. Some differentiation of lengths must take place, then, in the picking up and wielding of different sticks. But this discrimination is still only of lengths relative to himself. Moreover, if his use of tools were confined merely to brandishing them about, it is doubtful whether his attention would ever be attracted to the length of the stick as distinguished from its size and general shape. He would learn merely to choose sticks of certain sorts "on the whole," and to avoid others as generally unwieldy. But he does more than simply brandish the stick about. He *strikes and thrusts at things with it*, and this involves a more complicated action. A new factor has entered in, and a factor of momentous importance. To strike an effective blow with a stick, his movements must be regulated and controlled *both by the distance of the object and by the length of the stick*. What is necessary is not a single constant system of coördinated movements, as would be the case if the stick used were always of the same length, but a variable set of coördinations. If the stick is longer, he strikes at a greater distance; if it is shorter, he goes closer or reaches out farther. Here we have two factors, distance and length, each an independently variable element of a distinct stimulus-center, the object to be struck and the stick used, which must act correlatively in determining a successful response. The correlation which is necessary is, moreover, highly systematic. The result is that the animal or man who learns to strike effective blows with sticks or clubs of varying lengths, must learn at the same time to perceive the distance of the object to be struck and the length of the particular stick as objective properties, *i.e.*, as relative to each other and not simply as relative to himself.

This new power of perception is reinforced in other ways. As his use of sticks and clubs becomes extended, occasions arise when the stick he may happen to have will not do. Let us suppose, for example, he wishes to get some fruit hanging high out of his reach, where he cannot climb. The stick he has is too short; if he is to reach the fruit he must have a longer stick. He must learn to choose his implement with reference to the purpose in hand. He chooses, that is, not merely the stick which is "usable" in the sense of being wieldable by him, but the stick whose length is relative to the distance to be reached or spanned. He learns to attend to the length as a determinate and variable feature, and *he perceives it in terms of the distance to be reached*. So too he learns to see the distance of an object not merely in terms of the movements of his own body in reaching it, but *in terms of the length of the stick he must choose*. Distance becomes embodied, as it were, in perceived length, and perceived length becomes perceptually representative of distance. Moreover, as the indirect dealing with implements becomes extended, it is not merely the distance of the object from himself that comes to be perceived in terms of length, but distances of objects *from each other*. Whether it is in the construction of rude shelters and wind-breaks, in throwing logs across a stream, or in other ways, the fact remains that "distance-apart" becomes discriminated and objectified by its correlation with length as well as does "distance-away."

Of course the account we have just given is highly schematic. For the sake of analysis we have considered length in isolation from other properties, such as size and shape, hardness and softness. These must gradually have emerged together as the interrelated features of the independent objective world. These are the *primary qualities* constitutive of a permanent "reality," in contrast with the *secondary* qualities of the changing world of "appearance." Consider shape, for example. An animal whose behavior is confined to direct action on things, perceives shape only as an undiscriminated feature of familiar objects. That is, the apparent shape

221

is one characteristic among others by which an object is recognized. But the shape is not discriminated as the object of selective attention, because it exercises no independently variable control over response. The most that it does is to modify to some extent the movements in seizing or grasping. An object with rough projections may be seized by one of these; an object that has sharp points or edges must be seized in such a way as to avoid injury, etc. But generally speaking, shapes exercise no distinctive or systematic control over behavior; shape in itself "means" nothing particular to the dog or to the rabbit. But to the man who has come to depend on natural implements, shape is an important matter. The shapes of things stand out as physical properties charged with interesting dynamic potentialities. Think of the characteristic differences of the club with the bulging end, the sharp-pointed stick, and the sharp-edged stone. The club hits a smashing blow when it is swung, the pointed stick pierces soft things when it is thrust at them, and the sharp-edged stone cuts or scrapes. Each shape must be wielded in a particular fashion, and it produces its own particular kind of effect on other objects. A characteristic shape, accordingly, comes to mean something definite and something objective.

Much the same thing is true in regard to size. Size has always been an important aspect of things even for very simple animal organisms. But until the stage of implement-using and indirect dealing with things, size generally was little more than an immediate affective quality. Large things were immediately more desirable than small things, or they were more to be feared. At most they meant greater effort to move or to go about than smaller things, as does the large stick or stone to the dog. The physical properties of size are discovered only when things are used in relation to each other. The larger object will act, for instance, as a stable support for the smaller, but not *vice versa* (though differences in shape also play a part here). The bigger stone is harder to throw, and it will not go so far for a given effort of throwing; on the other hand, it smashes things up more when it hits, etc. The big movable object fills up a bigger hole, or covers more surface; more things can be placed in it, etc. The hard material not only "feels" different in the hand and resists direct pressure, but it does greater execution as a missile or weapon. The soft thing may not only be chewed or crushed in the hand, but it may be pierced or cut with a pointed or sharp-edged stick.

Space Perception in the Child.

THAT the capacity to perceive these properties as objective qualities of things does develop through the actual using of objects in relation to each other,[1] we have direct evidence in the play of little children. The child who has already learned through grasping and handling and moving about among things to discriminate distances and sizes with reference to his own posi-

---

[1] This statement is, perhaps, ambiguous. There is a sense, of course, in which the capacity for this perception is inherited by the child. It is *native* to the human being as it is not to the dog, for example. Yet it must be developed in each child through his intercourse with the physical world. See the supplementary note, pp. 181-188.

tion and movements, is yet wholly unable to appreciate these physical properties as manifested in the relations of things to each other. The writer's child who tried indiscriminately to put any one of her nest of blocks inside any other, simply did not "see" the one as bigger than the other. She undoubtedly had some perception of size—she would not, for example, have tried to pick up a block at all if it were as large as herself, and she knew how to adapt her grasping movements to the size of the block she was trying to pick up. But to perceive one of the blocks as "bigger" than another in the full and objective sense, is to see it as a possible container of the smaller, and the smaller as an impossible container of it. It is this objective perception of size and shape that the child is building up in its persistent play with blocks and every other small object; just as earlier it is the perception of distance-from-himself and subjective size he is building up in his grasping at things and his creeping about among them. When he begins to creep he is just as ready to creep out over the edge of the stairway or verandah, as he is later to put the big block inside the small one. He is incapable of seeing the stairs below as "below," until he has learned to adjust the movements of his body to changes of level. To see the stairs as "below" is to see them as something he must cautiously creep "down" after a particular fashion. Even when this is learned, he does not yet perceive the stairs as objectively below, that is, as a place down which playthings will fall, etc.

Along with the growing perception of the sizes of blocks, there is developing the capacity to see their shapes also. For long the child has no perception of the flat side of an object as a stable base, nor of a corner as an unstable one,[1] nor of the round ball as something that rolls. He tries aimlessly to "do" things with his blocks. Soon his efforts grow less random; he tries to stand them up, to pile them on top of each other, etc., but it is only after incredible persistence and patience that he gets the "hang" of them. At first, indeed, he cannot even be said to "try" to do anything at all, any more than the four-months-old baby who clutches at the dangling ball can be said to "try" to grasp it. The sight and touch of the pile of blocks rouse in him vague longings, just as the sight of the dangling ball excites the baby to an aimless stretching out of arms. By accident, at first, he brings two blocks together in a way that pleases him. Some chance combinations please him more than others, and he learns to repeat his performance.[2] He learns, in effect, to imitate himself, just as he earlier learned to imitate himself in uttering pleasing sounds. From imitating his own performances to obtain a pleasing result, he passes to imitating the performances of others. Thus he learns to build "piles," and later "houses."

In all this play the spatial and physical properties of things are gradually emerging into view—thrown into relief, as it were, against each other. The square or cubical block is a conditional stimulus to the placing of it in certain specific combinations with others so as to

[1] The chimpanzee apparently is incapable of acquiring this power of perception. Compare Köhler, *op. cit.*, p. 163.

[2] It is not intended to imply that this learning takes place by simple trial and error and without "insight."

make a stable structure. The long blocks are possible pillars and beams to support roofs, span doorways, etc. Of course it is not the play with blocks alone that develops the child's perception of physical properties. He is busy all day long with all sorts of aimless investigations and essays. He pulls at dangling ends and unties shoes; he fills up holes and chinks and scoops them out; he pokes and digs and scratches and smashes with anything he lays hands on.

It is evident that no extensive use of natural implements, much less the making of tools, could have taken place among beings who were not endowed with an instinctive love of constructive play. The actual use of implements in the business of life is a very complicated sort of behavior. It is made up of a great number of elementary acts, which enter as constituents into the larger complex activities. If these simple constituents were not capable of becoming what we have termed complete acts, *i.e.*, of yielding satisfaction in themselves, they would not become perfected through practice, and the fundamental perceptions essential to them would not be clearly differentiated. Just as the play of kittens in stalking, crouching, and springing on each other and on small moving objects develops skill in the proper coördination of successive movements, and, as the essential complement of this, the perception of direction and movement in relation to themselves; so the child's play in striking and digging, opening and shutting, piling and building, develops as its necessary complement the perception of the objective primary qualities.

Köhler's Experiments with Chimpanzees.

KÖHLER's delightful and illuminating account of his experiments with chimpanzees casts a flood of light upon this subject. Chimpanzees represent a transitional stage in the use of tools, and consequently a comparison of their accomplishments and their failures—particularly their mistakes—with those of human beings is able to reveal much of what is psychologically involved in the indirect dealing with things.

The experiments show clearly that chimpanzees are able, with certain limitations, to discriminate the length of a stick in relation to the distance of the goal to be reached. Very often a stick or other implement much too short will be picked up and brought up to the bars as if to be used. But often when the critical spot is reached, the animal, after a glance from the distant fruit to the stick, will drop it in evident disappointment without making any attempt to reach the fruit with it. It is to be noted, however, that in these cases, while the animal evidently does see the length of the stick relative to the distance of the goal, it is still in terms of *distance from himself.* To perceive the length of an object in terms of the *distance-apart* of two other objects is a more difficult achievement. There is some evidence that the most gifted of Köhler's apes, Sultan, when watching the performance of one of his companions, was able in a sense "to see the task to be carried out from the standpoint of the other animal." Thus on one occasion after watching the futile efforts of Chica, whom Köhler was vainly trying to teach to make a "double stick,"

Sultan took the two pieces, fitted them together to make the longer stick, and pushed it through the bars to Chica. [p. 177.] It is not at all clear from this behavior, however, that Sultan perceived that the pieces of stick were "too short to reach from Chica to the fruit." His behavior seems to indicate no more than recognition on his part of the general similarity of Chica's situation to his own and the expectation that the procedure which had helped him gain the fruit would also help her. The fact that chimpanzees find it much more difficult to "make detours" with sticks or other implements than with their own bodies is further evidence that the discrimination of spatial properties relative to one's own body is on a different level from the discrimination of the spatial properties of objects in relation to each other.

The perception of distance-apart would seem to be closely bound up with the perception of *shape*, and this is very limited in the chimpanzee. Even after considerable experience the clever Sultan remained somewhat uncertain how to proceed in order to pull a T-shaped stick, or one with a crook, through a narrow opening. In general one might say that the shapes which the chimpanzee perceives are vague and confused as compared with the distinctness and clearness of the shapes we perceive. Thus an orderly coil of a few turns of wire was treated by the chimpanzees much as we tend to treat a "confused tangle" of string, *i.e.*, they pulled at it aimlessly and blindly instead of taking hold of the proper end and *uncoiling* it in a regular way. [pp. 119 f.]

Perhaps the most interesting point in this connection,

brought out by Köhler, is the striking lack of what he calls "static sense" in chimpanzees. This is shown especially in their "building," but also in their use of "jumping-sticks." They seem, for example, incapable of distinguishing the larger, broader end of a pole or board as a more stable base when they set it up to climb, and are as likely to put the small end on the ground as the large one. After they had learned to put a box under the goal to climb up on when the fruit was out of reach, they showed the greatest difficulty in learning to pile a second box on top of the first. "They then drag it up (Tschego) or carry it just to the first box and all of a sudden stop and hesitate. With uncertain movements they wave the second one to and fro over the first (unless they let it drop to the ground immediately, not knowing what to do with it, as Sultan once did) and if you did not know that the animals see perfectly well in the ordinary sense of the word, you might believe that you were watching extremely weak-sighted creatures, that cannot clearly see where the first box is standing. Especially does Tschego keep lifting the second box over the first and waving it about for quite a while, without either touching the other for more than a few seconds. One cannot see this without saying to oneself: 'Here are two problems; the one ("put the second box up") is not really a difficult task for the animals, provided they know the use to which boxes can be put; the other (*"add one box to the other, so that it stays there firmly, making the whole thing higher"*) is extremely difficult.' For therein lies the one essential difference between using one box on the ground and adding a second to the first. In the *former* case, on the homogeneous and shapeless space, which does not claim any special requirements, a compact form is put down on the ground, which, being all over the same and of no special shape, needs no special treatment; or else it is just dragged along it (till underneath the objective) without being taken off it at all. In the *latter* a limited body of special shape is to be brought into contact with another like it, in such a way that a particular result is obtained; and this is where the chimpanzee seems to reach the limit of his capacity." [p. 152.]

Köhler believes that this inability to deal intelligently with shapes, and in particular to build stable structures, is due chiefly to the limitation of the chimpanzee's "visual insight." [p. 158.] That there is a limitation of "visual insight" the present writer would heartily agree, but there is a certain difficulty in the statement that the lack of visual insight is the *cause* of the inability to build. The capacity for visual perception and for intelligent behavior are strictly *correlative* to each other—they are two aspects of the functioning of a unitary nervous organization—and neither is, strictly speaking, the *cause* of the other. They develop together, and neither can exist without the other. After all, it is only the behavior that is evidence for the presence of the insight. There is probably no real difference of opinion in this matter between Köhler and the present writer, but only a difference of emphasis. What is emphasized in these pages is that the perception of objective qualities, size, shape, etc., develops only *with the capacity for the indirect dealing with things.*

Speech and the Use of Tools.

THAT the more discriminative and analytic use of tools by human beings is dependent on the development of conception and the use of language may be assumed. Just how far, and in what particular ways, the indirect dealing with objects may be developed without the aid of speech, we have no means of knowing at present. Are the evident limitations under which the chimpanzee suffers in his building and handling of forms connected with his inability to use language? We cannot answer. How is the child's capacity for indirect dealing at different stages related to the degree of his language development? We are almost equally ignorant. That the two are closely connected we may suspect from the fact that certain forms of speech-disorder carry with them a distinct loss of spatial (and temporal) discrimination. These are extremely difficult problems, and their solution must await further experimental research. There are, however, certain theoretical distinctions which it is important to make, if only to set specific problems to research.

An object which is selected by an animal for use as a tool (using the term "tool" in its widest sense), may be adapted only in the loosest way to the use to which it is to be put. Thus the stick or club which the gorilla uses is probably not selected with reference to its particular shape and size. As a rule, we may suppose, he picks up one that is handy and generally wieldable—one that is "good on the whole." A fox terrier dog will learn to bring sticks or other objects to be thrown for him to fetch. He takes great delight in this sport, and whenever he sees his master at liberty, will come bringing up some object and deposit it at his master's feet, hopefully waiting for it to be picked up and thrown. It is very instructive to see what the dog will bring on such occasions. No stick which he can tug is in his eyes too big, nor is any discoverable splinter left of a used stick too small. He of course identifies the object he brings by the smell, and prefers any fragment with the familiar smell to any other object. A dog known to the writer was accustomed to fetch tennis balls in this way. In the course of time a ball would begin to get torn, and the dog could never resist the temptation to complete the destruction. He would then pick up a fragment, even the tiniest shred, and bring it confidently up to be thrown. Now bringing a ball to be thrown is not, to be sure, what we ordinarily mean by using a tool, but it is analogous in that the dog's behavior is controlled by two objects in their relation to each other, the master and the ball. Of course the dog has no way of gauging his master's ability to throw. But this is just the point we wish to illustrate. The dog has no way of distinguishing the properties of an object which make it "throwable," and so remains incapable of exercising any discriminative choice.

With chimpanzees the case is evidently somewhat different. When conditions are unfavorable, e.g., if no stick is at hand, or if the animal is in a state of emotional excitement, he will, as we have seen, pick up the most absurd objects to use as "sticks." But under more favorable conditions the chimpanzee does discriminate *lengths* and will evidently choose a stick with reference to this property. We find in the chimpanzee, then, the beginnings of a different sort of behavior, *i.e.*, that which is based upon an analytic discrimination of the specific properties of things. It is present, however, to a very limited extent. Even length is definitely discriminated only with reference to "distance-away" from the animal, while almost no analytic discrimination of *shape* is evident. A chimpanzee might, for example, learn to unlock a door with a key. He might learn to choose a smaller key for a smaller lock (just as Sultan definitely chose the smaller end of the stick to fit into the end of the piece of bamboo in making the "double-stick," p. 134); but he probably would be unable to choose a key whose shape matched the shape of the aperture in which it was to be inserted. The man (or animal) who has learned to do this and similar things has reached a distinctly higher level of intelligence. He is capable of regulating his behavior with reference to distinct and variable properties of objective things. What the man looks for and chooses is a determinate shape or size or consistence, or a determinate combination of these in specific relations, and not an unanalyzed whole.

The Making of Tools.

WHILE choice of definitely appropriate implements exhibits this sort of discrimination, it appears in a clearer and fuller form in the *making* of tools. The term "making" is, to be sure, somewhat ambiguous in this connection. It may cover such a simple case of "improvement" as the breaking off of twigs and other projections on a branch, or the biting a board in two, as Köhler's chimpanzees did when in need of a stick. In such cases as these there is probably no analytic discrimination of the particular properties the implement must have to fit it for the task in hand. The chimpanzees, however, did seem to make on occasion definite efforts to *lengthen* the stick when it was obviously too short, although this statement of their aim is probably too definite. In moments of confusion even the more intelligent animals might vainly seek to improve the stick which would not quite reach by holding another firmly alongside it, or by holding two sticks, accidentally placed end to end so that they looked "longer," firmly at their place of junction and hopefully reaching for the distant fruit. Such mistakes as these show that the discrimination of *length* as the essential property was uncertain and confused. By far the greatest achievement in tool-making was that of the clever Sultan. This animal actually succeeded in fitting one piece of bamboo into the hollow end of another and so making a serviceable double-stick. It is significant, however, that if the two pieces of bamboo were lying crossed or in a position visually different from the end-to-end one, he became confused. Even in his case I think we must say that *length* was not completely objectified as a distinct property.

Are chimpanzees capable of tool-making in the sense of *shaping* an object? Here we must probably give a negative answer, for Sultan's achievement in this direction is at best somewhat ambiguous. He was given a

234

piece of bamboo and a narrow board whose end was too wide to fit into the hollow end of the bamboo. "Sultan seizes the board once more, but now works at it with his teeth, and correctly too, from both edges at one end towards the middle, so that the board becomes narrower. When he has chewed off some of the (very hard) wood, he tests whether the board now fits into the sound opening of the tube, and continues working thus (here one must speak of real 'work') until the wood goes about two centimeters deep into the tube." [p. 137.] What he has to do is to make the piece of board *small enough* to go into the opening and stick there. There is no question of *shaping* the end of the board to *fit* the round opening of the tube. At least there is no analytic discrimination of *shape* from *size*. It is only in the more highly developed tool-making, such as we find among men, that shape operates as a functionally independent factor. It emerges as a clearly differentiated property of things along with their static and dynamic relationships. Even the rude chipping of a stone would probably be beyond the powers of the chimpanzee. What we are here concerned with, however, is not the limits of the powers of the chimpanzee, but an analysis of what is psychologically involved in different sorts of behavior.

Let us consider a little more closely the case of truly *sharpening* a stick *to a point*. (Sultan did not do this.) Here, instead of the preliminary act of hunting about for a stick of the proper size and shape, there is substituted the highly adaptive act of scraping with another instrument, itself specifically adapted to its use.

The end of this new act is the production of a definite objective property, specifically related to a further objective end. The property of "pointedness" is cognized not merely *in its relation to the ultimate act of thrusting into a soft object,* but *in its relation to the preparatory act of scraping with a sharp stone, etc.* The "pointedness," being thus the center of two sets of responses (or shall we say a member of two configurations?), thrusting and scraping, acquires a greatly increased functional independence. It is accordingly the object of a clearer and more discriminating attentive scrutiny. It is attended to for itself as an end of action.

The Conceptual Control of Behavior.

TOOL-MAKING appears, it is true, like other higher activities, as a factor in a larger whole and not as an end in itself. But the distinctive making of tools implies, it is clear, the emergence of a new kind of end. At the lower level, behavior is directed toward the end of bringing oneself into a desired relation to objects, or of bringing objects into such a relation to oneself that they stimulate one in a desired way. But in the act of shaping a tool, the end of the act is determined not by its direct relation to oneself, but by the relation of the shaped tool to some further objective end. Now it is evident that the performance of such an act as this depends on the capacity for a larger organization of behavior than has hitherto been necessary or possible. The shaping of the tool is a separate act, relatively complete in itself. It may be separated by a considerable interval of time from the use of the tool. But it is, of course, a part in a larger whole, a means to a further end. Such behavior is *purposive* in the complete sense of the term. Not only is there from the beginning of the course of conduct an anticipation of the end and of the attendant satisfaction, but there is prefigured also a plan of the successive stages. Behavior which is thus directed toward bringing about a determinate objective state of affairs, and which is controlled by the objective relations of things and events to each other in independence of their relation to the acting organism, is behavior which is controlled by *conception*.

In our account of the complete act (*i.e.*, the organized response terminating in a pleasant or unpleasant state of the organism), we maintained that the unity of the act depends upon the anticipation of the affective outcome from the beginning of the response; and that the function of this anticipation is to reinforce or inhibit the act in progress. In simple sensori-motor behavior this anticipation shows itself in overt movements of response, like mouth-watering or bill-wiping (as in the case of Lloyd Morgan's chick). In more complex behavior controlled by the "image," the end is anticipated in what M. F. Washburn has called "tentative movements." Thus the dog that is hunting for the stick that has been thrown is all *ready* to pounce and seize even as he runs. He shows this readiness by premature pouncings which must be inhibited to allow the search for the proper-smelling stick to proceed. Even before the stick is thrown, there is a "set" of the organism for the satisfying seizure of the stick in his jaws. It is this preparation in advance for the final stage, this incipient

237

pleasant seizing, which acts as a determinant of the performance of the earlier stages of the act: the waiting for the ball to be thrown, the running about in search of it. It is as if the sensory stimuli coincident with the final pleasant stage were already present. Now when the end of the act is the establishment of a direct relation between the organism and something in the environment, the culmination in a consummatory reaction, the course of the response may be adequately controlled by tentative movements anticipatory of this consummatory reaction. But the end of tool-making is no consummatory reaction. When the act of sharpening a stick is successfully accomplished, the end is marked by the actual perception of the sharpened point. This highly analytic perception is a very different thing psychologically from the perception of a stick in one's jaws. If it is to be represented by an "image," such an image must have the functional value of a concept, *i.e.*, it must represent what is general and abstract—an objective state of affairs. We shall try to show later how the tentative movements of articulate speech perform this function of conceptual representation.

PART III

The Rôle of Speech in the Life of the
Individual

CHAPTER XII

Some General Considerations

In Part I we were concerned with speech primarily as a social phenomenon. Speech serves the same social function as the animal cry, *i.e.,* it coördinates the actions of the members of the group. When speech is regarded in this objective fashion, its evolution from the cry becomes comprehensible. Speech does indirectly and in a highly complex way what the cry does directly and simply. The typical language-forms—the declaration, the command, and the question, the sentence itself with its functional parts, the subject and predicate made up of distinct words—may be exhibited as arising through differentiation and specialization from the simple cry. The factors which brought about this evolution we found to lie primarily in changed conditions of group life which made necessary a higher degree and a more flexible sort of coöperation within the proto-human group.

But such a profound development in the life and organization of the group must have involved an extension and modification of the psychological capacity of the individuals. Indeed, it is only individuals already endowed with a specific psychological organization who could have responded by the achievement of language to such changes in social conditions as we have assumed. In order to comprehend how the evolution of speech from the cry is psychologically possible, it was necessary in Part II to consider certain fundamental psychological problems. We have been particularly concerned with the evolution of intelligence, and what this has involved, on the one hand, in the evolution of behavior, and on the other hand, in the increasing objectification of the environment. We are now ready to draw the threads of our argument together and to analyze, in the light of its evolutionary development, the part which speech plays in the life of the individual.

Typical Character of Speech-Development.

In this chapter we shall take up briefly certain general considerations in regard to language, which will be dealt with more fully in the succeeding chapters. In the first place, we have to note that the transition from the animal cry to human speech is a typical case of mental evolution. The development of intelligence we have seen to be closely correlated with an increase both in the complexity and indirectness of behavior. Acts which at a lower stage appear as mere factors, inseparable from the responses in which they are elements, acquire functional independence. This means not only that they come to be performed as ends in themselves, but that they make possible the organization of behavior in more complex and variable courses of conduct. The animal cry is merely a factor in a type-response. It "expresses emotion"—that is, it varies only with the affective appeal of the situation as a whole. Speech is in a high degree functionally independent. It may, or may not, express emotion; but its articulate language-structure is determined by the objective features of the situation rather than by the affective state induced in the speaker. Not only is speaking an end in itself, but it enters as a factor of some sort into almost all human activities. The cry serves to call out a specific type-response in those who hear it, directed either to the animal uttering the cry or to the situation which called it out. Speech, on the contrary, may arouse not only every emotion of which man is capable, but it acts as a conditional stimulus to any act or combination of acts which he is able to perform. The cry, again, is a response to the situation as a whole; it represents a low degree of objectification of the environment. Speech is analytic; it is in effect a distinctive response to the objective features as such. The features which are singled out for naming are highly conditional and indirect determinants of primary behavior. Hence speech represents a highly objectified situation. If a man is able to say to his neighbor, "There is a fire on that mountain," it is because such an objective condition is one to which he is capable of responding in a great variety of ways and toward which he may take a great variety of affective attitudes. So also the fact that he has distinctive verbal responses (names) for *fire, mountain*, etc., is due to the cognitive status of these objective elements as constantly identifiable but varying factors in many situations, having systematic relations to one another. Of course, the fact that the fire on the mountain is something to which he himself may behave in a variety of ways is not a sufficient condition of his ability to proclaim the event. The fire and the mountain and the occurrence of the one on the other must be objects of *common* interest, *i.e.*, possible objects of common or reciprocal action. He utters the speech *to someone,* because of the bearing of the given situation on the attitude and acts of that other. So too the ability to hear and understand such a speech depends on the ability to cognize objects not only in their direct bearing on one's own response, but in their indirect bearing on the responses of others. What is discriminated in speech is that which demands *indirect* treatment through the instrumentality of others. It is the social object common to both speaker and hearer which alone is capable of being named.

Analogy between Language and the Tool.

LANGUAGE, like the tool, is primarily an instrument to be used for the accomplishment of objective *ends.*[1] It provides an indirect way of dealing with things. It has,

---

[1] It is true that language continues to perform the simpler function that Malinowski has called "phatic communion." That is, it serves commonly enough merely to keep us in affective *rapport* with one another. We pass the time of day with our neighbor merely as an expression of our good will and to arouse and maintain a friendly attitude on his part. But it is worth observing that a nod and a smile serve this purpose as well as language. Indeed, the language we use on such occasions tends to become highly conventional and stereotyped. "How are you?" and "It's a pleasant day," are language-forms which have become atrophied because they have come to perform a simpler social function than that to which language proper is adapted. It was in the performance of a more complex function than that of phatic communion that language evolved its characteristic structures. Furthermore, when language is used to influence a person's feelings with reference to some enterprise or event, the end accomplished is an *objective* one, in the sense in which the term is used in these pages. In such a case the feelings of the person spoken to are *objects* in so far as they are cognized in their bearing on something further. They are means or obstacles, and not merely pleasant or unpleasant manifestations on the part of another.

accordingly, a cognitive status comparable to that of the tool. That is to say, its successful use depends on the capacity for discriminating objects (including other human beings) in their relations to one another, and independently of their direct relation to the person who is speaking. Moreover, language, like the tool, and unlike the limb, is something objective to, and independent of, the individual who uses it. It is a factor which he finds in his psychological environment, and to which he must adapt himself. It has a structure of its own, which he must learn to take account of in his use of it. Like the physical properties and structure of the tool, the structure of language is relative to the nature of the objects in connection with which and *on* which—if such a term be permissible—it is used. There is a technique of language, just as there is a technique of a tool; and the better this technique is mastered, the more extensive and the finer are the uses to which it may be put.

Analogy is useful because it brings into view characters which might otherwise remain unnoted. But while it may yield a clue, it cannot take the place of a direct analysis of the phenomenon under consideration. There is, we believe, a fundamental and fruitful analogy between language and the tool; but language is, after all, very different from the tool and much more than the tool. On the one hand, it is much more general in its use than any tool. It does not, like the spear or the saw, produce simply one sort of effect on one class of objects, but it produces the greatest variety of effects on all sorts of objects, through the agency of other human beings. It is an instrument by which human nature itself may be played on, to evoke not only every act of which man is capable, but every emotion and sentiment as well.

Speech as a Specific Mode of Response.

ON the other hand, although language is vastly more general in its use than any tool, it depends on the development of the specialized structure which functions in articulate speech. For the modifications of mouth, throat, and larynx, which make speech possible, are specifically adapted to vocal articulation. The human hand, on the contrary, is rather a generalized than a specialized organ. It is true that the hand itself is used in gesture language, and that proto-language was probably more dependent on gesture than is any language known to history. Nevertheless, the evolution of language proper has been the evolution of articulate speech. Moreover, and this is more important, the use of language by the individual has involved the development of a new and specific mode of behavior. To call a thing by a name, to make a statement about it, is a way of directly responding to that thing, although it is also an indirect way of dealing with it as well. Speech, as a new and distinctive mode of response, involves a specialized psychological development. It is as if the older psychological organization of the individual were no longer able to meet the increasing demands of life, and so a new function had to be created, which should not only supplement the older functions, but effect a new organization of them as well. For this is what speech does. We may compare speech to the precious metal, gold, which was originally a mere commodity, having its own immediate value, but which, partly as a consequence of this, has become a medium of exchange for all other commodities as well, thus effecting a vast systematization and extension of the whole economic life of society. So speech marks the appearance of a new type of psychological organization. A higher level of integrating centers is added to the nervous system, making possible a vast extension in the range of human behavior.

How speech is able to effect this extension and reorganization can only be understood through an examination of it as a specific mode of response. What is peculiar to speech is that it is a direct response to what is *objective*, to what *is*, in independence of the particular relation which this bears to the individual who is speaking. All other ways of responding to things—all primary behavior—are responses to things-in-their-setting.[1] It is only the "hyphenated" object, as described by the pragmatists—that is, the object-in-its-setting— which can on any particular occasion be eaten or handled or wielded. Its position, its properties, its relations to other features of the concrete situation may be—and are—conditional and partial determinants of the response; but none of these, as such, can be the object of a response of the primary sort. We cannot eat an apple without eating the apple-held-in-the-right-hand,

[1] It is of course true that speaking always takes place in a setting, or context, and that what is said is always more or less dependent on the context in which it is said. The distinction which is here drawn between speech and primary behavior is not an absolute one, but it is very real and important. The relation of speech to its context has already been discussed in the chapter on *Predication*, and it will come up again in the following chapters.

SPEECH: ITS FUNCTION AND DEVELOPMENT

etc. We cannot even see its red color except as the red-of-the-apple. In short, all our primary behavior to things is to particular things in concrete settings. But through the secondary behavior of speech we may directly and specifically respond to *the apple*, as distinguished from its particular setting. When we say, "The apple is red," it is to the apple as such that we are responding. We may make the same response no matter what the actual situation of the apple may be. Nay, more, we discriminate the *class* of apples as such in a direct speech response and say, "Apples are juicy." Or we may single out a single property of the apple and respond to it directly, without any reference to the fact that it happens to be a property of apples; as when we say, "Red is complementary to green."

It may perhaps be thought that merely verbal response of this sort, since it often produces no effect upon its object, can be called a "response" only in a figurative sense. An action which is directed toward a thing, but which has no "come-back," has no possible *raison d'être*. Even if we suppose such a mode of action to have come into existence, it could not enter as a factor into the system of behavior. Nevertheless, speech is a response, although of a unique sort. It is true that we may idly talk of things without producing any observable effect on anything except ourselves. But speech is not normally idle. It is potentially capable of bringing about all sort of consequences, varying with the circumstances in which the speech is uttered. Speaking of something is a direct response in that it specifies directly; but by reason of this very directness, its consequences are indirect and conditional. Its very utility lies in this fact. Moreover, the more analytic and abstract speech becomes, *i.e.*, the more specifically we may respond to the elements of the objective world, without regard to the particular setting in which they may be at the time, the greater both in extent and fineness is the potential effectiveness of speech.

CHAPTER XIII

The Animal Cry as a Mode of Response

In order to substantiate these general observations and to make them clearly intelligible, we must once more return to the animal cry and the resemblances and differences which it exhibits when compared with speech.

The Animal Cry as an Acquired Response.

The cry is in part an instinctive response to a type-situation, in part an acquired response learned by imitation under the conditions of group life. It is well known that the calls and songs of certain species of birds are not fully acquired by individuals that are brought up in isolation from their kind. More important, however, in the present connection is the fact that, even when the cry, as uttered, is simply characteristic of the species, the appropriate occasions for its utterance have in large measure to be learned by the individual. W. H. Hudson remarks that a young dove, hatched and reared among pigeons, remains as fearless of man as the birds on a desert island.[1] It has not the instinctive endowment to enable it to respond to the warning cries of its foster parents; and since it never hears the warning cries of its own species, it has only its own individual experience to teach it what is to be feared. A fledgling robin, which was once reared in the writer's family, remained entirely without fear not only of human beings,

---

[1] *The Naturalist in La Plata*, pp. 91 f.

but of its natural enemies, dogs and cats. A bird properly brought up learns from the warning cries of its parents what to be afraid of, and is thus prepared as it grows older to warn others of danger.

The call given by the young when hungry, or the variant given in fear or in acute distress, is originally no more than an expressive movement made under the influence of the emotional state. But it brings the mother with food, and the comfort and security of her presence; and gradually it comes to be given with the expectation of the food or of the mother's brooding warmth, or of deliverance from danger, as the case may be. The baby, who at first cries as the expression of any discomfort, comes to cry—with a distinctive wail —*for* his bottle, or *to be* taken up. The blond ringdove that gives the nest-call when he has found a satisfactory site, is inviting his mate to join him, *i.e.*, he continues to give it until she comes. So the mother hen that catches sight of a hawk circling over her brood and clucks to them in alarm, *expects* them to come, as is evidenced by her uneasy regard of them, the fluffing-out of her feathers to cover them, and her insistent sounding of the call until the last fluttering chick is safe beneath her wings. In short, the animal cry comes—in varying degrees, according to the species—to be given not merely as a simple direct response to the stimulus which excites it, but as an act directed toward the eliciting of a desired response on the part of others. Otherwise, indeed, it could not be *learned*, but would necessarily remain on the level of a purely automatic reaction. The success or failure of the cry as a mode of response,

which alone can reinforce or inhibit or regulate its occurrence, is precisely its success or failure in influencing
the acts of others in such a way as to bring relief or
satisfaction to the one that gives the cry. It is true that
in order to be successful it must be given as a response
to the appropriate situation. The alarm cry must be
given under properly "alarming" circumstances. The
nest-call must be given as a response to its own sufficient stimulus, etc. In other words, the cry as given must
maintain its *double* character as a response to a specific
situation and as an act directed toward others.

The Cry as Heard.

THE cry as heard acts originally as a stimulus to a
specific affective state—sexual excitement, fear, anger,
maternal solicitude, etc. But if these arousals of emotion are to be useful, and not a mere waste of energy,
they must issue in response *toward something*. How is
this accomplished? It is evident that the auditory stimulus of the mere sound cannot by itself adequately determine conduct. The cry of fear, for example, rouses
fear and the tendency to flight; but flight to be useful
must be flight *toward something*, or *away from something*. Where the danger itself is perceived, its perceived situation determines the direction of the flight;
but the cry of alarm does not in itself indicate the position of the danger, nor the direction in which safety is
to be sought. The cry must, then, usually be supplemented by other stimuli. This supplementation occurs
in various ways. If a bird is on the ground when he
hears the alarm cry, he flies *up;* if a tree is near, he flies

to the tree. The perceived features of the situation in which the cry is heard, act, that is, as supplementary determinants of the response. Moreover, the previous experience of the hearer may modify the character of the total situation to an indefinite extent. If a bird is near a house, where men and cats may be expected, for example, the bird will fly not simply up, but away from the house. The immediate surroundings in which the animal finds itself when the cry is heard always determine to some extent the form which the response takes. What the cry itself determines is the type of the response.

Among the more important of the perceived features of the situation in which a cry is heard is the animal which utters it. The cry is originally only one element in the total affective response made by the animal, and for this reason it is important he be seen as well as heard. Thus it makes a great difference *what* individual is giving the cry. The cry of distress given by her own perceived young acts on the mother as the same cry from other young does not. So the cry of the mate is responded to distinctively. It is true that the call of the mate or other well-known individual may have peculiarities by which it comes to be recognized even when the giver is not otherwise perceived. But in such a case the cry itself is perceived as the cry-of-the-mate, etc. In addition to the perception of the cry as the cry of a particular individual, it is always heard as coming-from-a-particular-place. This may serve merely to announce the presence of the giver in that place, but it may also aid in locating the object to which the cry is a response. If the giver of the cry is within visual range, the cry commonly serves to attract the attention of the hearer to him; and his seen attitude and behavior—the direction in which he is looking or running—indicates to the hearer the position, and perhaps also something of the character, of that which caused the cry. A dog that hears another bark in the distance, for example, will first run to the spot whence the barking comes; if he then sees the other dog running or jumping, he will run in the same direction, looking to see what the other is barking at.

We must, then, distinguish two factors or elements in the cry as heard: (1) the kind of cry, or the cry as such, *e.g.*, alarm or challenge, (2) the setting or context in which the cry is given, including the individual perceived as giving it, and the circumstances in which he gives it. It is these two factors together, *plus* the perceived features of the situation in which the hearer finds himself, which are the complete determinant of the latter's response. The cry itself, apart from its total context (as we may call these supplementary factors taken together), is always an incomplete stimulus, although it plays a distinctive rôle in determining response. This rôle it is important for us to analyze. In the first place, the cry as such serves to define or characterize the situation as a *specific sort* of situation. It rouses a specific affective attitude. The cry of alarm which rouses the hearer from sleep normally excites fear, even though that fear be vague and wholly undirected at first. The context in which a specific kind of cry is heard may differ from occasion to occasion, but the cry tends to bring out the same general affective attitude. There are exceptions to this. There may be two alternative kinds of response to the same sort of cry; *e.g.*, the challenge call which precedes attack may call out either reciprocal hostility or submission. But even in such a case, the cry serves to characterize the situation; for it is, in effect, the announcement of an impending event of a distinctive sort, and thus prepares the hearer in advance.

Representative Character of the Cry.

In the second place, the cry as such has a *representative* function. It not only characterizes the situation which is partly perceived—as the mother bird's warning cry endows the appearance of the approaching man with "fearfulness" in the eyes of her young—but it *supplements* a perceived situation by representing features which are not, but may be, perceived by the hearer. This is the case when the "opening bay" of the leader of a pack of hounds announces the sight of the quarry, or when the nest-call of the dove announces the finding of a suitable nesting-site.

The important thing for us to note is that in such cases the cry as such, apart from its context, acts as a partial substitute to the hearer for the actual perception of the situation which called it out. The situation as perceived is a complete determinant of response; it is concrete and particular. The situation as represented by the cry is an incomplete determinant of response. The representation is abstract and general. That is, the cry is a substitute for the situation perceived by the giver of the cry *only so far as the perceived situation is like any other situation of the same sort.* The cry represents a kind of situation and not a concrete particular situation. It represents the situation, moreover, as an unanalyzed whole, as felt rather than as cognized. How the representative function of speech differs from that of the animal cry will be considered later. What we have to notice here is that the cry already performs a function of representation and that what it represents is the general and not the particular. It is the *perceived context* which alone can give particularity. Profound as is the difference between the representative function of speech and that of the cry, there is, nevertheless, as we shall try to show later, a parallel between language and the cry in this fundamental respect.

CHAPTER XIV

The Transition to Speech

THERE are very good reasons for supposing, as we saw in Part I, that language proper as it exists everywhere today, *i.e.*, in the form of sentences composed of words, was preceded by a simpler stage in which there were neither distinct word-elements nor explicit predication. This simpler stage, where speech is confined to the utterance of unanalyzed and uncompounded sentence-words, is passed through by the child and is also exemplified by certain forms of Indian signalling. We attempted to show in a schematic way under what general social and environmental conditions, and in the service of what social needs, the transition took place from the animal cry to this primitive form of human speech. In giving this genetic account we were regarding language from the social rather than from the individual standpoint. Yet we were forced to recognize that the evolution of speech from the cry must have been dependent on a much larger development, as a result of which man's simpler and more instinctive modes of behavior as an arboreal animal were broken down under stress of new conditions, and replaced by more complex and varied behavior. In the light of the preceding analysis of cognition, we are now able to see that this transition from cry to speech, while of peculiar importance, is a *typical* extension of the previous evolution of intelligence. It exhibits the same characteristics which we have discovered to mark its course from the beginning.

On the side of behavior, evolution has meant, on the one hand, the breaking-up of the larger type-response into separable elementary acts. These elementary acts appear first as factors in many larger complete acts. Then, through the very fact of their having a multitude of varying connections, they acquire what we have termed functional independence, and come thus to be performed, in play or otherwise, as secondary complete acts. Life thus becomes richer and more diversified both in its ends and in the means by which its ends are attained. On the other hand, this differentiation of what were originally independent factors makes possible their reorganization into larger complex wholes. This alternative differentiating-out of elements which become functionally independent, and their reorganization into new and larger complexes, are constantly repeated as psychological evolution proceeds.

On the side of the environment, this development of behavior involves, and is correlative to, the process which we have termed progressive objectification. The situation, which is the complete determinant of response, itself undergoes a differentiation. The primitive affective qualities attaching to the situation as a whole become diversified and at the same time distinguished from the perceived features of the situation. As partial determinants of response, indirect and conditional in varying degrees and modes, *objects* emerge, which are cognized rather than felt. These primitive objects, which at first are centers toward which specific acts are directed, become progressively differentiated, as possible means and obstacles, into more indirect and conditional determinants of many acts. At the same time, this increased conditionality takes on systematic form, and distinctive properties and relations of the primitively vague objects come into view. Finally, as the necessary complement to the indirect attainment of ends through the instrumentality of the other members of the social group, and the indirect dealing with things involved in the use of tools, the objective order of reality appears and the world becomes truly known.

The Differentiation of Speech-Behavior.

A CHIEF feature of the evolution of speech from the cry is the differentiation of the two fundamental forms, the proclamation and the command. We have already seen the importance of this differentiation of the speech-function in making human coöperation possible. The proclamation, as distinguished from the mere cry, does not arouse a specific type-response in all members of the group. It is potentially a conditional stimulus to a wide variety of behavior, both on different occasions and on the part of different individuals. It thus makes possible both a greater flexibility in the adaptation of group-behavior to the situation, and the coördination of more varied acts on the part of individual members. The command, on the other hand, is potentially a direct stimulus to any functionally independent act or any organized complex of such acts. Neither the proclamation nor the command could develop without the other. They are necessary complements to each other, and together constitute an adequate instrument for the control and coördination of social behavior.

The cry, as we have shown, has a certain double character. It is, particularly when called out by external conditions, at once a specific response to a situation and an act directed toward another member of the group. The development of the cry into the complementary proclamation and command depends upon a differentiation of these two characters of the primitive cry. The proclamation is primarily a specific response to a situation, and only secondarily an act directed toward the hearer with the end of influencing his behavior. Or, rather, perhaps, the proclamation is *directly* a response to the situation, and *indirectly* a means of acting on others. The command, on the contrary, is primarily an act directed toward another in order to influence his behavior. Since the command is always actually given in view of, and with reference to, the existing situation, it is secondarily and indirectly a response to the situation. Thus, while the proclamation and the command show a differentiation of function, each still retains the double character implicit in the cry.

The Sentence-Word as a Response to the Object of Perception.

FROM the beginning, the sentence-word differs from the cry in that it is a response to the situation as *perceived*, or otherwise cognized, and not as *felt*. What the sentence-word singles out for response is not the unanalyzed situation-as-a-whole, but some objective feature of it, which is for some reason of especial interest to the speaker. The feature thus singled out by verbal response, while it is of especial interest, is not of itself sufficient to determine primary behavior. It is an element which may appear in many other situations, and which has a constant though conditional value. What constitutes the identity of an object of perception is, as we pointed out earlier, precisely this conditional constancy. The "same" object of perception does not yield the same physiological stimuli, nor does it call out the same movements of response, on all occasions. Its identity is the identity of a *system*, composed of regularly varying stimulus-patterns on the one hand, and of response-elements on the other. In proportion as this system is loosely organized, the identity is imperfect, and its objectivity is of a low order.

"Identity" is, of course, a term strictly applicable only to objects of highly conceptualized cognition. Before the psychological environment is thus conceptualized, there is no hard and fast line between objects which are "like" each other and different appearances of the "same" object. Even for the thought of the more primitive peoples of today, the "identity" of an object with itself is much looser and vaguer than for our thought, as Lévy-Bruhl has shown. The world perceived by men at the beginnings of speech must have been much vaguer still in feature and outline, more charged with the primary meanings of feeling and less with the secondary meanings of cognition. But for a perceived world to exist at all, there must be some constancy from situation to situation, some "sameness" recognized, however vaguely.

Now it is these vaguely "same" features which are singled out as the objects of the first specific response of speech. What speech does is to furnish a specific and direct response to the object of perception, which up to this point has been merely a conditional determinant of response. A man, for example, will call out "Wolf!" or "Fire!" as the occasion demands, instead of uttering a mere cry of alarm. Moreover, he may call "Fire!" not for purposes of alarm, but to proclaim the welcome discovery of fire, or to announce his accomplishment of kindling one. It is the *tone of voice* which makes the utterance of the sentence-word a cry of alarm or an ejaculation of satisfaction or triumph. Now if fire were merely an object to be feared, as it is to most animals, and one over which men had no control, there would be no need of proclaiming its presence by a name; a cry of fear would suffice. But since fire is to be feared under some circumstances and welcomed under others, and especially since it may be controlled and made use of in various ways, a distinctive response, such as language alone can give, becomes necessary. To the speaker, the ability thus to respond to an object by a distinctive act of naming, endows it with a new particularity of being. The constancy of the name consolidates the unity of the primary response-system already in existence. An object which calls repeatedly for the same verbal response thereby acquires a sharper and clearer identity, acquires sameness as distinct from likeness-on-the-whole. Through being specifically named, an object is discriminated from the context in which it occurs, as well as from other objects similar to it. Its objectivity is itself consolidated and heightened.[1]

The influence of speech on the objectification of the world makes itself felt not only through the act of speaking, but through the act of hearing and responding to the speech of others. As heard, the sentence-word like the cry is representative. Its representative capacity is very different from that of the cry, but it has the same fundamental basis in the fact that it calls out a response to the objective stimulus of the utterance of the speaker. That is to say, it is the function of the proclamation to direct the attention of the hearer to what the speaker is talking about, and in some way to control his behavior with reference to the state of affairs that called out the speech. The proclamation acts within certain limits as a substitute for the actual perception of what is proclaimed; or it leads to an expectation of, and a preparation for what the speaker announces to be present.

As we saw in Part I, proclamations are of various sorts. When what is proclaimed is the presence of some object unperceived by the hearer, he is led either *to expect* to see or hear or otherwise perceive it, or in some other way to take account of its presence. If the proclamation is what we have termed predicative, *i.e.*,

---

[1] The influence of the name upon the recognition of identities and differences is not less marked in the case of highly advanced thought. Identity of name obscures for us today differences which it is important to discriminate both in our practical dealings with the world and in our thinking about it. And differences in name equally obscure identities of property, or relationship, or process, which demand recognition in our treatment. The importance of adequate terminology for science and philosophy does not need emphasis here.

if it calls attention to, or announces, some property unnoticed by the hearer, of an object already within his
field of perception, it equally leads to an expectation
of perceiving that property, or acts as a substitute for
the actual perception in its influence on the hearer's
behavior. The same thing is true if the proclamation is
the announcement of what the speaker has done or is
about to do. The hearer is thereby led to act (within
certain limits) *as if* he had already seen the speaker
perform the act, or to prepare himself in advance for
the speaker's impending performance of the act. We
shall consider in a moment the limitations of this function of representation.

First we wish to emphasize the fact that what the
sentence-word represents is something objective, something cognized rather than felt. The cry is a representative of the unanalyzed situation; the sentence-word represents some factor in the situation as already analyzed
in perception. What is thus represented by primitive
speech presents itself to actual perception under a variety of appearances and calls for a variety of responses.
It contains, nevertheless, let us repeat once more, a core
of "sameness," of identity with itself, in the midst of
this variety. It is this "sameness," vague as it is, which
makes possible the representation of the perceived object by the spoken symbol.

*Dependence of the Sentence-Word upon the Perceived
Situation.*

In Part I we showed how the use of uncompounded
sentence-words is restricted in its social utility. Such

rudimentary language can be used and understood only with reference to the particular situation of the speaker, or the hearer, or both. It is largely for this reason, we remarked, that a stranger unfamiliar with the life and daily habits of a little child finds it so difficult to understand his prattle; and that even a member of the family often fails to grasp the significance of what the baby is saying if he does not see what the baby is doing. For the same reason, too, the single Indian signal of "discovery" is sufficient when a hunt is in preparation or an enemy party is expected (*i.e.*, when the situation as a whole is already determined), while the "discovery" signal must be supplemented by the specific signal for "game" or for "enemy" if the situation is not yet determined. It is this limitation in the function performed by speech of this primitive sort that necessitates (or permits) the largeness and looseness of meaning which its terms exhibit. The same term means indiscriminately an object, an action performed on the object or by the object, a person connected in some way with the object, or some property of the object. That is to say, the term abstracted from its context and considered by itself has all these meanings. But for the speaker as he uses it, and for the hearer as he hears it, it is not ambiguous, for the reason that it is always used with reference to a concrete context which gives it particularity of meaning.

Analysis of the Sentence-Word.

THE articulate utterance is not simple. It consists of the complex of sounds which constitutes the "word" itself, plus the tone in which this complex is uttered—the "expression." The complex of articulate sounds tends to remain the same from occasion to occasion; it is the response to what is *objective* in the situation. Thus in the example just used, the articulate complex "fire" remains the constant response of the speaker to the objective phenomenon of fire. The tone and manner of utterance, on the other hand, varying as they do with the occasion, constitute the speech as a response to the particular fire, *i.e.*, the actually perceived fire. The success of the speaker in bringing about the desired behavior on the part of those he speaks to, depends on his ability to make this discrimination in his speech. It is essential that he call "fire" only when it is a case of fire, and that he use only the tone and expression appropriate to the particular occasion.

The hearer who is spoken to always hears the speech as a factor in a concrete setting. He hears the "word" as uttered by a particular speaker in a particular voice. At least he must so hear it to understand its significance and take account of it in his behavior. The speech as he first hears it may be indeterminate in one of these respects. He may not be sure of its source, and he looks and listens to see *who* is speaking, and *where*, before he acts further. Or he may not catch *what* is being said, and he listens again for a repetition to distinguish the "word." The tone and expression are less likely to be doubtful, but one sometimes, for instance, hears a child exclaim something without being sure whether he is calling in distress or glee. The fact that the hearer can thus attend specifically to these distinct factors in the total speech, is evidence that each has some degree of functional independence, and that its bearing on the hearer's conduct is distinctive and determinate.

It is undoubtedly easy for us to exaggerate the independence of the word as an entity. Even in language proper, which contains sentences composed of separable words, we are far too prone to think of the "word" as self-sufficient—independent of, and somehow prior to, the sentence in which it occurs. This tendency on our part is largely due to the influence of the printed symbol with which we are so familiar. It breeds in us a fallacy against which we must be on our guard in our efforts to understand and analyze language. It is particularly misleading when the language we have to consider is the proto-language of the one-term sentence-word. In a sense it would be true to say of this stage of language development, that it contains no *terms* at all; and that it is inexact to assert that the meaning of its terms is not fixed and definite, but variable and loose. On the contrary, what should be said is that what is actually spoken and understood at this stage—the actual meaning conveyed from speaker to hearer by the use of the sentence-word—is more specific and more concrete than what is conveyed by the highly organized sentence composed of highly specialized words.

Here again we have to note the familiar features of the course of mental evolution. The utterance of the articulate word as compared with the cry is functionally independent since it is relatively free from the control of emotion in the speaker, and also since the acts it stimulates in the hearer are equally independent of his emotion. Moreover, if we consider the articulate complex itself, *i.e.*, the term, apart from the tone and context, we find a further differentiation of function. Tone and term vary independently. At this stage, however, the term cannot function independently of the tone and context. Apart from them its meaning is incomplete and indeterminate. Speaking intelligently and understanding what is heard are dependent on perceiving. One can speak only of what is immediately about one, and with reference either to what one is doing or about to do oneself, or to what another is doing or about to do. It is not until the stage of complete predication is reached that language becomes truly independent either as a mode of behavior or as an organized system of symbolic representation.

The Use of Sentence-Words by the Child.

WE have already remarked how the little child very early shows a tendency to point to objects which arouse his interest, and how this pointing often becomes a social game because it attracts the attention of others who give sympathetic responses. This early pointing is apt, we may recall, to be accompanied by a "vocal gesture," a cry which equally serves to attract attention to the interesting object. Under the influence of his elders, the child learns to vary the vocal gesture with the object, and repeats over and over the "names" of different objects, pointing at them, and looking to his companion for approval and sympathy. The child takes delight in the performance of this new activity, just as he has taken delight in his coos and gurgles, but the success of this activity is measured by the approval and confirmation expressed by his companions. So far as we are aware, this sort of play is peculiarly human; the anthropoids do not exhibit it. Like other sorts of play, it is essential to success later in carrying on the serious business of life. Indeed, in the child this new form of activity becomes almost at once more than play. The child would not learn to speak unless he made use of his "words" to get what he wants. Now it is obvious that his success in using this instrument depends on his ability to discriminate clearly the different features of his environment by giving the appropriate verbal response to each. He must learn to attach to each object, act, etc., its proper "name." This marks a new level of response; first, because it is highly indirect in its results—the object named has no "come back"—and secondly, because the verbal response is from the first *analytic;* it is a specific and direct response to an *element* in the situation, as the cry is not. This is true of no other sort of behavior. Manipulatory behavior can be *modified* and *varied* adaptively to variations in the elements of a situation, but it remains a response to the concrete situation as a whole. Pointing may discriminate a single object in the situation; but it cannot *specify*, because it does not change its form according to the kind of object. The full potentialities of the verbal response are not, of course, exploited in the beginning. The sentence-word is analytic; it specifies some feature of the given situation from the start; but just what it specifies on a given occasion is determined by the nature of the situation.

Social Status of the Objects Discriminated by Speech.

LET us consider a little more closely what features of
the objective world it is that are singled out for this
discriminatory verbal response. For not everything in
the world has a name. Even in our modern world, which
has been combed over and teased out by the subtleties
of civilized language, there remain aspects and nuances
which escape fixation in speech; which are not only
directly, but even indirectly, indescribable. Much more
widely was this true of the world within which primitive speech grew up. For language singles out for specification only those features which are, in a peculiar sense,
common to the social group. The verbal response
attaches itself to the objective features upon which
coöperative action *pivots*. Whatever is peculiar to the
individual does not need, nor can it receive, specification in language. Moreover, what may be common to
many individuals merely as individuals, because they
are alike, cannot be effectively specified by language,
except in so far as it excites common interest. I may
specify verbally features of my world which are equally
features of yours; but unless such verbal response on
my part calls out some answering behavior from you,
directed to what I have been talking about, there is
nothing to mark the success or failure of my speaking.
It is only through the *convergence of action* upon the
objects of verbal response that language becomes standardized, and its terms freed from ambiguity and vague-
ness of meaning.

Where language has become highly developed, it is

of course possible to establish or correct the meaning of terms without resort to primary behavior. I may discover from the verbal context of a new term what its "meaning" is, and we may agree upon *definitions*. But this is possible only because we are in possession of a language rich in a vocabulary already standardized through practical coöperation. This substratum of primary words denoting the objects and acts of daily practical life is like the gold or silver money upon which an indefinitely vast and complex system of paper currency may be based. The language-system like the financial system is solvent so long as its abstract terms, like paper money, remain exchangeable somewhere and somehow for the gold of intrinsic value.

Since it is characteristic of the sentence-word to point to and represent some *objective* feature of the situation, it is only in an environment which has already undergone a high degree of objectification that language is possible at all. Language is the peculiar instrument for controlling the indirect behavior of tool-using men in a highly organized social group. The features singled out for "naming" are pivotal points on which coöperative action turns, rather than centers to which specific acts are directed. They stand out because they are centers for the intersection of many crossing lines of behavior. But with the development of language, they are selected as the independent points to which a certain specific act is directed—the spoken word. A new and sharpened attention is fixed upon them. At the level of implicit predication, what is named by the sentence-word is distinguished only momentarily and partially from its background. The sentence-word is not in itself the name of either object, or property, or act, as such, but only of the imperfectly differentiated whole which these form. On occasion the sentence-word specifies now one of these aspects and now another, according to the particular exigencies of the case. As elements they are still only conditional determinants of response, but in a delimited field. It is not until predication becomes explicit that the elements of this delimited field themselves gain the independence with which the specific naming endows them.

As language develops it acts like a sculptor, carving into ever sharper relief the features of the objective human world. What is at first vague in its outline and contours, becomes gradually more distinct. The world is for the first time genuinely individuated. Objects stand out in their particularity from a vaguer background. At the same time likenesses and differences become distinguished and accentuated. As the world becomes individuated, it becomes classified.

But speech means far more than the attaching of specific verbal responses to objective elements. The learning of distinctive names for things and acts is indeed essential to language. But this primitive "naming," although it marks the appearance of a new type of response of momentous importance, does not constitute speech any more than words constitute language. The ability to respond directly to a thing or act by name is the beginning, but merely the beginning, of a highly complex organized activity. It is only as the functionally differentiated elements of the complete sentence that true words come into existence. It is the using of *sentences*, then, that we must examine as a form of individual activity, in order to determine the part it plays in the higher processes of thought.

CHAPTER XV

The Complete Act of Speech

THE evolution of the complete sentence from the sentence-word we have already considered in its social aspect. The appearance of explicit predication we found to be conditioned by the need for an extension of concerted action beyond the limits of the situation already perceptually determinate for the group as a whole. The great social advantage of explicit predication lies, on the one hand, in the enlargement of the field of possible coöperation it effects, and, on the other hand, in the increase in the adaptiveness of the group action to the structure of the particular situation. It both extends and analyzes the field within which concerted behavior takes place.

Now this development of the organized activities of the group is correlative to a commensurate development on the part of the individual. If men were heretofore confined, in their common enterprises, to the limits of their perceived surroundings, it was because they had not developed the individual capacity for anything more complex. To speak in complete sentences is to act in a new way. It is, in the first place, a far more independent act than the utterance of the single sentence-word. It is less closely bound up with the immediate primary behavior on the part of the speaker. But a more important claim to novelty lies in the fact that its immediate *end* is different. Its fundamental function still remains the control of primary behavior. But this control now tends to be exercised indirectly. The response which the complete act of speech directly elicits from the hearer is a verbal *reply* or *rejoinder*. This is as much as to say that the sentence is a unit of *intercourse,* an element in *conversation.* The specialized forms of the sentence—the declarations of different sorts, the question, the command—arise to serve complementary uses. They represent, indeed, typical parts played by different interlocutors. It is by remark and rejoinder, question and answer, that conversation proceeds. Each of these characteristic forms of speech plays its distinctive rôle, and each must be understood in relation to the others. We shall return presently to the closer consideration of the psychological importance for the individual, of the evolution of this give and take of verbal intercourse. But first we must discuss, more fully than we were able to do in Part I, the phenomenon of conversation as a social enterprise.

Conversation.

THERE is something very like conversation foreshadowed in the cries and calls of animals. For many of the cries of bird and beast tend to bring out answering calls from mate or other companions. This vocal interchange is from the first a sort of "phatic communion," which helps to cement the bonds of common life. But it often plays a more specific rôle. We may recall Craig's account of the interchange of coo and caress which a pair of ringdoves goes through with in choosing a nesting-site. This not only strengthens the tie of mutual affection, but it acts as a direct preparation for their common task of nest-building. A more familiar example of this sort of proto-conversation is to be found in the mutual behavior of two hostile animals. The challenge-call and counter call, and the long interchange of expressive behavior which so often follows, serves primarily to prepare the combatants for conflict. They feel out each other's determination and strength. But it may also act as a substitute for the real fight and itself decide the issue.

The true conversation of speech differs from this prototype in fundamental respects, which are, perhaps, already sufficiently familiar to the reader. It is carried on in relative independence of other forms of expressive behavior; it operates through conventional symbols instead of instinctive cries; as an instrument of social coordination it is vastly more complex and flexible and indirect in its functioning. In spite of these differences, however, human conversation continues to perform the primitive social functions of its animal prototype. It keeps men *en rapport* with one another. It serves to establish mutual sympathy and understanding, or to foster suspicion and hostility. Indeed, all of the multifarious affective relationships in which human beings may stand to one another are furthered, destroyed, or transformed by verbal intercourse. Through it reciprocal status is established and maintained, and common sentiment fostered. In short, conversation weaves the changing pattern of the fabric of social values which underlie our common life and without which society would be impossible.

But it is not to the control of the affective springs of human relationship that the development of the structure of language is due. The forces which have created sentence structure and the representative symbolism which this involves have arisen from the impingement of concerted action upon an *objective* environment. And it is equally in the guidance of social action in and upon the world in which men live that the complex structure of conversation has been fashioned.

Conversation is primarily the preparation for concerted or socially determined action. It plays a part in organized group life comparable to that played by the perception mediated by distance-receptors in the life of the individual. As looking and listening make it possible for the individual organism to anticipate the results of actual contact by a wide variety of adaptive behavior, so talking over a remote or complex situation makes it possible for the social group to concert action in far more complex and indirect ways for the attainment of indefinitely remote ends. Like perception, conversation prepares the response which is to follow by determining— or "constituting"—the situation. These two processes proceed *pari passu* and are reciprocally determinative. The individual sees or hears in terms of what he is to do, and he prepares to act with reference to the situation which he discerns. In the conversation which precedes concerted action on the part of the group, these two processes become embodied, as it were, in the declaration of presence or predication, on the one hand, and in the announcement of intention and the command, on the other.

As conversation develops, it tends to fall into two complementary parts, or phases. The first is the determination, through analytic description, of *what* the situation is in which action is to take place. The second is the formulation of a plan of action. Let us particularize. One member of a hunting group, perhaps a scout, makes an announcement; another member supplements this with a further piece of information. These give rise to questions on the part, let us say, of the leader; and these in turn elicit replies which serve to add further interesting details. In the light of the situation whose relevant features are thus set forth in language, someone suggests a course of action. This is elaborated and perhaps modified, as further questioning reveals difficulties to be met. Finally the common course of action as thus sketched out in language is agreed upon, and specific commands are issued by the leader. It is not altogether fanciful to compare this process of preparation for group action to the psychological process which takes place in the attentively perceiving individual. The sensory excitation does not directly and immediately issue in overt action, but leads first to various tentative movements, which, like the announcements of intention, sketch in advance a rough outline of the behavior which is to follow. These tentative movements react upon the sensory centers until, through mutual action and reaction, sensorium and motorium reach a harmonious adjustment, and the organism is oriented for overt response.[1]

Factors of Conversation.

LEAVING aside the analogy with perception, let us observe certain outstanding features of conversation. The first of these is the essential correlativity—or the functional interdependence—of the statement of matter-of-fact and the statement of intended action. The announcement that a given state of affairs exists, or that something is thus and so, is made primarily because of its possible bearing on the behavior of another. The announcement of intended action is made with reference to a situation presumably known in its essential features by both speaker and hearer. The temporal order may be reversed and the announcement of intended action be made first, to be followed by the announcement of relevant fact; but the essential relationship of the two phases of conversation remains unaltered. For example, a child comes in and says to his mother: "I am going to play tennis with John." "But your sister has your racquet." "Then I shall ask Father to lend me his. Where is he?" "He is in the library, but wipe your feet before

---

[1] It is of interest to compare the account of conversation given above with what Köhler has to say about "learning with insight" and its criterion. This criterion is, it will be recalled, "the appearance of a complete solution with reference to the whole lay-out of the field." The pause in which the animal scrutinizes his surroundings until their details slip into place to form a unitary configuration (compare Dewey's "constitution of the stimulus") is like the conversation which sketches in language the field of social action. That the period of the animal's scrutiny is also the preparation of his response is evidenced by the suddenness and continuousness with which the overt action takes place.

you come in." As conversation develops and becomes increasingly an end in itself, these phases acquire functional independence. The correlativity of stated fact and proposed action tends thus to become obscured. It remains, nevertheless, fundamental.

The next point to claim our attention is the *question*. We observed earlier that the question is a specialized form of speech whose specific function it is to elicit directly a *verbal* response. The question already exists in a rudimentary form at the stage of the sentence-word. But it is not until the appearance of complete predication, that the question becomes fully differentiated. In its rudimentary form it marks mere hesitation and uncertainty. It is uttered with a sharp rising inflection and may be answered by signs of affirmation and negation—primitively attitudes which tend to confirm or to inhibit the course of action with reference to which the question has been asked. But with explicit predication there arises a new form of question, which is complementary to the complete declarative sentence. This is the *what* question—with its variants, the *who*, *when*, and *where* questions.[1] This question is not asked with the same sharp rising inflection. Its interrogative character is marked instead by a specific interrogative *word*—pronoun, adjective, or adverb. This is in effect an empty verbal frame to be filled in by an appropriate *name*. Consequently, this form of question cannot be answered by a mere sign,

---

[1] It is noteworthy that the *what* question appears at a definite stage in the linguistic development of the child. We have all been victimized by the incessant demands of some two-year-old for our response to his reiterated question, "What's that?" The asking of this form of question tends to degenerate into a sort of mechanical verbal game.

but calls for a distinct act of speech. The response to the primitive question could influence primary behavior in only two alternative ways—either by confirming or by discouraging the questioner in the behavior with reference to which the question was asked. The verbal reply to the completely developed question, however, controls primary behavior conditionally and hence in a great variety of possible ways.

There is another type of question which is equally indirect in its control of primary behavior. This has the form: "Is that an antelope?" "Is the water cold?" "Do you intend to leave for home tomorrow?" A query of this sort resembles the primitive question in that it may be answered by a mere sign, as well as by the verbal *yes* or *no*. But the nod and the shake of the head, while they may have their genetic sources in the primitive attitudes of approval and disapproval, now mark specifically *assent to* and *dissent from* what is *said*. I may give an affirmative answer to your question although I disapprove of the enterprise in view of which you have made your inquiry.

Correlative to the verbal dissent which is expressed in the negative *reply*, is the negative form of the *declaration* which denies a specific matter of fact. "The pasture is not swampy." "There are no fairies." The appearance of verbal assent and dissent is the last feature of conversation which calls for special notice here. In addition to the specific *act* of speech by which one replies affirmatively or negatively to a question, or by which one positively affirms or denies a particular matter of fact, there is also an *attitude* of assent or dissent

284

which one takes toward statements made by another. At an early stage of language development, where the proclamations of different sorts and the direct command are not clearly differentiated, there is little distinction between the attitude of assent to what is said and the acceptance of it as determining one's immediate action. At this early stage the announcement is made with reference to the immediate situation, and the one to whom it is made either acts on it at once or not at all. Since primitive speech controls behavior immediately, acceptance of what is said is equivalent to preparing for, and committing oneself to, the appropriate action. But the evolution of explicit predication causes, or permits, a greater indirectness in the control of primary behavior. The ultimate primary action which is the indirect end of speech is mediated by conversation, reply and rejoinder. Consequently one may assent to what another says and remain still uncommitted to any particular line of conduct. In the typical conversation which leads up to coöperative action, *agreement* must be reached as to *what the situation is* in which action is to take place, before the plan of action itself can be concerted. Furthermore, it becomes possible to assent to the statements of another as to what the situation is, and to reject his proposal for common action. Finally, as conversation develops into an independent form of social life, and especially as the two phases already discussed acquire functional independence, agreement as to what is to be *said* comes to be an end in itself. One's success in speaking comes to be measured in terms of the verbal *assent* one elicits from others.

The psychological importance of this capacity for assent and dissent we shall discuss in a later chapter. It is in the evolution of conversation as a social enterprise that we shall find the clue to the development of the higher intellectual activities most distinctive of man.

CHAPTER XVI

Human Perception

Perception as a Preparation for Speech.

As the animal looks at the world about him he perceives its features in their immediate bearing upon his own impending responses. This is true in a sense even of the chimpanzee which learns to see the length of the stick in relation to the distance-away of the fruit. For he sees the stick as a means to *the immediate reaching of a particular banana.* Perception even in human beings remains bound up with the preparation of immediate response; but what sets human perception apart is the fact that the response for which it prepares may *be the act of speaking itself.* Now this affects the object of perception, not simply because speaking leads up to a more indirect primary response, but because the act of speaking is itself a new sort of direct response to what is perceived. I am familiar, for example, with the house in which I live. The door yonder I see as the one I must open to go out on the side-porch; that corner as the one I sit in to catch the fading light in the afternoon, etc. But let me try to describe the plan of the house to a possible tenant, and all these features take on unfamiliar aspects and fifty new features spring into view. Or I try to tell a new cook just how she is to prepare a certain favorite dish I have made myself a hundred times, and the process takes on a surprising intricacy and strangeness. When we observe things attentively in order to describe them in language, they undergo a characteristic transformation. Their features acquire a greater fixity and clearness, unsuspected details stand out, and vaguely sensed relationships are thrown into relief.

Much the same thing happens if we are told beforehand what it is that we are about to see or hear. The verbal specification rouses definite expectations. It moulds in advance the features we are to discern, and, it may be, transforms them into something which would never have appeared to our uninstructed vision.

Influence of Language on the Psychological Environment.

THIS transforming and creative power of language is shown most clearly, perhaps, in the *epithet*. It is not for nothing that epithets are said to be hurled, for they do real execution. Give a dog a bad name—and he is transformed as if by an evil spell. The current vocabulary of every generation and community has its set of stock epithets and descriptive phrases with which persons and things, acts and incidents, come to be branded and their public status established. It is thus in large measure that the feelings and sentiments of the community are directed and canalized, that prejudices are fostered, and conventions maintained. In acquiring the vocabulary of his day, each adolescent youth is being fitted with a set of variously colored spectacles, through which he is to look at the world about him, and with whose tints it must inevitably be colored. It is peopled with "reds" and "reactionaries," "flappers" and "lounge-lizards," "live wires" and "morons." It is a world in which "pep" and "efficiency" and "personality" are desirable and in which "inferiority complexes" are to be dreaded.

But language is not wholly composed of epithets and *clichés*, nor does it influence merely attitudes and prejudices. It arms men as well with a dissecting instrument by which the structure of the world about them is laid bare. The language which every child learns is composed of nouns and verbs, adjectives, adverbs, and prepositions. The sentences in which his elders encourage, restrain, and guide every impulse and act of his daily life are composed of subjects and predicates. Consequently he is introduced from his earliest months into a world already individuated and articulated. He sees persons, toys, and chairs as *objects* having *qualities;* and he perceives himself and others engaged in distinctive and identical *acts*, like eating and riding and playing. Moreover, as each object that emerges to his view has, centering in and about it, characteristic acts and qualities, so the *name* which belongs to it, and which serves to mark it as the very object which it is, has its familiar verbal context. Its name is used habitually along with a more or less fixed set of adjectives and verbs and prepositions. The apple is "round" and "red." The dog "barks" and "jumps." Knives are "sharp" and "cut." The stairs are climbed "up" and "down." Hence, when the familiar name is applied to a new object, it carries its verbal context with it and endows the new object in advance with the familiar qualities and relations of the old. If we may revert to the simile of the spectacles, the lenses we acquire with language are not merely colored, but blocked out in more or less regular designs, so that the world we see through them is *patternized* to our earliest view.

The ability to speak, then, to attach names to things and to make statements about them, does not leave unaltered the world which we see and hear. Perception remains primarily a preparation for direct primary response toward things, but there is superadded the capacity for a more detached and disinterested sort of scrutiny, in which the response that is "constituted"— to use Dewey's term—is not a bodily act, but the utterance of a descriptive word or phrase. We look at things to see in a new sense "what" they are. Even when the descriptive epithet, the verbal tag, is not spoken, its utterance is prepared in tentative movements, so that all our attentive scrutiny of things is informed by speech. Human perception is, then, *conceptualized* to an indefinite degree. Compared to those of men, the percepts of animals are "blind"—to use Kant's expression—being without concepts. Yet since perception, even in us, continues to play its primitive rôle of preparing our grosser bodily adjustments to things, of controlling first of all our merely individual and private relations to the world in which we have our being, its content is by no means wholly describable in language, or brought under conceptual rubrics fixed by social conventions. Its immediacy and givenness always escapes complete subjection to the dominance of language. The world of each of us is not completely objectified, but retains a privacy which is inexpressible to ourselves and incommunicable to others.

We may find a homely illustration of this in the reply of the darkey cook, who when asked for the recipe of a certain delicious cake of her own responded: "Oh, I take a good-sized piece of butter, and cream it with sugar until it is just right, and then I add enough flour and milk and eggs to make a good batter, and bake it in a quick oven." However far in our sophistication we may carry the analysis of the acts and processes of our daily occupations, there always remains a margin where we are like this worthy woman in our immediate and incommunicable recognition of the "rightness" of the look and feel of textures and consistencies and combinations.

CHAPTER XVII

Conception and Purpose

Dependence of Conception on Speech.

IT has been impossible to consider the transformation which speech has wrought in perception without referring to the new and distinctly human function of conception. What is this new function? How is it bound up with the capacity for speech, and what part has it in the psychological economy of the individual?

We have already anticipated to some extent the answer to these inquiries in our discussion of the use and making of tools. Conception appears, we discovered, in the guidance of acts, which, like the sharpening of a stick to a point, have as their end the bringing about of an *objective* state of affairs, rather than one which is determined by its direct relationship to the immediate needs of the individual. The little child who builds a "big tall" pile with his blocks, is already doing something which no animal can do, and which he can do only by the aid of concepts expressed in the words "big" and "tall."[1] The constructive play of little children

---

[1] Köhler's accounts of the constructive play of chimpanzees is of interest in this connection. The high-water mark seems to have been reached by the gifted Nueva. A favorite occupation—which is strikingly like the performance of a child—was dipping water out of the butt and pouring it back, watching meanwhile with the greatest interest the drops that trickled down the sides of the cup. Of more significance were her efforts at "weaving" and "tying things together"—although the description of her play in these terms is not accurate. Köhler writes: "She had a special fancy for knots; for

marks, as we tried to show earlier, a stage in intellectual development as distinctive as the earlier grasping-stage. It is through the indirect dealing with one thing by means of another that the primary qualities first come to be discerned. The child's growing perception of these objective properties is, however, greatly sharpened by his learning to use names descriptively. "Sharp" and "blunt," "round" and "square," "wide" and "narrow," first come to be features upon which attention may center in the indirect manipulation of things. But the possible extension of such manipulation would be limited if speech did not lend its aid. For in becoming the objects of the specific response of naming, these features acquire fixity and independence. They attract *analytic* attention. They are singled out for observation and their mutual relations thrown into relief. The fact that one knows the names of objects, like "round" or "square" or "oblong," enables one to look at the shape of a par-

instance, she thrust a strip of banana leaf through a wire mesh, laboriously drew the end back through another mesh, tied the two ends together, and continued in the same way, either by slipping one end of the leaf through the knot, or tying the ends again. I often thought that she was about to begin a deliberate, though rudimentary, constructive effort, a form of manual craftsmanship, but she could never be induced to continue these efforts on any plan, however easy. When I prepared for her a wooden frame with a few loosely inserted strips of leaf, she turned aside and devoted herself to her own knots; the slightest pressure towards anything stable and 'productive' extinguished her joy and interest at once, and she let the frame fall in sullen displeasure." *The Mentality of Apes*, p. 324. Similar as this play of Nueva's undoubtedly is to the early constructive play of the child, there is, I venture to think, an important psychological difference introduced when the child begins to guide his efforts by words. Nueva was not trying to tie a "knot" in the same sense that the child tries to build a "tall pile" of blocks, much less in the sense in which the child later tries to build a "house."

ticular object as distinguished from its size and color, and to compare it with the shape of another object beside it.

If the theory which we are now about to advance is sound, the development of the child's capacity for constructive play is closely dependent on his speech development. If the child did not learn the use of language, he probably could not advance beyond the aimlessness which marks the beginnings of this play, and there would be no possibility of the development of truly purposive behavior such as is peculiar to man. Unfortunately, so far as we know, there have been no experimental researches into the relation between the period of constructive play in the child and his speech development, and our statements must remain to some extent speculative. There is evidence, however, that the more serious speech defects carry along with them disabilities of behavior of various sorts. We may mention in particular some cases cited by Dr. Henry Head.[1] One individual suffering from a motor affection of speech was able, for example, to imitate the acts of another provided he was not standing opposite. The "looking-glass" reversal necessary when the other person was facing him was quite beyond his powers. Another individual, suffering from a similar disorder, could carry out the *oral* command to touch the right ear with the left hand, etc., but was unable to do so when the command was *pictorial*. Dr. Head concludes that the ability to perform such acts depends on the ability to use the words

[1] "Papers on Aphasia and Kindred Affections of Speech," *Brain*, 1915, XXXVIII.

"right," "left," "eye," "ear," etc. Again, a similar patient could not draw a plan of a familiar room, putting bed, bureau, etc., in their proper relations to one another. But when a partial plan of the room was drawn for him, on which some of the objects, *e.g.*, the bed, were indicated by dots, he could point to the spots where other objects in the room belonged. This is interesting in the light of the theory advanced in these pages, that in its primitive stages, and until complete predication is fully developed, speech can function only in dependence on immediate perception. The partially made diagram could be completed with the aid of such language ability as the patient still had, but the ability to make the diagram *de novo* with no spatial orientation, required the aid of normal speech. In general, it may be said that the evidence from pathology shows clearly that acts involving the apprehension of both spatial and temporal order, are intimately bound up with a normal capacity for the use of language.[1] Although a good deal of investigation of speech defects has been carried on, much of it has been comparatively fruitless, owing to false psychological preconceptions. The subject is vast and complex and offers a most fruitful field for research.

Verbal Anticipation of the End of Action.

In the analysis of the complete act, we tried to show that the final stage, particularly its affective outcome, is anticipated from the beginning, and that this anticipa-

---

[1] In this connection see an interesting article by von Woerkom, *Journal de psychologie*, XVIII, année 8-9.

tion serves to guide the performance of the earlier stages of the act, and to bind them together into a single whole. Where the act is complex, it falls into distinct stages, each of which is similarly guided by the anticipation of its outcome, which has acquired a secondary affective quality. As behavior becomes more complex, and relatively long series of partial acts become united to form a complete act, it is evident that the anticipatory fulfilment of the outcome must somehow be prevented from getting in the way of the performance of the earlier stages. It must remain tentative, or become in some way representative. Let us consider a little more closely the nature of this anticipatory fulfilment. In the case of an act like seeing-reaching-eating, it consists in such gross bodily adjustments as mouth-watering, or, in the opposite case, of retching and nausea. It is an actual adjustment of the organism, adapted to the presence of a specific stimulus. At a higher stage, it may not be such a primary consummatory reaction as eating that is anticipated. It may be the holding of a given object in the mouth or in the hand; or it may even be the perceptual enjoyment of a particular smell or sound or sight. In this case, there is an anticipatory adjustment of the distance-receptor, *e.g.*, the visual apparatus—and hence, in some degree, of the whole organism—to the sensory stimulus it habitually receives under these conditions, and to which the course of action in progress is leading up.[1]

[1] According to M. F. Washburn's theory of the image, this anticipatory adjustment of the receptor involves an excitation of the sensory centers. So far as such sensory excitation does occur, it is part and parcel of the anticipation of the outcome of the act in progress, and serves,

Now it is evident that the behavior which is controlled by the anticipation of a particular bodily adjustment of the primary sort, *i.e.*, by an image, is very limited in its scope. In general, what the image controls is behavior resulting in the adjustment of the individual to what is already existent in the environment, and not in the production of a state of affairs objective to him. So far as a change in outer conditions is brought about by behavior of this type, it is a change that is of immediate concern to the individual, or a direct means to such an end. Of this sort, for example, is the destruction or driving away of an enemy, the hunting of prey, etc. Very little of the behavior of even the higher animals is directed toward the accomplishment of changes in the environment. Most of it results merely in the establishment of favorable relationships of the organism to objective conditions, or in inducing specific attitudes and activities in other members of the group. The *image* (in the sense in which we use the term), just because it is bound up with a particular response of bodily adjustment, can control only a direct sort of behavior, *i.e.*, behavior which is determined by the relation of things *to the actor*. Behavior which is indirect, in that it is determined by the objective relation of things or of persons *to each other*, and which issues in the production of an objective state of affairs of mediate utility or interest to the actor, must be controlled by something other than the image.

It is speech which makes possible this higher kind of

if we are right, the function of controlling the unfolding sequence of its stages.

behavior. *The anticipatory bodily adjustment to the outcome of the act is replaced by the anticipatory utterance, overt or tentative, of some word or phrase which names or denotes the result aimed at.* The verbal response is, as we have been at pains to show, unique, in that it constitutes a specific response to what is objective. For this reason it is able to guide behavior to the production of an objective outcome, such as sharpening a stick to a point, or piling blocks into a determinate structure. The verbal response has grown up as the instrument for controlling response in others, and is to the hearer a conditional determinant of response. Accordingly, when uttered to oneself in this anticipatory fashion, it serves to mobilize in advance the system of activities connected with the object or condition named. The sentence-word with its ability to represent what is objective, and at the same time to include within its denotation both object and acts, is precisely adapted to this function.

It is not to be assumed, however, that the anticipatory verbal response need entirely replace the perceptual *image*. The image indeed may continue to function, but the image which is mediated by the act of speaking is a new thing. It is transformed by speech just as perception is transformed. Just as the individual in learning how to speak learns to *see* objective properties like the pointedness of the stick, so the image, although it remains the image of what is concrete and particular, *e.g.*, of *the stick at a certain distance and in a certain position*, has come, nevertheless, to represent what is objective and universal, *i.e.*, it is the image of a *pointed* stick. Because the same verbal response of naming is called out equally by all the differing sights and "feels" of the pointed stick, it may come to evoke any of the corresponding images. But whatever particular image may be evoked, the act of speaking transforms and universalizes it.[1]

Whether in the higher stages of psychological development the perceptual image is wholly replaced by anticipatory speech responses, we shall not pretend to decide. That question must await further empirical investigation. It seems clear, however, in view of the increasing independence of speech with reference to other forms of response, that it comes to exercise a very extensive independent control of behavior.

Verbal Anticipation of the Course of Action.

BUT we must go further. From the beginnings of speech in the sentence-word, behavior has reached the new level of conceptual control. It is now directed to *objective ends*. But since these are to be reached for the most part by indirect means, behavior becomes truly *purposive*. While language remains at the stage of the primi-

---

[1] It will be recognized by the reader that this treatment of the image bears a close analogy to the theory of the general idea set forth by Berkeley and Hume. It is true that they meant by "idea" a mental entity whose *esse* is its *percipi*, while "image," as the term is here used, is an objective phenomenon defined in terms of its function in controlling behavior. The solution they reached of the problem of universality, namely, that the universality of an idea is constituted by representative *function*, is wholly incompatible with their subjectivism, as it is with all subjectivism. That they were led to accept such a solution, in spite of its fundamental inconsistency with their metaphysical dogmas, and that Hume in particular was led to recognize the dependence of abstract thinking upon language, is very significant.

tive sentence-word, behavior is already purposive in a rudimentary way, since the outcome is prefigured in the anticipatory verbal response which names the outcome of the act. But it is not until predication is developed in the complete sentence that behavior becomes purposive in the full sense of the term. The sentence-word denotes, without distinguishing, the end and the acts which lead up to it. The language of complete predication permits *both end and acts to be specifically denoted and hence distinguished*. The end to be reached is not simply prefigured by a vaguely inclusive descriptive term, but it may be analyzed and its essential features delineated. Furthermore, the series of acts which must lead up to this end may also be announced in advance. The saying over to oneself what one is about to do is a preparation for the primary acts that are to follow. It is not simply that each act is individually and separately prefigured and thus prepared, but the *serial organization* of behavior is thus preëstablished by speech. It is this indeed which is chiefly characteristic of purposive behavior.[1] The complete act in its simplest form is purposive in the sense that its progress is determined by the anticipation of the end to be reached, as well as by the antecedent condition from which it starts. Completely purposive behavior differs from this simple sort, in that the prefigured end and the antecedent condition reciprocally determine beforehand in a progressive fashion an organized series of intermediate acts. The organization of these intermediate acts is,

[1] The writer has found R. B. Perry's article, "A Behavioristic View of Purpose," *Journal of Philosophy*, 18, p. 85, very suggestive.

moreover, to a greater or less degree, *conditional*. Not everything is cut and dried in advance down to its last details. For the outcome of each stage is anticipated only in outline. As each stage is completed, and the prefigured outline is filled in, it forms a new starting-point for a fresh determination of the remaining stages. The advantage of this flexibility in the carrying-out of human purposes is evident. What we wish to make clear is the peculiar fitness of language to control such behavior as this. The primitive naming of the desired outcome is not simply a denoting of the object or condition aimed at, but also a *connoting* of the acts connected with this object or condition. Now as language develops, and substantive and verb, for example, are differentiated, the connection of objective condition and human activities is not lost. It is rather, as we have so often tried to make clear, just the fact that things become the pivots upon which an increasing number of acts hinge, that endows them with objectivity. It is for this reason that the prefiguring in speech of an objective outcome which is desired—the very act of describing it in language and dwelling upon its anticipated features—serves as the *conditional* preparation for appropriate behavior. But this preparation of overt conduct is indirect. The framing of the descriptive sentences leads first to further verbal response—the announcement in language of the acts to be undertaken.

Internal Conversation as a Preparation for Action.

WE are dealing with an enormously complex subject, and our only hope of understanding it at all lies in schematizing it in a more or less adequate fashion. The complete analysis of even a simple case of human purposive behavior is beyond our reach. But we can at least exhibit in a rough way its salient features in their close dependence on speech.

The announcement of intention we have seen to be a primitive form of language. It has its direct source in such animal cries as the cry of attack. The development of purposive behavior attaches directly to the development and differentiation of the primitive announcement of intention. While its primary function, like that of all language forms, is the control of the behavior of others, it has a tremendous repercussion on the psychological development of the individual. Animal cries tend to occur as the accompaniments of more general expressive behavior. The cry of attack, for instance, is originally an element in the emotional "winding-up" of the organism to the pitch of action. In general it may be said that the numerous cries which accompany or precede definite acts come to be more or less integral elements in these acts. It is, then, one of the functions of vocal utterance from the beginning to serve as a preparation for primary action. But, needless to say, if it were not for the indirect consequences of the influence of the cry upon the behavior of others, it would remain comparatively ineffective with reference to the individual. The first of these indirect consequences is due to the mutual interaction of the cry as uttered and the cry as heard. If a given cry as uttered becomes anticipatory of the performance of a given act by oneself, the same cry as heard comes to be a representative of similar behavior in others. While this leads to a certain objectification of both the cry and the act, it does not of itself go very far. In the sentence-word the process is carried farther. The same verbal utterance which serves to announce a specific intention on the part of the speaker, may also be used to command the performance of the same act on the part of others, or to proclaim that a third person has performed or is performing it. But it is through the development of explicit predication that the announcement of intention is clearly differentiated as a language form and becomes at the same time objective and free—acquires, that is, those characteristics which fit it to be the instrument of completely purposive behavior.

It is important for us to keep clearly in mind here the account which has been given of the social forces which brought about the development of the complete sentence. It will be recalled that the differentiation of subject and predicate in the primitive proclamation of discovery arose in order to specify clearly what was not open to direct observation by both speaker and hearers. It was also owing to the need of concerting action with reference to what is not perceived by all, that the distinctive sentence forms—declaration, question, and command—attained true linguistic differentiation. In particular it is to be borne in mind that *conversation*— the mutual interplay of these diverse forms of speech— arose as the necessary instrument for the preparation of concerted action toward what is remote. It is as an essential component of primitive conversation, and in the service of this social end, that the announcement of intention has attained its perfected form. It is not too much to say that it is to the definite announcement of intention that primitive conversation naturally leads up. The declaration that a given state of affairs exists, the question and reply that serve to analyze and make explicit the important features of the remote situation, are all preliminary to common action; but they are in themselves so highly conditional in their bearing on primary behavior that a more direct and definite verbal preparation is needed before group action can begin. Between the verbal announcement of the end to be reached and of the conditions of action, and the actual beginnings of action, there is the mediating *announcement of intention*—the formulation in language of the acts to be performed in their proper order.

The Autonomy of Speech.

BUT, it may be asked, how is language fitted to perform this mediation? Why is it easier or more natural to formulate in language the steps necessary to reach a given end, than it is to proceed to take these steps without more ado? The answer is that the one linguistic act is the natural correlate of the other. The announcement of intention takes place normally *with reference to a determinate statement of conditions*. The very meanings of the two statements are connected. Language grows up as an organic whole. This does not mean simply that the various linguistic *forms* reciprocally imply each other, although this is a significant fact. But beyond this, the organic nature of a language means that any particular sentence, phrase, or word has determinate,

305

albeit complex, connections with other particular sentences, phrases, and words. The essential constitutive relations of the things we cognize in the world, and the acts we perform to, or with, or on them, are reflected in the structure of language. But while the basic structure of language is ultimately determined by the interrelations of things and human acts, it develops an organic structure peculiarly its own, relatively independent and autonomous.

It is the development of this autonomous structure of language which is at once cause and effect of the freeing of the activity of speech from other bodily behavior. It is because words and phrases and sentences have this independent and intimate interconnection with each other, that men may converse together freely and independently. Conversation becomes an occupation with its own internal criteria of success and failure. But while speech becomes increasingly an end in itself, it does not on that account cease to be an instrument for the control of behavior. On the contrary, its very independence and autonomy increases a thousand-fold the sweep and subtlety of its dominance of action.

The objection may perhaps have occurred to the reader that our argument has put the cart before the horse. How, it will be asked, could conversation take place as a preparation for concerted action unless the individuals were already capable of forming purposes and making plans? This objection is plausible, but not really sound. The ability to carry on conversation, at least of a developed sort, is of course dependent on the individual capacity for purposive behavior. It is also true that social coöperation of an "intelligent" sort can be carried on only by rational individuals. There is undoubtedly a reciprocity of social and individual achievements and powers. But the analogy of the egg and the hen does not hold completely. There is a certain priority here of the social to the individual. Each human being finds the instrument of language ready made for his use, and it is *through his learning to make use of this* that he becomes a rational being capable of forming and carrying out purposes. Language is a *social* product, at once the fruit and the source of coöperative activity. But this is not a denial of the fact that the individual's ability to plan and to think, although due to his social inheritance of language, should not be in turn essential to the pursuit of the social activities of his time and of his verbal intercourse with his fellows.

The Habit of Internal Speech.

THE little child, as we have seen, spends many hours and much energy in vocal *play*. It is far more agreeable to carry on this play with others, and indeed if the impulse were not encouraged by his elder companions it would soon become abortive. But the little child indulges in language-play even when he is alone. He talks to himself while he is occupied with his toys and the other affairs of childhood. When he does not talk aloud, he continues to talk to himself silently. Internal speech, fragmentary or continuous, becomes the habitual accompaniment of his active behavior and the occupation of his idle hours.

The advantage of this habit of internal speech is not

merely the gaining of facility through practice in language. The habit of verbally responding to the things about one works a transformation of the powers of perception and reveals the features of a new world. It also prepares and makes possible purposive behavior. The objective and dynamic interconnections of things and acts and events are taken up and embodied in the structure of the living language which is the child's social inheritance. Just in so far as he learns to use the language of his people, and the autonomy of that language becomes a part of his own nature, he is the master of a new power. Speech not only brings the distant end to closer view and permits him to taste in advance its delights, but it reveals to him the road he must take, and sets his feet upon it. In language he finds preserved the experience of the race. It is true that his power to tap this vast reservoir has its source in his own experience of eye and hand and limb; but through speech thus fostered he may indefinitely transcend his own individual limitations and take full possession of his racial inheritance.

To be more explicit, the habit of internal speech causes a desired outcome to be verbally represented. The verbal response, in the first place, mediates an anticipated enjoyment which provides the impulse toward action. But, secondly, the act of verbally describing the outcome leads, through the autonomy of language, to a verbal rehearsal of the course of action appropriate to the attainment of the end thus represented. This verbal preparation takes the form of a silent conversation carried on with one's self in which, as in the conversations carried on aloud with others, questions arise to evoke in turn their own answers, until the course of overt action is traced out in advance.

The verbal formulation, while it has been reached through the independent exercise of the speech function, has nevertheless its vital connections with bodily action. When the formulation of the intended action has been carried to its natural conclusion—determined, be it remembered, by criteria internal to language—the bodily acts represented and mobilized by speech are released, and their course conditionally controlled throughout. We say *conditionally* controlled, for, as we have previously tried to show, what language represents is the act as objective and universal. The act as it occurs is, of course, concrete and particular, and must consequently be determined in detail by the actually perceived situation of the moment. It is, after all, only a schema of concrete action that speech can prepare. As action proceeds, the abstract schema gets filled in from stage to stage by the representative imagery of the anticipated acts themselves, and then by the realized accomplishment. It happens, too, that this progressive filling-in may initiate a modification of the later stages by calling for fresh verbal rehearsal and consequent changing of the verbal schema of action. Each end reached may mark a fresh beginning in the light of which the end needs new definition. Thus it is that language, through the objectivity and universality of what its terms represent, on the one hand, and the autonomy of its structure, on the other, reveals the distinctive ends of human conduct and endows their pursuit with rational purposiveness.[1]

[1] It has, perhaps, occurred to the reader that the theory here advanced of the objectification of the environment could easily be paralleled by a theory of the evolution of values from simple affective qualities. The conceptualized *end* of purposive action no longer possesses, or need not possess, simple affective quality. It has *value*. Its value represents the objectification of affective quality, just as its cognized properties represent the objectification of sensory qualities. Values, too, are social phenomena, dependent on language for their apprehension. It is also true that it is only in a world of appreciated *values* that *objects* can be known.

CHAPTER XVIII

Memory and Imagination

Primitive Memory as Anticipation.

THE development of human purposive behavior is intimately bound up with the development of other psychological capacities, which are themselves directly dependent on speech. Notable among these are memory and imagination.

Memory, in a very general sense of the term, is indeed a primitive endowment of animal organisms. But in man memory becomes so enlarged and transformed that it is almost a different function. As we have seen, memory appears at first in the service of immediate action. At this stage, it is not so much a revival of the past, as an anticipation of the future. Past experience influences the present because the outcome of an act which has already been performed is more readily anticipated. The anticipated outcome of the act is memory, inasmuch as the form that it takes is determined by past experience. What is anticipated is what has been previously experienced. But, so far as the evidence goes, animals do not recall the past except as it has direct bearing on the present, and as an immediate aid to the behavior that is going forward; and then the past is recalled merely as an anticipated future. Perhaps it may be supposed that the dog lying quietly on the hearthrug is reliving scenes of his past and enjoying again in retrospect the pleasures of past rabbit-hunts.

That is the sort of thing a man in a similar situation is apt to be doing. But that the dog does so is very doubtful. There is no direct evidence that he is doing it; nor so far as we know is there any indirect evidence except the uncertain analogy with ourselves. Moreover, so long as the dog is awake, he remains very much alive to what is going on about him, ready to be roused to action by any interesting occurrence. But a man who is engaged in reminiscence has his attention elsewhere; he is in varying degrees oblivious to his present surroundings, and is not easily roused to action. It is true that a sleeping dog often seems to be *dreaming* of chasing something. His legs move as if running, and he twitches and growls with excitement. But this need not be a recalling of the past, although it is doubtless dependent on experience. More probably, it is an abortive, or incomplete, present experience of running or chasing, subject to Freudian interpretation in terms of suppressed desire.

We are prone to think of memory, in the sense of the recall or reliving of the past, as a very simple and primitive phenomenon. But in reality it is, we venture to affirm, very complex and far from primitive. The recall of the past *as* the past, the reliving of former experience in an independent act, is, we believe, confined to human beings. It is through speech that memory and free imagination arise in differentiated forms. The same development of psychological organization which makes it possible freely to recall the past in memory makes it also possible to experience in imagination scenes and events which have not and never will occur, as well

312

as to live through in anticipation the experiences which are to occur. Reminiscence and day-dreaming have grown up together in the enlarged capacity for life with which speech has endowed man.

Dependence of Human Memory on Speech.

THE normal human being carries on more or less continuously a sort of running commentary on all that he perceives and does. Internal speech, fragmentary or connected, is the accompaniment of all his activities. We have already discussed the transformation in the world of perception that is wrought by the habit of verbal response. A similar transformation takes place in his own behavior as experienced by him. His own acts are not merely felt, but cognized as objective events. The objectification of one's own behavior is of at least equal importance with the objectification of the outside world. There is a great deal that might be said upon this point, but we are now interested in the bearing such objectification has on memory.

Free memory is a direct consequence of the freedom and independence of the activity of speech. Internal speech is not only an accompaniment of other activities and occupations; it is also an occupation in itself. Man goes on talking to himself when he is otherwise idle; and when he is busy he may carry on silent, or even audible, conversation which is independent of the bodily acts he is performing. Now it is evident that the course which this independent speech will take is determined by many circumstances. While much of it may be as nearly as possible aimless—like the aimless bodily activities, which, according to Watson, bulk so large in the life of all animals—it is usually determined more or less directly by *desire*. The imaginative rehearsal, through the mediation of internal speech, of actions leading up to and constituting the consummation of desired ends, is a frequent occupation of leisure. It differs from planning in that it does not attach directly to the concrete circumstances in which one is placed, as well as in the fact that it does not initiate and direct an immediate course of conduct. While imaginative activity of this sort may usurp the place of real and complete life, it normally performs a function of incalculable importance. No less than planning itself, it prepares for action. But while planning is a direct preparation for a particular course of action, imagination is a conditional preparation for contingent action. Possible sequences and combinations of behavior are practiced in advance, so that if and when such exigencies arise, one has a reserve of appropriate alternatives of action on hand. The importance of such habits of imagination on the formation of character is incalculable.

Memory like imagination is often controlled by desire. Satisfactions and delights actually enjoyed in the past are desired afresh, and this desire may lead to a reminiscent living over the past as it occurred. When a cherished hope has been frustrated or a purpose defeated, the rankling desire may cause the past to be relived with emendations. Up to a certain point one may recall and imaginatively repeat the actual course of events, and then complete it in imagination to a happier outcome. Memory is always selective, and the line between reliving the actual past and remoulding it nearer to the heart's desire is not always clear. The advantages and disadvantages involved in habits of this sort are fairly obvious, and we shall not pause to enlarge upon them.

It has seemed worth while to call attention to the dominant rôle played by desire both in memory and imagination, because the classic treatment of memory has tended to reduce it to a quasi-mechanically determined repetition of past experience.[1] When it is thus conceived, the difficulty of distinguishing memory proper, or reminiscence, from habit is well known, and is even notorious since Bergson's dramatic presentation of it. Other things being equal, it is undoubtedly true that, if a given sequence of acts has once occurred, the recurrence of the first act tends to initiate the whole former sequence. But other things are so rarely equal, and the play of affection and desire is so constant, that association as such can obviously account for very little.

The Recall of the Past.

LET us now consider a little more closely the part that speech plays in the recall of the past. An experience when it occurs is accompanied throughout its course, let us assume, by a sort of running commentary of internal speech, which, though fragmentary in itself, is more or less integrally bound up with all that is going forward. Now if later on some occurrence by its relevancy serves to initiate some part of the former verbal response, the completing of this internal re-

[1] Hobbes and Condillac are notable exceptions.

sponse is induced, not simply by mere habituation, but by the additional fact that language is an inherently connected thing. There is a certain *autonomy* of speech. The phrases and sentences internally formulated are connected through their meaning. The following of one upon another is not a mere matter of chance, nor does it form a simple mechanical sequence. Furthermore, the verbal response which accompanied the original experience was integral to it; the primary behavior that took place was to an indefinite extent guided and controlled by the accompanying speech; what was perceived was equally moulded by the same agency. Consequently, when the same speech reactions recur, they tend to revive along with them an incipient repetition of the bodily movements, and even of the induced sensory stimulations, which they originally mediated.[1]

[1] The general agreement of the account here given of the dependence of memory on speech with M. F. Washburn's theory of "tentative movement systems" will be evident to anyone familiar with *Movement and Mental Imagery*. The tentative movements of articulation involved in internal speech belong to both simultaneous and successive movement systems. The autonomy of speech rests upon the fact that the movements of articulation form a permanent system, or set of systems, which may function independently of their connections with the system of other bodily movements involved in what we have termed primary behavior. Thus the "meaning" of a word or a phrase is largely conditioned by the fact that the movements employed in its utterance belong to complex simultaneous systems of articulatory movements. But, while the systems of such movements may function independently, they are connected with the systems of tentative bodily movements, and it is through these latter connections that speech is able to direct and control primary behavior. We should like to call attention especially to the application Washburn makes of her theory (pp. 144 ff.), in accounting for the difference between the two forms of memory, a difference which had been urged by McDougall—as well as by Bergson—as evidence of the essential inadequacy of a naturalistic psychology.

Our memories of past events are verbalized to an indefinite degree. We remember *that* such and such an incident occurred under such and such circumstances. We remember, in short, to a greater or less degree, in terms of propositions. But along with this memory of what we may term "facts," there goes a filling-in of more immediate imagery. It is only certain bits of the "facts" that appear thus concretely filled in, while other parts of the remembered factual events lack detail and vividness. Thus we may be able to state positively *that* an event occurred, and we may enlarge verbally upon this fact, describing certain features in detail, and yet be unable to go beyond a bare general statement in regard to other features. Moreover, if we try to enlarge beyond a certain point, we find ourselves at a loss, just as we do in describing in words the fullness of what is present to the senses.

It will be recalled that among the primitive forms of the animal cry, we found the cry which serves as the announcement of completed activity—the accomplishment of something of emotional interest, like the triumph over an adversary. As speech develops, the announcement by the speaker of what he has just done or enjoyed or suffered persists as one of the distinctive forms of the proclamation, having its own distinctive social function. The dog that has been kicked or hurt by someone comes whimpering to his master to beg for sympathy. This behavior results, of course, from a "hang-over" of his emotional state, but the fact remains that the presence of his master often seems to revive symptoms of distress which had begun to disappear. The child behaves in a similar way. M. Bloch, we may recall, records the incident of his child coming to him in tears, saying "Mon-mon," after her brother Raymond had been teasing her. Those of us who are familiar with the behavior of little children will have no difficulty in recognizing this as a typical childish act. The sentence-word announcement of one's past experience may also be made in order to inhibit, or otherwise influence, the behavior of another, and not merely to rouse an affective attitude toward oneself like sympathy or admiration. The rehearsal of the past as a means of directly controlling the behavior of others is, then, a primitive function of speech, and one which has grown in scope and importance with the evolution of the structure of language. At first it is only the immediate past which is thus rehearsed, and then only when it has some direct bearing on the present situation. But with the appearance of complete predication, the range and freedom of the rehearsal of the past are increased. We have already seen in Part I the importance of the celebration of tribal deeds in fostering group-solidarity.

It is through the internalization of this form of speech that memory develops. It is, of course, true that in a sense even a simple announcement to another of what one has just experienced involves an act of memory. But the internalization of the act transforms it psychologically. It is when the movements of speech take place *tentatively* that they form those organized systems which are essential to all the higher mental functions. We are not to think of the internalization of the rehearsal of the past as an event altogether subsequent to primary language development. As each stage of overt speech is reached, it becomes internalized in turn; and it is largely owing to the psychological effects of this internalization that further development of speech as a social instrument is made possible.

The Objectification of One's Own Behavior.

WHEN one is able verbally to recall bits of past experience as present exigencies make them relevant, it is evident that one's chances for successful action are greatly increased. Behavior becomes "intelligent" in a new sense. Again, if one is able through internal speech to relive the past in a free act of reminiscence, it is evident that this repetition serves to reinforce the effects of the experience thus relived. Its lessons get stamped in. It is a common observation that one may go through a dangerous or critical situation and remain emotionally calm while the need for action lasts. It is only later, in reliving the experience in memory that one feels fully either the fear or the grief or the joy, as the case may be. Now this may be due in part to physiological causes. But there is a further reason why one does not always "realize" fully the "meaning" of events as they occur, and while they are demanding immediate primary response. When they are recalled, it is through the medium of tentative movements which are members of highly organized systems. We have already had occasion to mention the fact that speech enables us to *objectify* our own acts. It is in verbal recall that this process is carried furthest. One's remembered acts are recognized as objective events belonging to a causal order. Hence they *might* have taken place differently or had other consequences than those actually experienced. Moreover, internal speech occurs in the form of a conversation carried on *with oneself*. One recites one's deeds to oneself as if they were the deeds of an *alter ego*. As thus objectified, one approves or condemns them. One's past, as thus set forth in memory, often appears in a very different light from that of its original experience. It is internal conversation that makes self-criticism possible, and it is in the process of self-criticism that standards and values are moulded.

Memory and the Conceptual Order.

IF our general theory of the dependence of human memory on speech is sound, the recall of the past is intimately bound up with the *conceptualization* of experience. This has very important theoretical consequences. It has long been a particularly knotty metaphysical problem, recently agitated anew to the confusion of the behaviorists, how, even if a revival of the past takes place, it is, although a *present* experience, yet experienced *as past*. This has been a metaphysical problem because the difficulty of dealing with it psychologically, or, rather, naturalistically, has led many thinkers besides Bergson to take refuge in a special metaphysical entity, conceived *ad hoc*. We do not pretend to solve the problem in detail, but our general faith in the method of natural science, and our conviction of the dependence of the phenomenon of memory on speech, leads us to venture the following general considerations.

MEMORY AND IMAGINATION

It has been very widely held that the cognition of temporal relationship rests ultimately upon memory—upon the ability to relive one's personal past experience in the present, and yet as distinguished from the present. This faculty of memory has commonly been regarded as one—or even *the*—distinctive trait of mind as such. Now it is our opinion that memory in this sense is not prior to the development of the conceptual order of temporal relations in general. The common opinion in this matter is bound up with the traditional view that we begin with our personal subjective experience and gradually interpret, or construct, an objective order in its terms. This view we regard, it is needless to state, as thoroughly false. The time order is developed —or discovered—as is the space order: *through our indirect dealing with the things of the outside world.* Duration and temporal position are primary qualities. Important events occur in regular sequences and to these our indirect behavior must be accommodated in definite and complex ways. Speech enables us to discriminate and objectify these dynamic relationships of events and of our own acts. The growth of a conceptual schema, embodied in the structure of language and sharing its autonomy, is essential to the remembering of the past *as past.* We do not mean that all this linguistic and conceptual development took place first, and that afterwards men acquired the faculty of memory. But we do mean that the ability to remember developed *pari passu* with this conceptual organization and in the closest dependence on it. That the growing capacity for remembering was also essential to the development of language and of all distinctively human behavior is also true. But that memory is an ultimate and unanalyzable endowment of the human mind, we deny.

Is there an ultimate feeling of "pastness," as is so often alleged? We do not pretend either to deny or to affirm the existence of ultimate "feelings." But, although they have been invoked—and introspectively "discovered"—in the interests of theory, they serve the purposes of theoretical description and analysis no better than any other metaphysical quiddities and powers.

CHAPTER XIX

Belief and Thought

It remains to give some account of the relation of speech to the higher phenomena of cognition—belief and thought. The subject is too vast a one to be adequately treated in these pages. We shall only attempt to show in a general way how these forms of cognition have arisen, and to analyze their function in terms of our theory.

The Beginnings of Belief and Thought.

We find the matrix of both belief and thought in that primitive interchange of speech which precedes and prepares common action in a situation demanding analysis. This primitive conversation, in what we may call its complete form, has two phases, or stages. The first phase is the establishment, through formulation in language, of the essential features of the objective situation relevant to the occasion. In very simple cases, a single announcement may serve to characterize the situation sufficiently. But in more complex cases, it is necessary that a more particular description be given. Questions may be asked to elicit further details, and supplementary statements made by different individuals. Conversation is not always initiated, of course, by an announcement of presence. It may be an announcement of intention on the part of one individual, which meets with opposition on the part of others. Difficulties are raised by the statement of existing circumstances, which tend to inhibit or modify the proposed action. Or it may be that a command is given which is unwelcome, or which presupposes a state of affairs which must be denied to exist; and a counter statement of facts may be given.

When a mutually satisfactory verbal formulation of the situation has been made, the plan of action has still to be determined. This is the function of the second stage of the conversation; and, as we have seen, the development and internalization of this stage are the origin of conscious purpose.

In the evolution of conversation we meet again what we have so often observed to be characteristic of the evolution of behavior. Activities, which in their origin are but factors or stages of a single responsive act performing a single function, come to acquire later a relative independence of each other, and to perform distinct, but mutually dependent, functions. Let us consider how this differentiation of what we may term the primitive form of complete conversation takes place.

It is evident that on different occasions either the one or the other of these two stages of preliminary conversation may become the more important and tend to overshadow the other. The description of the situation in all its essential features may have been easily reached and be before the group, but there may be a variety of possible ways of meeting it. In this case conversation has still the difficult and important function of reaching a formulation of intended action which is satisfactory to all. It is conversation of this sort—where the emphasis is on the second phase—which is the prototype of the formation of purpose by the individual through internal speech.

On other occasions, the important step is to reach an adequate formulation of what the situation is. The description already given may be vague or incomplete at points where a greater clearness would be determinative of appropriate action. Or the reports made by two individuals in regard to a distant situation may be incompatible. Before a plan of action can be formulated, it is clear that a relatively complete and definite formulation of the situation must be reached, and one which is internally consistent in the sense that it does not tend to call for incompatible courses of action. Furthermore, one and the same statement of facts must be accepted as the basis for the formulation of a plan of action by all the actors, unless, indeed, everything is in the hands of a leader who is followed blindly.

Belief and thought attach directly to that phase of primitive conversation whose end is the formulation in language of the relevant objective features of the situation. It is of course true that reflective thought may also enter to any degree in the formation of purposes and in the rational planning of action. And it is equally true that the endeavor to form a plan of action may prompt and lead to further analysis of the situation, by directing attention toward features hitherto unrecognized. What we have called the two phases of conversation are mutually dependent in their origin, and continue to determine each other reciprocally. Any development of one phase inevitably reacts on the other. Yet there seems to be a more direct connection of purpose with the second stage, and of belief and reflective thought with the first.

Belief and Expectation.

BELIEF proper is confined to human beings. Yet it bears an evident resemblance to the *expectation* which is common to both animals and men. We expect the water which we see, to feel "wet" and "cold" when we wade into it. So the dog or chimpanzee that has seen his reflection in a mirror *expects* to see or lay hold of the animal lurking behind it. Expectation of this sort, however, without which distance-perception could not function, is a much simpler phenomenon than belief. The expectation of the impending wetness and coldness of the water, which manifests itself in a shrinking or an anticipatory bracing of the body, is scarcely equivalent to the belief "that the water is wet and cold." Nor can the chimpanzee that snatches behind the mirror with the evident expectation of catching the animal that he sees there, properly be said to believe "that a chimpanzee is behind the mirror." The object of belief is a matter of fact, which may be formulated in the propositional form, "that x is y." The object of the more primitive expectation is perceptual presence. We believe that the water is wet and cold even when we are not on the point of stepping into it, and when we cannot see it. A belief leads to specific expectations on appropriate occasions—it is a *conditional* determinant of expectation.

BELIEF AND THOUGHT

The Social Character of Belief.

BELIEF is socially determined. What we believe rests only in part upon our own individual experience. It is always in some degree directly or indirectly dependent on the testimony of others. Even the sense-perception, which, we must agree with Hume, is essential to all belief, is itself socially determined to an indefinite extent. Now there is a sort of expectation among animals which is likewise dependent on the acts and attitudes of others. It is expectation of this sort, roused by the behavior, and particularly by the cries of others, which is the true prototype of human belief.

The development of belief, like that of memory and imagination, is intimately bound up with speech. Belief proper, as distinguished from expectation, appears, we hold, in the acceptance of the announcements of others as determining one's own attitudes and acts. In its more primitive form, belief functions only in connection with what is actually seen and heard, and it leads with relative directness to primary action. But as complete predication appears and conversation develops, belief loses the immediacy of its connection with both the perceptual present and direct primary action.

Now while it is the function of speech to control the behavior of others, an announcement does not always, even at a primitive stage, lead to action on the part of the one to whom it is addressed. Whether it does so or not depends on a number of conditions. Chief among these is probably the affective or emotional state of the hearer. No response at all may be made if what is announced has no bearing on the immediate concerns of the hearer. It may likewise be ignored or definitely repudiated, if the course of action it tends to incite runs counter to a course of action in which the hearer is deeply engaged, or if it suggests an obstacle to the satisfaction of cherished desires. On the other hand, the announcement of a state of affairs favorable to the desires of the hearer is likely to be eagerly welcomed and acted on.

Not less important than the affective attitude toward *what* is said, is the attitude toward the *speaker*. Men speak with varying degrees of authority not only when they command, but when they state facts. The prestige of a speaker depends on his social position, his personality, and the personal relation in which he stands to his hearers. Some men are notoriously untrustworthy, while others have particular motives for deceiving on a given occasion.

In addition to these emotional and affective determinants of belief, are what in a general way may be called its intellectual conditions. A statement may be made by another which directly contradicts what one has seen with one's own eyes. Or it may be incompatible in a less explicit and direct way with one's *presumptions* in regard to the situation in question. We have already seen that speaking always takes place in a concrete situation and that it is dependent on a context of presumptions. Now it is these presumptions—what is already more or less vaguely taken for granted—which determine not only the "meaning" of what is said, but its *acceptability* as well. They form from the beginning (although one cannot properly speak of a beginning) a more or less organized whole of interrelated groups, which are correlative to the organized modes of action of the individual. Just as no act can be performed, at least by a normal person, which is wholly at variance with the organized system of behavior, so no perception can be formed which has no place in a predetermined perceptual schema, and no statement can be accepted as determining action which is not compatible with the organized system of presumptions. We shall have occasion to revert to this subject later.

The Act of Assent.

ALL these factors—and others as well—which are operative in determining the effectiveness of an announcement in arousing appropriate behavior in the hearer, enter into the phenomenon of belief. To believe a statement, however, is not simply to be aroused to one of the courses of action which it naturally tends to suggest, nor is it even to hold oneself in readiness so to act. In belief proper one is indeed conditionally committed to action, and this commitment remains a characteristic of it; but the peculiar commitment of belief occurs through the mediation of speech. A proposition which is believed is accepted or *assented to*. Now *assent* and *dissent* are fundamentally acts of speech, which appear along with the affirmative and negative forms of the sentence when the stage of complete predication is reached. The attainment of complete predication marks, as we have seen, a critical stage in man's evolution, both socially and psychologically. With the evolution of the complete sentence, speech becomes an independent

329

act. But, as usual, its independence is at once cause and effect of the greater scope and indirectness with which it has come to perform its primary function in controlling behavior. Belief attaches directly to the verbal act of assent which follows upon a statement. It is part and parcel of the growing autonomy of language which is essential to its increased scope and power.

The verbal act of assent marks a conditional commitment to action. But, as language develops, the action to be undertaken is commonly prepared by further speech, either through talking to others or internally to oneself. Thus assent to a statement comes to lead directly to the making of further statements, or, in other words, to further appropriate speech behavior. This speech may be the formulating of possible plans of action, especially plans of action leading to pleasing outcomes. Nothing is commoner, when an interesting statement is made and assented to, than the embarking in imagination on plans of possible enterprises on the strength of the new information. When the original statement is believed, these verbal rehearsals are not mere pleasing flights of fancy, but positive preparations for action contingent upon the realization of other suitable conditions.

Assent to a statement leads also to one's repeating the statement to others, to the end of suitably directing their action with reference to the state of affairs asserted to obtain. Or it may lead upon occasion to the giving of specific commands, or to the utterance of warnings, etc. At a higher level of development, the action to which belief in a proposition commits one is almost entirely the action of speech itself. The relation of the more abstract beliefs to the life of common action becomes so indirect as sometimes to be practically negligible. Yet men do believe and disbelieve such abstract propositions with even greater ardor and tenacity than they usually display toward the more concrete beliefs of everyday life. Such beliefs are often held with passionate conviction. In the common phrase men "commit themselves" to them. But this commitment, with all its deep engagement of emotion, need not, it is interesting to note, issue in any overt behavior implied by the content of the belief. It does indeed lead to action of a sort, namely, the proclaiming of the belief to others and the defense of it in argument. Without stopping to raise the difficult problem of the psychological character of *implication,* it is to be noted that assent to one proposition carries with it conditional assent to other propositions, and is itself, in turn, implied in assent to other propositions. It is in the assertion of these other propositions, the urging of them in debate and argument, that belief in abstract propositions is apt to exhibit itself. For language becomes to an indefinite degree autonomous. Conversation grows to be a form of social activity so indirect in its influence on the primary behavior of men that it is nearly independent in its procedure. Conversation is a social enterprise capable of bringing out the whole gamut of human emotions in its participants. It is a means of conflict and achievement, in which the most humiliating personal defeats are suffered and the most glorious victories won. It constitutes a life apart, superimposed upon the more primitive life of bodily action. It contains within itself, to an indefinite degree, the criteria of success and failure.

It has sometimes been held, most notably by William James, that a belief which has no specific consequences for action, no "cash value" in terms of particular ideas, is essentially meaningless—a mere empty verbal form. Now it is undoubtedly true that there are so-called beliefs of this sort, in which a verbal formula is maintained that has gathered round it a halo of sentiment. Political and religious creeds are often of this sort. They are believed in the sense that they are verbally maintained. Sometimes they do indeed have a "cash value," for all the passions of partisanship may cluster around their profession and men may fight in their defense. But such deeds of blind and fanatic violence scarcely constitute the "meaning" of the verbal creeds and formulas which inspire them, but express rather the feelings with which they are held. For it is not the distinctive nature of what is said to be "believed" that inspires such acts, nor have the indiscriminate deeds of blind passion any appropriateness to the content of the belief. The emptiness, or meaninglessness, of an alleged belief is not measured by a failure to issue in primary action, nor is its "meaning" constituted by the acts which it may inspire. As a matter of fact, no believed proposition taken by itself is capable of determining any specific act, nor does it independently imply any other proposition. It is only a conditional determinant of either the primary acts that are ascribed to it, or the secondary assertions in language of other propositions. The pragmatists have been so impressed with the profound and important truth that belief and thought are fundamentally connected with the life of action, that they have generally failed to do justice to the extreme indirectness of the relationship. Largely owing to their failure to take account of the instrumentality of language, they have greatly oversimplified their treatment of the phenomena of cognition.

Further Aspects of Belief.

WERE our purpose to give an adequate analysis of belief, there are many questions which it would be necessary to answer, and many distinctions which we should have to make. Belief is not a scientific term, but it is used to cover loosely a number of closely related phenomena. To say that belief is a conditional commitment to action mediated by speech is no sufficient definition of belief, although it may be a step in the direction of such a definition. How, for example, is belief to be distinguished from suggestion? For suggestion, as Pierre Janet has so interestingly shown, is also a commitment to action mediated by speech.[1] It differs from belief largely in the fact that it leads to action more directly; it is a less conditional commitment, and depends less on elaboration in the form of internal speech. It is evident that no adequate account of belief can be given without the most

---

[1] *Les medications psychologiques*, Vol. I, pp. 213-228. The reader will find that there is much in common between the position taken in these pages and Janet's incidental discussion of language in his treatment of suggestion.

careful analysis of suggestion and other pathological and quasi-pathological phenomena.

Belief in a proposition as such must be distinguished from belief in a proposition as asserted by some other person or persons. It is evidently a very different thing psychologically to believe a proposition on its own merits, so to speak, from what it is to accept it because of the prestige of the person who asserts it. Beliefs may be in very different degrees "rational convictions." Just what a rational conviction is psychologically, it is extremely difficult to say. Judging from current psychological analyses of other people's beliefs, one might be led to suppose that a genuinely rational conviction, like Kant's moral act, never has existed and perhaps never will exist.

The beliefs of different individuals in the same proposition differ enormously from each other as psychological phenomena. Its acceptance by one person may be determined very directly and simply by the influence of desires and feelings, with very little assimilation of it to other beliefs. In such a case it may lead comparatively directly to action, but the scope and variety of behavior it is capable of controlling are very limited. The defense of the believed proposition in discussion may be warm and stubborn, but the repertoire of arguments is small. On the other hand, the acceptance of the same proposition by another person may be reached only after long processes of preparation by internal speech, as a result of which it becomes assimilated to his other beliefs. Such a person may be slow and hesitating in carrying his belief into overt action, but the possible range of its application to behavior is greater. Moreover, the long process of reflection which preceded its acceptance has prepared a great variety of things to be said not only in its defense but in its criticism. In many cases, indeed, where two individuals profess belief in the same proposition, such different consequences for behavior, both in speech and in primary action, are involved, that we may well question whether they really believe the same thing or not.

Again, there is difficulty in deciding to what extent readiness to carry a belief into primary action is essential to believing it. One may be rationally convinced of the truth of a proposition, and yet balk quite irrationally when it comes to committing oneself to important action on the strength of it. It is one of the interesting and instructive consequences of what we have called the autonomy of speech, that the life of reason and the life of action may be so far divorced. Individuals with the superb balance of a Stefansson are rare. He, it will be remembered, reached the conclusion that the polar seas were not, as was universally held, devoid of life, but that lower forms of animal life, and consequently, also seals and polar bears, were to be found there.[1] This conclusion was reached by a complex course of reasoning, but it was not supported by any direct evidence. Yet Stefansson was willing, on the strength of this reasoning and in the face of the utter disbelief of almost every other supposedly competent person, to risk his life in a journey into the polar sea without carrying provisions. It is a human achievement of the highest

[1] See *The Friendly Arctic*.

order. Many other men have dared equally, but few have dared on the strength of mere reason as did Stefansson. Now suppose other men agreed with him in his reasoning, and were willing to stake their scientific reputations on the existence of seals in the polar sea, and yet were unwilling to risk their lives on it—would we be warranted in denying that they really believed it after all?[1] It is evident that belief may be of many degrees, and that rational conviction does not always determine primary action.

It may be of interest to compare Stefansson's behavior with that of the two men who accompanied him. The belief on the strength of which they were willing to make the supreme venture was not, like Stefansson's, a rational conviction that seals were to be found in the unknown regions. Rather it was the belief that Stefansson himself was a man to be trusted. They believed in the existence of seals not as a rationally inferred fact, but as vouched for by their trusted leader.

It is outside our purpose to carry the discussion of the complex subject of belief further. We have been

[1] Such a question would be very difficult to decide, for there would be many complex factors to be considered, such as the physical strength and the daring that goes with it, ambition and other traits of character, etc. Of course, no belief or set of beliefs, however firm its rational foundation and however sincere the conviction with which it is held, can by itself lead to action. Every action of even the most rational being has its springs in feeling and desire. When all this is said, however, there is, we hold, a difference in individuals in the degree to which the life of reason is a thing apart from the life of practical action, or in the degree to which their daily acts are determined by rational considerations. One cannot read Stefansson's works without being impressed by the unusual extent to which his actions were controlled by beliefs based upon independent reasoning.

interested to show that while belief has its genetic source in the animal expectation based on the expressive acts and attitudes of others, it is only with the appearance of speech that it becomes distinguished as belief proper. It is to be specifically connected with the acceptance of, and the assent to, statements made by another. It is in the light of this relationship that we can understand the *social* character of belief on the one hand, and, on the other, its fundamental relation to behavior. Its growing independence of the influence of the authority of others, and the growing indirectness of its relation to practical life, are intimately bound up with the development of conversation and the increasing autonomy of speech as a human activity.

Thought and Purposive Behavior.

THINKING is closely connected, both genetically and functionally, with purposive action. But not all planning of action constitutes thought in the sense in which the term is here used. Thinking represents a further stage in the indirectness with which speech performs its primary function of controlling behavior, and a further stage in its own development into an independent human activity complete in itself. In brief, thinking is a *re*-formulation of the conditions and of the ends of action, which makes possible a further reformulation of the steps leading from one to the other.

We have already discussed the rôle of the concept in mediating purposive action. The ends of men's acts are envisaged by them through the *name*, or verbal description. It is through naming that it becomes possible to direct behavior to the attainment of objective ends (*e.g.*, sharpening a stick) by use of indirect means (*e.g.*, tools or the services of other men). The naming of the end, together with the naming of the existing condition of affairs in which the end is to be attained, prepares the naming of the acts which must be performed to reach the end. Now in a primitive state of culture, the ordinary ends of life are comparatively few in number and fixed by custom. Furthermore, they are usually reached by familiar and customary modes of procedure. For this, thought is not necessary, although speech is. It is through the aid of verbal direction and correction that each generation acquires the arts of its ancestors, and through the aid of internal speech that he carries them on throughout his life. But however complete and rigid custom has become, it never suffices to direct one's acts in all their details, nor, more importantly, in every emergency. Conditions vary and change, and the old formulas do not fit the case. But language is a flexible instrument. The familiar situations and ends of life are recognized through the mediation of familiar and habitual forms of verbal characterization. But there are other possible ways of characterizing them as well, and some which, for the unusual occasion, may be more appropriate than the familiar ones. What is new or unusual attracts attention, and an experienced failure of familiar ways of action arouses still more attentive scrutiny. The aroused attention calls out first the preparatory response of *re-naming*. One has a more or less extended vocabulary at one's disposal, and one tries out fresh verbal characterizations. These lead in turn to tentative rehearsals of different modes of procedure. It is this trying out in internal speech of new and modified procedure based on a reformulation of the conditions and ends of action, which is the simplest form of thought.

This reformulation may be initiated in more than one way. Action arises either as a response to external conditions and events perceived by oneself or announced by others, or through the inner impulsion of habitual and customary needs. Thus the announced presence of unexpected game may sometimes initiate hunting; and sometimes a hunt is undertaken because food is needed, when no game has been sighted. But it is evident that the occasions and the ends of action are reciprocal. If the getting of game were not a customary end, the presence of game would not initiate hunting; and if the presence of game were not a frequent occurrence, the need of food would not initiate the search for it. It is in similarly distinct and related ways that thinking is initiated. A state of affairs arises which is recognized as unusual and demanding unusual treatment. The immediate need is to ascertain what sort of a thing it is— to find an appropriate verbal characterization for it. It shows itself on examination to possess certain familiar properties, or to be on the whole similar to some familiar sort of thing. The verbal characterization which it thus receives is one which is relevant to the possible needs of the individuals concerned, for one is naturally prepared to see qualities and relations which are of importance and interest.

Again, it may be some end of action which calls for reëxamination and reformulation. A fresh characterization of an end, the discerning in it of new properties or elements or of formerly unseen likenesses to other things, forms a fresh point of departure for the reformulation of the given conditions of action, and consequently for a new tracing of the steps necessary to attain the end. Particularly important is the characterization of the end in more objective or more general terms. For the more it is freed in conception from the particular setting of the given occasion and from its immediate relation to specific hopes and fears, the more do its relations to other objective conditions and events emerge. It becomes envisaged as the outcome of impersonal objective agencies. The way is thus opened for greater indirection, and hence for greater flexibility, of procedure in its attainment. The reformulation of the ends of human conduct has been one of the most important accomplishments in the history of civilization. For example, the re-conceiving of health and disease by Alcmaeon, in terms of a balance of the constituents of the body, not only brought the different ailments under a single unifying category, but it opened the way to a new and systematic practice of medicine. Of course such a reformulation of an end of action comes about as a result of very complex conditions; but the point we wish to emphasize is, that when it occurs it brings with it a fresh organization of its conceptual field and a resulting extension and improvement of possible ways and means.

BELIEF AND THOUGHT

Conversation as an Independent Activity.

THE process of thought can arise only in a world already verbalized and so in some form conceptualized. Thought does not create an organization of the world *de novo;* that is the work of simpler agencies. Thinking modifies the crude organization it finds and makes it more systematic. So far we have spoken of thinking as incidental and subservient to purposive behavior. Undoubtedly it does so arise, and undoubtedly much thinking continues to be of this simple sort. But, like so many other activities which have arisen as factors in a larger whole, it has, in accordance with the usual process of evolution, gradually freed itself from its subservience to other ends and become a complete and independent activity in its own right.

It is individuals who think, just as it is individuals who remember and imagine and form purposes. But just as these latter processes have arisen through an internalization of speech which is originally carried on by the social group, so thinking also arises through the carrying-on of internal conversation. But thinking is a particular kind of internal conversation, and to understand it we must examine its prototype in the conversation that is carried on by the group.

Conversation in its simplest form is a direct preliminary to concerted action. Through announcement, question and answer, proposal and counter-proposal, the conditions of action are determined and laid before the group in representative form. Now while all that is said in such conversation is inspired by the immediate interests of the occasion; and while the very meaning of the sentences uttered is in part determined by the concrete context in which they are spoken; neverthe· less, because the terms of language are inherently representative of what is objective and universal, the conversation is more than a mere preparation for the particular action of the given occasion. It is indirectly a preparation for other occasions. Because of these traits, conversation may, like play, be advantageous even where it does not directly prepare for any further action. In part, perhaps, through evolutionary modifications of the human organism, men have acquired a taste for "idle" conversation and discussion, just as they have acquired a taste for the constructive play of early childhood. Discussion of imagined or remembered common enterprises, in which they are criticized and reconstructed, becomes a social occupation. The criterion of success in this new activity is the *reaching of agreement*. For the individual it may be a contest in which he who succeeds in gaining the assent of others comes out ahead.

Through conversations of this sort there emerge more clearly defined and more objective standards of success and failure. The give and take of criticism and defense tends to cancel out the influence of individual desires and feelings, which may color each one's utterances. Furthermore, the verbal agreements reached influence later action, and are confirmed or corrected through the success or failure their application brings. Assent to assertions made in the course of conversation comes to be less influenced by the prestige of the speaker, and more by the fitness of what is said. Or, prestige in discussion comes to be differentiated from personal prestige of other sorts. The wise counsellor is distinguished from the hero in battle. Of course we are here schematizing a very complex process of development, which must have taken place gradually and amid many influences. Conversation did not undergo this development in independence of the development of internal speech and thought. Nevertheless, while there is and always has been a certain reciprocity, yet it is conversation which has been the prototype of thought, and it is in the give and take of discussion that the objective standards of rationality have been determined. The particular sort of conversation to which thought most naturally seems to attach is the discussion which has for its end the formulation of the conditions of possible action, and, ultimately, the conditions *of the conditions* of action. This end is attained, so far as the particular conversation is concerned, when a mutual agreement has been reached.

Thought and the Reorganization of Beliefs.

THOUGHT is the process by which beliefs are at once modified and organized. Belief is thus a simpler and more primitive phenomenon than thought. Without a starting point in belief, thought could get no purchase, or, rather, it could not even begin to be. Although this was shown long ago by the curious dialectic of the Megarians, its truth has not always been fully appreciated. In particular, it has been assumed that the elaborate and often fantastic beliefs of savages are a sort of crude but inherently rational theory formulated to explain the

343

mysterious phenomena of nature. Animism, for example, has been called a primitive philosophy of nature. We know now that this cannot possibly be the truth of the matter. Such an intellectualistic way of accounting for and interpreting primitive beliefs is exactly on a par with the explanations of social organization and the state in terms of an original contract. There was social organization before there were contracts and unreflective beliefs before there were theories.

We have already tried to show how human perception is transformed by the ability to speak. The language which the child inherits as part of his social endowment constitutes a veritable *a priori* form of cognition. His perceptions of the world about him, moulded as they are by language, are to an indefinite degree *"représentations collectives."* So too are the beliefs which he inherits along with his mother-tongue. As social animals, men have always had organized ways of acting. The activities of wolves in a pack make up a sort of system, while the behavior of our domestic dogs is almost ritualistic, so true is it to prescribed form in all its details. The organization of behavior is a necessary condition of successful coöperation. While this organization among lower animals is based upon what may roughly be termed instinct, in man it rests upon language-moulded tendencies. It is custom and not instinctive habit that determines the form of coöperative activity. Custom undoubtedly has its roots in complex social instincts, just as speech has its roots in instinctively made and understood inflections of the voice. But it represents a different level of development. The organized system of customs, which enables the group to maintain itself from generation to generation as a distinctive unit carrying on coöperative activities, has its correlative system of sentiments and beliefs. Belief we have just seen to be a conditional commitment to action, represented and made possible by assent to some verbal formulation of matter of fact. Beliefs come into existence as members of a more or less organized system. *They constitute a sort of psychological projection of the system of customary modes of action which make maintenance of the group possible.*

Since the human group, like the individual, must live in the midst of an environment to whose factors it must adapt its actions, its beliefs must in some degree represent the objective natural order. But the simpler and more direct the means by which social ends are attained, the wider may be the divergence between belief and reality. It is a constant source of amazement how men were able throughout so many thousands of years to support the burden of magical and religious superstition. Those elaborate and monstrous systems of belief cannot possibly be accounted for on any simple theory that beliefs are determined by their successful "working" in practice. The cost of magic and religious superstition in human suffering and misguided effort has been appalling, and it does not seem to have been compensated for by commensurate advantages. Primitive societies existed and thrived in spite of them rather than because of them. How, then, could they have been evolved if they were not useful? it may be asked. But we have learned that in the field of organic evolution we cannot explain all the phenomena in terms of simple utility. Much less can this be done in the more complex field of social evolution. The truth is, however, that some more or less organized system of beliefs and sentiments is an absolute necessity for the carrying-on of social life. So long as group solidarity is secured by some such system, the particular beliefs which enter into it may to an indefinite degree lead to behavior ill-adapted to the objective order of nature. Of course a point may be reached, and very likely has been reached at times in the past, when the burden of false beliefs has been too great, and societies have collapsed under the weight of harmful practices.

But when all this is admitted, the fact remains that magical and crudely religious beliefs which exercise a deep and widespread control over the lives of men can be maintained only when the state of the arts and crafts is low, and particularly when it is stable. Increase and improvement in the arts of life, advance in the indirectness and consequent efficiency of methods, must inevitably bring about a more adequate system of conceptions and beliefs concerning the instruments and processes employed. Dewey has well argued that progress in knowledge has been conditioned upon the preoccupation of thought with the instruments of action. This is indeed typical of all psychological development, as we have seen repeatedly.

We have said that the systems of primitive beliefs are not the work of thought. This statement needs to be guarded. While the beliefs of savages—which are of course far from being primitive—are not "philosophies" or theories, thought has nevertheless played its part in determining their fantastic pattern. We may compare them to the eoliths, or early chipped flints, which are artifacts, not in the sense that they were fashioned entire by men's hands, but in the sense that the shapes they now have are due to slight chippings here and there made to improve the natural shapes they originally had. So the earliest work of men's thought, as of their hands, was the refashioning bit by bit of what was already partly fashioned for use by other agencies. Just as speech can have significance and force only in a perceptual context, and can at first formulate in language only those features of the situation which call for explicit attention on the given occasion, leaving unsaid what is already presumed, so belief arises as the explicit formulation of only certain features of what is already vaguely anticipated and expected. Before man's ancestors had any explicit beliefs, their behavior was guided by rudimentary systems of anticipations. And just as the evolution of language has been conditioned by the gradual replacement of the perceptual context of speech by a presumed language context, so the evolution of beliefs has taken place through the gradual formulation in language of those vaguer expectations which have been the matrix of all belief. For every explicitly formulated belief which controls human behavior, there are a whole set of implicit expectations— of what has been taken for granted without definite formulation, but is ready to be formulated as the occasion demands. The progressive formulation of the presumed context is in effect the transition from the simple organization of expectations to the more complex system of beliefs. But it is more than a mere translation of a preëxisting system. Reorganization is necessary, and the development of a new type of system. It is this gradual working-over of the old system which thought effects in answer to the demands of expanding activity.

Thought and belief, like language, are essentially social phenomena. They belong primarily to the group and not to the individual. And yet it is of course true that it is the individual, and not the group, that actually speaks and believes and thinks. So custom is primarily and distinctively the custom of the group and not of the individual, while yet it is the individual who in his behavior practices and exemplifies the custom. The individual can become a member of the group in which he has been born only through a process of education, as a result of which he acquires the language and customs of his people and assimilates their beliefs and modes of thought. The process of education consists in the development of a psychological organization of the individual himself. In learning to speak, the structure of the language with all that this carries with it becomes incorporated in his own person. But while each individual is thus an embodiment of the group-organization, he represents a particular rendering of it. Individuals differ from each other in social status and in organic endowment. While each shares the common ends and pursuits, he has his own private activities, and these differ from and even conflict with those of others. Philologists tell us that with each generation that learns the mother-tongue, it undergoes slight changes of accent, vocabulary, and idiom. So, as each generation takes over and assimilates the sentiments and beliefs of its fathers, these become modified.

The individual, like the group, must develop a certain psychological organization in order that he may carry on the complex and systematic activities of human life. As, at a lower level, habits must not conflict with each other, so the more complex ways of behaving must be mutually compatible. The natural world in which the individual lives is an objective order. It is this order of external nature which is the *fons et origo* of the psychological unity of the individual. His ways of behaving must be organized first of all to match the order of things. In addition, they must be ordered to match the existing social organization, which is itself a reflection of the primary order of nature. Lastly, the ways of individual behavior must be so ordered as not to conflict with one another; they must lie down together.

Recent developments in the field of psycho-pathology have made us familiar with some of the various ways in which a working compromise between conflicting tendencies may be reached, as well as typical ways in which it may fail of realization. It is as if the organization of the individual could take place at different levels, depending partly on the native capacity of the individual, and partly on the degree of tension created by the circumstance of this life. Sometimes suppression occurs; or continuity is completely lost and a division of the psychological organization takes place. Suggestion and various forms of automatism also are partial low-level adjustments. Generally speaking, what is too complex, or too much in conflict, to permit of inclusion in the working-system, gets cut off in some more or less effective way.

At a higher level, the reconciliation is effected by what is known as "rationalization." This occurs when the ends that control the process of organization are the relatively immediate and simple ends of the individual —his desires, his *amour propre,* his prejudices, etc. The falling back on "rationalization" is not, like the phenomena just mentioned, pathological. It is quite normal, and undoubtedly occurs more or less in the thinking of every individual. When one has recourse to "rationalization," one secures a real unity, but one secures it through one's failure to assimilate the more objective standards built up in coöperative enterprise.

Discussion as a Social Enterprise.

WE have tried to show how the whole course of the evolution of behavior and its correlative "mental" phenomena has been marked by the reaching of successive levels. On the one hand, as we pass from the simplest animal organism onward, we find stages of increasing indirectness in the attainment of the primary ends of life. On the other hand, with each increase in the indirectness of behavior, there have emerged new ends of life itself. As the psychological environment has been progressively objectified, it has come to include more and more of the objective order of nature, and to coincide more and more nearly with it.

The development of speech and of the tool marks the attainment of the distinctively human level. With them for the first time the primary qualities of things emerge, and the objective physical order appears. But the process of evolution does not stop with the rise of language, nor with the attainment of what we have called complete predication. The fashioning of the earliest tools marks the attainment of a new and distinctive kind of behavior; but it is only the beginning of a new evolution, superimposed, as it were, upon the foundations of the old. Just as the sharpening of sticks and the chipping of flints by hand have been succeeded by the making of tools and machines to make other tools, until so indirect and complex has become the process of production that almost all the instruments and tools in use are manufactured by other machines; so has speech by successive stages become so indirect and involved in its organization, that it is only tentatively and with great difficulty that we are able to discern its primary function and the factors which have governed its evolution. While, like the using of tools, it is in its origin and essence a new form of indirection in the attainment of the primary ends of life, it has come to constitute a relatively independent human function, serving its own ends, autonomous and self-regulating to an indefinite degree. In its capacity for turning and re-turning back upon itself, reflecting in its own features again and again the successive stages of its own development—like ever reduplicated images in opposing mirrors—it stands alone among human functions.

We have had occasion repeatedly to refer to the autonomy of speech. Conversation has various autonomous forms: the interchange of greetings, the recounting of past deeds and events, the telling of imaginary tales, discussion and argumentation, and finally, all literature and all science. Conversation is not only the great instrument for securing social solidarity, but in its various forms it constitutes many of the major human activities, and is the source of the most distinctive of human satisfactions. Internal speech plays no less important a rôle. From the planning in direct preparation for primary action, it becomes, in divergent forms, the medium for the reliving of the past in memory, the enjoyment in imagination of a world of delights, and of achievements and triumphs unattainable in the course of primary living. Each of these expansions of individual life has its prototype, as we have tried to show, in some form of conversation, and has, in turn, reacted upon and transformed the social activity from which it sprung and from which it receives constant nourishment.

The Autonomy of Internal Discussion.

IN the activity of thinking itself, speech reaches the highest and most typical of its autonomous functions. The form of conversation from which thought springs is the discussion, which has for its end agreement among the participants regarding some specific conditions of common action. In its earlier form this type of conversation has for its end the common assent to propositions which serve as commitments to more or less immediate action. In its later and more independent forms, its relation to conduct becomes increasingly indirect and conditional. The end of such autonomous argumentation

is the common acceptance of some belief hitherto un-
formulated or not formulated in acceptable terms. It
is a complete coöperative enterprise in itself, having a
beginning, a middle, and an end. It starts with premises,
partly presumed and partly assumed, which are either
categorically or hypothetically assented to, and proceeds
to a specific end, in the light of which the assumed
premises have been chosen. The end is agreement in
answering some question which has arisen from a dis-
agreement or incompatibility of beliefs. As this form
of discussion evolves, objective standards gradually
emerge by a very complex process, partly as a result of
the cancelling-out of the subjective tendencies of different individuals, and partly owing to the gradual and
indirect influence of success and failure in the enterprises
to which the beliefs thus reached commit men.

Thinking is the internalization of this form of conversation and its independent practicing by the individual. This is originally and primarily a rehearsal in
direct preparation for his active participation in the social enterprise of discussion. It serves also, although
more indirectly than has generally been recognized by
pragmatists, as a preparation for his own individual
primary action. Thinking, like discussion, is a complete
act and has its own end. But since it is carried on by
the individual with himself, the end cannot be agreement as such. As pragmatists have insisted, thinking
is always a purposive activity undertaken with reference
to specific conditions, and having always the end of resolving some specific problem. This end is the reaching
of a *belief* regarding some doubtful matter. But while

agreement with others may not openly determine the outcome, the process is controlled throughout by social pressure. It is the essentially *social* character of thinking which the pragmatists have failed to recognize sufficiently—a failure which has been partly responsible for their neglect of the real independence and autonomy of thought. The thinking process reaches its end when a verbal formulation is found which is at once relevant to the point at issue and objectively compatible with the assumed premises and the presumed context from which the process took its start.

We cannot pretend to offer here any adequate analysis of what constitutes *objective compatibility*.[1] The recognized compatibility of the formulation reached by thought with its premises is objective in so far as objective standards are assimilated by the individual. Not only are the premises that are accepted by the individual as his point of departure assented to by him in large part because there is general agreement on them, but the procedure which he follows is similarly prescribed. He follows, indeed, so far as his thinking is valid, an *a priori* standard of value. The formal validity of this standard, as well as the material validity of the specific conclusion reached, cannot be wholly consti-

---

[1] This subject is involved in the problem of the evolution of affection and sentiment, and, in particular, of valuation. This evolution is as intimately dependent on the function of speech as is the evolution of cognition. Valuation and conception are mutually determining psychological phenomena. A value represents an objectification of affective quality, parallel to the objectification which we find in a conceptualized property of a perceived thing. Valuation, like conception, is also a fruit of coöperation. The objectivity of values is constituted in large measure by their social character.

tuted by social agreement. No procedure could grow up, and no standard be adopted, which did not to some degree represent and correspond to the objective order of nature. But such correspondence is acquired only through the medium of coöperation, as a result of the indirect dealing with nature through the group. The individual's contact with reality is measured by the extent and adequacy of the social organization through which he operates.

Universals.

THERE is a sense, of course, in which everything denoted through language is universalized. But there are degrees, or rather, levels, of universality. The transition from the primitive sentence-word, dependent on the perceptual setting for its significance, to the more independent complete predication which names its subject, is a step to a new level of universality. When again, by a characteristic turning back upon itself, speech transforms an original predicate into a subject, or uses the name to denote the class as such and not a particular member, the abstract universal emerges, and a still higher level of universality and objectification is reached. It is to be noted that such language forms can arise only when speech has ceased to concern itself directly with primary acts and, through its increased indirectness, has acquired a virtual autonomy.

What men talk about originally are the concrete objects which are of importance in their simple activities of daily life. What get singled out for verbal response are, as we have already emphasized, those points in the

objective order upon which primary responses pivot—
the conditional determinants of response. Language provides a new form of *direct* response to what is responded
to only *indirectly* by primary behavior. But speaking is
also a new form of activity, and consequently is itself
conditionally determined in its procedure by potential
objects of a new kind. Just as there are points upon which
primary behavior pivots, so there are points upon which
the secondary behavior of speech pivots. But the very
form of the speech response, its freedom from the direct control which sensible things exercise over bodily
response, leaves it free from any limitation as to its
possible extension. One may talk about anything—tangible or intangible, concrete or abstract—but one can
only manipulate what is tangible and concrete. The
world of universals is precisely the world of those
things which may only be talked about. Hence it is a
world of unsubstantial entities. It is not in space and
time, because—unlike the world of concrete things in
their relation to primary behavior—it presents no inherent limits of place or occasion to the activity of
speech. Yet, disparate as is this world of universals from
the concrete world of sensible objects, it has its natural
connections with this latter. For just as sensible objects
are the conditional determinants of primary behavior,
so universals are the conditional determinants of speech
behavior, and hence conditions of conditions of primary
behavior. The world of universals is a more perfectly
ordered and systematic realm than the world of sense,
because it is the very embodiment of the order which
articulates and supports the latter. It forms a hierarchy,

or system of hierarchies, because language, from its very nature is capable of returning again and again upon itself, and of finding in its abstract terms specific modes of response to what are the conditional determinants of its activity at each successive level.

Fine! Quote it Dec. 26, 1935, before the P.A.A.R.A. assembled at Stanford.

Index

Piaget?